LUND STUDIES IN ENGLISH. III.
PROFESSOR EILERT EKWALL, Editor

MIDDLE ENGLISH SURNAMES OF OCCUPATION
1100—1350

WITH AN EXCURSUS ON
TOPONYMICAL SURNAMES

BY

GUSTAV FRANSSON

Lund
1935

Reprinted by permission of C. W. K. Gleerup, Lund
KRAUS REPRINT LIMITED
Nendeln/Liechtenstein
1967

Soc
CS
2505
F7
1967

Printed in Germany

Lessing-Druckerei Wiesbaden

PREFACE.

It is my hope that the present work will show the abundant material — still unworked — that is afforded by Middle English surnames and the many ways in which this is valuable for philologists and historians. In the Introduction, where this will be pointed out more in detail, I have included the results of my examination of a few of those questions that can be explained or elucidated by surnames. I also hope that these rich medieval sources, of which a small part is now offered, will be further explored in the future and receive an attention similar to that which is at present bestowed on place-names.

It gives me great pleasure to express my sincere thanks to my teacher in English philology, Professor EILERT EKWALL, at whose suggestion this investigation was undertaken and to whom I am much indebted for stimulating and valuable criticism.

My gratitude is further due to Docent O. S. ANDERSON, who has always shown great interest in my work and given me much valuable advice throughout the course of it. I have also to acknowledge my obligation to Fil. Mag. M. LÖFVENBERG for much valuable assistance.

For kindness shown me during my stay in London I am indebted to Professor A. MAWER, Mr J. E. B. GOVER, and Dr A. H. SMITH.

Finally, I want to thank my secretary, Miss E. HANSSON, and my brother ARNE FRANSSON for greatly facilitating the final stage of my work.

Lund, November 1935.

GUSTAV FRANSSON.

CONTENTS.

Bibliography	8
Abbreviations	15

INTRODUCTION
- A. Scope and Aim. Explanatory Notes 16
- B. A Short Survey of Middle English Surnames
  - 1. The Rise of Surnames 20
  - 2. Surnames in Latin and French 23
  - 3. Classification of Surnames 25
- C. Surnames of Occupation
  - 1. Surname and Trade. A Comparison 29
  - 2. Specialized Trades 30
  - 3. Names not Found in NED. Antedating 32
- D. The Heredity of Surnames 33
- E. Two Suffixes of Obscure History
  - 1. The Ending *-ester* 41
  - 2. The Ending *-ier* 45

MIDDLE ENGLISH SURNAMES OF OCCUPATION
- Ch. I. DEALERS, TRADERS
  - A. Merchant, Dealer 51
  - B. Pedlar, Hawker, Barterer 53
- Ch. II. MANUFACTURERS OR SELLERS OF PROVISIONS
  - A. Miller, Sifter 56
  - B. Corn-Monger, Meal-Monger 60
  - C. Baker, Maker or Seller of Bread 61
  - D. Cook, Sauce-Maker 63
  - E. Maker or Seller of Cheese or Butter ... 66
  - F. Maker or Seller of Spices, Garlics, Oil 68
  - G. Maker or Seller of Salt, Soap, Candles, Wax .. 70
  - H. Butcher, Poulterer 73
  - I. Seller of Fish 76
  - J. Brewer, Vintner, Taverner 77

1*

Ch. III. CLOTH WORKERS
    A. Manufacturers of Cloth
        1. Flax-Dresser, Comber, Carder 81
        2. Spinner, Roper
           a. Spinner, Winder and Packer of Wool .. 84
           b. Maker of Ropes, Strings, Nets 85
        3. Weaver or Seller of Cloth
           a. Weaver, Webster 87
           b. Maker or Seller of Woollen Cloth 89
           c. Maker or Seller of Linen or Hempen Cloth 90
           d. Maker or Seller of Silk, Pall, Curtains.. 92
           e. Maker of Sacks, Bags, Pouches 94
           f. Maker of Quilts, Blankets, Mats 96
           g. Felt-Maker, Worker in Horsehair 98
        4. Fuller, Teaseler, Shearman 100
        5. Dyer and Bleacher of Cloth
           a. Dyer, Litster 104
           b. Dyer with Woad, Cork, Madder 106
           c. Blacker, Bleacher, Washer 108
    B. Manufacturers of Clothes
        1. Tailor, Renovator of Old Clothes 110
        2. Maker of Cowls, Jackets, Pantaloons 114
        3. Maker or Seller of Hats, Caps, Hoods, Plumes 115

Ch. IV. LEATHER WORKERS
    A. Tanner, Skinner, Currier 119
    B. Saddler, Girdler 123
    C. Furrier, Glover, Purse-Maker 125
    D. Maker of Bellows or Bottles 127
    E. Parchmenter, Bookbinder, Copyist 128
    F. Shoemaker, Cobbler 130

Ch. V. METAL WORKERS
    A. Goldsmith, Gilder 133
    B. Coiner, Seal-Maker, Engraver 134
    C. Maker of Clocks 136
    D. Copper-Smith, Brazier, Bell-Founder 136
    E. Tinker, Pewterer, Plumber 139

    F. Blacksmith, Shoeing-Smith 142
    G. Locksmith, Lorimer 146
    H. Needler, Nailer, Buckle-Maker 148
    I. Maker or Furbisher of Armour 150
    J. Maker of Military Engines, Swords, Knives .. 152
    K. Maker of Bows or Arrows 154

Ch. VI. WOOD WORKERS
    A. Sawyer, Maker of Laths or Boards 157
    B. Carpenter, Joiner 158
    C. Maker of Carts, Wheels, Ploughs 161
    D. Maker of Ships, Boats, Oars 163
    E. Maker of Coffers, Boxes, Organs 164
    F. Turner, Maker of Spoons, Combs, Slays 166
    G. Cooper, Hooper 168
    H. Maker of Baskets or Sieves 171
    I. Maker of Hurdles or Palings 172
    J. Maker of Spades or Besoms 173
    K. Maker of Charcoal, Potash, Tinder 173

Ch. VII. MASONRY AND ROOFING WORKERS
    A. Mason, Plasterer, Painter 175
    B. Thatcher, Tiler, Slater 177

Ch. VIII. STONE, CROCKERY, AND GLASS WORKERS
    A. Miner, Quarrier, Stone-Cutter 181
    B. Lime-Burner, Tile-Maker 183
    C. Potter, Glazier 184

Ch. IX. PHYSICIAN, BARBER
    A. Physician, Surgeon, Veterinary 187
    B. Barber, Blood-Letter 188

EXCURSUS. TOPONYMICAL SURNAMES 190
    A. Surnames Ending in *-er* 192
    B. Surnames Ending in *-man* 203

A List of Compound Surnames 209
Index of Surnames 211

BIBLIOGRAPHY.

I. Sources.

AccR   Extracts from the Account Rolls of the Abbey of Durham. Surtees 99, 100, 103 (1898—1901).

Ass   Assize Rolls: *La:* Rec Soc La 47, 49 (1904—5). — *Li:* The Publications of the Lincoln Record Society 22 (1926). The Publications of the Selden Society 53 (1934). — *Nb:* Surtees 88 (1891). — *So:* So Rec Soc 11, 36, 41, 44 (1897—1929). — *St:* Salt OS 3, 4, 6, 7, 9, 10, 11, 12, 14 (1882 ff). — *Wo:* The Publications of the Selden Society 53 (1934). — *Y:* YAS 44 (1911).

Ass   Assize Rolls (unpublished) at the Public Record Office: *Ess:* 1255 (235 [1]); 1285 (249); 1341 (258). — *Ha:* 1272 (780); 1280 (1.[2] = 783; 2. = 787; 3. = 789); 1287—9 (790); 1305—6 (791); 1322—3 (792); 1325—6 (794). — *La:* 1292 (1. = 409; 2. = 415; 3. = 408); 1300—4 (417); 1323 (425); 1332—4 (428); 1338—9 (429). — *Li:* 1245 (482); 1281 (1. = 486; 2. = 491); 1286—9 (503); 1305 (508); 1317—22 (515); 1328 (516); 1332 (520); 1340—1 (521). — *Nf:* 1250 (562); 1286 (575). — *So:* 1305 (764); 1307 (766); 1320 (767); 1344 (771). — *Sx:* 1249 (909); 1263 (912); 1279 (915); 1288 (926); 1314—29 (938). — *Wo:* 1255 (1022); 1275 (1. = 1025; 2. = 1026); 1293—5 (1030); 1305 (1031); 1306 (1032); 1307 (1033). — *Y:* 1268 (1051); 1279 (1060); 1293 (1098); 1305—7 (1108).

BBA   Bridgwater Borough Archives 1200—1377. Ed. T. B. Dilks. So Rec Soc 48 (1933).

CDN   A Short Calendar of the Deeds Relating to Norwich Enrolled in the Court Rolls of that City (1285—1306). Ed. W. Rye. Norwich 1903. A Calendar of Norwich Deeds Enrolled in the Court Rolls of that City (1307—1341). Ed. W. Rye. Norwich 1915.

CLB   Calendar of Letter-Books Preserved among the Archives of the Corporation of the City of London. A—L. Ed. R. R. Sharpe. London 1899—1912.

---

[1] Number at the Publ. Rec. Off.

[2] This figure has been put in front of the name of the roll: *1.Ass* 1280. If the roll is printed, such a figure denotes the volume of the roll in question (e. g. 3.Wake), except for the assize rolls for *St*, where it denotes the volume in the series (Salt OS). Abbreviations for MS sources are in italics *(Ass, GDR, SR)*.

Court	Calendar of County Court, City Court and Eyre Rolls of Chester 1259—97. Ed. R. Stewart-Brown. Chetham Society N. S. 84 (1925).
CR	Court Rolls: *Ess:* Court Rolls of the Borough of Colchester. Vol. I (1310—52). Ed. I. H. Jeayes. Colchester 1921. — *La:* Rec Soc La 41 (1901).
CR Ramsey	Court Rolls of the Abbey of Ramsey and of the Honor of Clare. Ed. W. O. Ault. Yale Historical Publications IX (1928).
Cur	Curia Regis Rolls. Rolls Ser. 1922—32.
DB	Domesday Book. London 1783—1816.
Ellis	Ellis, H., A General Introduction to Domesday Book. London 1833.
Epi	Episcopal Registers, Diocese of Worcester. Ed. J. W. Willis Bund. Wo Hist Soc 10: 1—2 (1902).
FF	Feet of Fines: *La:* Rec Soc La 39, 46 (1899—1903). — *Li:* Lincolnshire Records. Abstracts of Final Concords (1193—1244). Ed. W. O. Massingberd. London 1896. The Publications of the Lincoln Record Society (1244—72) 17 (1920). — *So:* So Rec Soc 6, 12, 17 (1892—1902). — *St:* Salt OS 4, 11 (1883—1890). — *Sx:* Sussex Record Society 2, 7, 23 (1903—1916). — *Y:* Surtees 94 (1199—1214) 1897. YAS 42, 52, 62, 67, 82 (1218—1377) 1910—1932.
Free L	A Calendar of the Freemen of Lynn. Norfolk and Norwich Archaeological Society. Norwich 1913.
Free Y	Register of the Freemen of the City of York. Surtees 96, 102 (1897—1900).
GDR	Gaol Delivery Rolls (unpublished) at the Public Record Office: *Ess:* 1. = 1280—88 (18 a); 2. = 1281—1350 ff. (18 b); 3. = 1316—28 (18 c); 4. = 1310—24 (19). — *Li:* 1329—30 (32). — *Nf:* 1295—1302 (47); 1307—16 (48). — *St:* 1302—9 (62). — *Sx:* 1. = 1309—14 (111); 2. = 1310—21 (112).
GuildCC	The Register of the Guild Corpus Christi in the City of York. Surtees 57 (1872).
Hal	Court Rolls of the Manor of Hales 1270—1307. Wo Hist Soc 21: 1—3 (1910—33).
Inq	The Inquisitiones post mortem for the County of Worcester (1242—1326). Ed. J. W. Willis Bund. Wo Hist Soc 2 (1894—1909).
LWint	Liber Winton'. Appendix to DB.
New.Deeds	Early Deeds Relating to Newcastle upon Tyne. Surtees 137 (1924).
Nf Arch	Norfolk Archaeology or Miscellaneous Tracts. Published by the Norfolk and Norwich Archaeological Society. Norwich 1847.
OCW	Original Charters Relating to the City of Worcester. Ed. J. H. Bloom. Wo Hist Soc 19 (1909).

P	The Great Roll of the Pipe (1159—88; 1190—1200; 1230). The Publications of the Pipe Roll Society 1884—1934.
PMR	Calendar of Plea and Memoranda Rolls Preserved among the Archives of the Corporation of the City of London at the Guildhall. Ed. A. H. Thomas. Cambridge 1926—32.
RBL	Records of the Borough of Leicester. Ed. M. Bateson. London 1899—1905.
Rec Soc La	The Record Society for the Publication of Original Documents Relating to Lancashire and Cheshire.
Reg	The Register of William de Geynesburgh 1302—1307. Ed. J. W. Willis Bund. Wo Hist Soc 16 (1907—29).
RFC	The Rolls of the Freemen of the City of Chester. Rec Soc La 51, 55 (1906—8).
RG Prest.	The Rolls of the Burgesses at the Guilds Merchant of the Borough of Preston. Rec Soc La 9 (1884).
RH	Rotuli hundredorum temp. Henry III et Edward I. Record Com. 1812—18.
Salt OS	Collections for a History of Staffordshire Edited by the William Salt Archæological Society. Old Series.
So Rec Soc	Somerset Record Society.
SR	Lay Subsidy Rolls: *Cu:* 1332: Cumberland Lay Subsidy. Ed. J. P. Steel. Kendal 1912. — *Db:* 1327: Derbyshire Archæological and Natural History Society, Journal 30 (1908). — *La:* 1332: Rec Soc La 31 (1896). — *Lo:* The London Lay Subsidy of 1332. In Finance and Trade under Edward III by G. Unwin. Manchester 1918. — *So:* 1327: So Rec Soc 3 (1889). — *Sr:* 1332: Surrey Record Society 18, 33 (1923—1932). — *St:* 1327, 1332: Salt OS 7, 10 (1886—9). — *Sx:* 1296, 1327, 1332: Sussex Record Society 10 (1910). — *Wo:* 1275, 1327, 1332, 1346: Wo Hist Soc 1 (1893—1902). — *Y:* 1297, 1301: YAS 16, 21 (1894—7).
SR	Lay Subsidy Rolls (unpublished) at the Public Record Office: *Ess:* 1319 (107/10); 1327 (107/12); 1332 (107/17). — *Ha:* 1327 (173/4); 1333 (242/15a): 1340 (173/13). — *La:* 1327 (130/5); 1341 (130/15). — *Li:* 1327 (1. = 135/10; 2. = 135/11; 3. = 135/12; 4. = 135/13; 5. = 242/63); 1332 (1. = 135/14: 2. = 135/15; 3. = 135/16). — *Nf:* 1329 (149/7); 1332 (149/9); 1337 (238/111). — *So:* 1327 (169/5); 1333 (169/6). — *Y:* 1332 (211/7a); c1346 (206/47).
Surtees	The Publications of the Surtees Society.
Wake	Court Rolls of the Manor of Wakefield. YAS 29, 36, 57, 78 (1901—30).
Wo Hist Soc	Worcestershire Historical Society.
YAS	The Yorkshire Archæological Society. Record Series.
YMB	York Memorandum Book. Surtees 120, 125 (1912—15).

II. Other Works Consulted.

AEBISCHER, P., Sur l'origine et la formation des noms de famille dans le canton de Fribourg. Biblioteca dell'Archivum Romanicum, Ser. II: Linguistica, n:o 6, Onomastica. Genève 1924.
BARDSLEY, C. W., A Dictionary of English and Welsh Surnames. London 1901.
—, English Surnames. London 1915.
BJÖRKMAN, E., Nordische Personennamen in England in alt- und frühmittelenglischer Zeit. Halle 1910. Stud. z. Engl. Phil. 37.
—, Scandinavian Loan-Words in Middle English. Halle 1900—2. Stud. z. Engl. Phil. 7, 11.
—, Zur Englischen Namenkunde. Halle 1912. Stud. z. Engl. Phil. 47.
BOILEAU, É., Le Livre des métiers. Histoire générale de Paris. Paris 1879.
BOWMAN, W. D., The Story of Surnames. London 1932.
BRIESKORN, R., Bidrag till den svenska namnhistorien. Uppsala 1912.
BT = BOSWORTH, J. and TOLLER, T. N., An Anglo-Saxon Dictionary. Oxford 1882—1921.
BÜCHER, K., Die Berufe der Stadt Frankfurt a. M. im Mittelalter. Abhandlungen d. Königl. Sächsischen Gesellschaft der Wissenschaften LXIII. Phil.-Hist. Klasse 30. Leipzig 1914.
BUCHON, J. A., Livre de la taille de Paris (1313). Collection des chroniques nationales françaises, t. 9. Paris 1827.
BÜLBRING, K. D., Altenglisches Elementarbuch. Heidelberg 1902.
BÄHNISCH, A., Die deutschen Personennamen. Aus Natur und Geisteswelt 296. Leipzig 1910.
CAMDEN, W., Remains Concerning Britain. London 1870.
CARSTENS, K., Beiträge zur Geschichte der bremischen Familiennamen. Marburg 1906.
CHADWICK, D., Social Life in the Days of Piers Plowman. Cambridge 1922.
COTGRAVE, R., A French and English Dictionary. London 1673.
COULTON, G. G., The Medieval Scene. Cambridge 1930.
—, The Medieval Village. Cambridge 1925.
DAUZAT, A., Les Noms de Personnes. Paris 1925.
DICKENMANN, J. J., Das Nahrungswesen in England vom 12. bis 15. Jahrhundert. Anglia 27 (1904).
DU CANGE, CAROLO DU FRESNE, Glossarium mediæ et infimæ Latinitatis. Editio nova a L. Favre. Niort 1883—87.
EETS = Early English Text Society.
EKWALL, E., English River-Names. Oxford 1928.
—, Names of Trades in English Place-Names. In Historical Essays in Honour of James Tait. Manchester 1933.
—, The Place-Names of Lancashire. Manchester 1922.
English Gilds. Ed. Toulmin Smith. EETS 40 (1870).
EWEN, C. L'ESTRANGE, A History of Surnames of the British Isles. London 1931.

FAGNIEZ, G., Documents relatifs à l'histoire de l'industrie et du commerce en France. Paris 1898—1900.
—, Études sur l'industrie et la classe industrielle à Paris au XIIIe et au XIVe siècle. Bibl. de l'École des hautes études 33. Paris 1877.
FORSSNER, TH., Continental-Germanic Personal Names in England. Uppsala 1916.
FREEMAN, E. A., The History of the Norman Conquest of England. Vol. 5. Oxford 1876.
FRITZNER, J., Ordbog over det gamle norske sprog. Kristiania 1886—96.
GÉRAUD, H., Paris sous Philippe-le-Bel, d'après des documents originaux et notamment d'après un manuscrit contenant le rôle de la taille imposée sur les habitants de Paris en 1292. Collection de documents inédits sur l'histoire de France. Paris 1837.
GODEFROY, F., Dictionnaire de l'ancienne langue française. Paris 1881—1902.
GROSS, C., The Gild Merchant. Oxford 1890.
GUPPY, H. B., The Homes of Family Names. London 1890.
GÖTZE, A., Familiennamen im badischen Oberland. Heidelberg 1918.
HALL, J. R. C., A Concise Anglo-Saxon Dictionary. 3rd ed. Cambridge 1931.
HARRISON, H., Surnames of the United Kingdom. London 1912—18.
HEUSER, W., Altlondon mit besonderer Berücksichtigung des Dialekts. Osnabrück 1914.
HEYNE, M., Das altdeutsche Handwerk. Strassburg 1908.
HOLTHAUSEN, F., Altenglisches etymologisches Wörterbuch. Heidelberg 1932—34.
JESPERSEN, O., A Supposed Feminine Ending. In Linguistica. Copenhagen 1933.
JÓNSSON, F., Tilnavne i den islandske oldlitteratur. Kjøbenhavn 1908.
JORDAN, R., Handbuch der mittelenglischen Grammatik. Heidelberg 1925.
KAHLE, B., Die altwestnordischen Beinamen bis etwa zum Jahre 1400. Arkiv f. nord. fil. XXVI. Lund 1910.
KEMBLE, J. M., The Names, Surnames, and Nicnames of the Anglosaxons. In Proceedings at the Annual Meeting of the Archaeological Institute of Great Britain and Ireland 1845. London 1846.
KLUGE, F., Nominale Stammbildungslehre der altgermanischen Dialekte. 3. Aufl. Halle 1926.
KLUMP, W., Die altenglischen Handwerkernamen. Angl. Forsch. 24 (1908).
KOBERNE, J., Die Familiennamen von Burkheim am Kaiserstuhl sprachgeschichtlich untersucht. Neubreisach i. Els. 1927.
KUSCHE, W., Ursprung und Bedeutung der üblicheren Handwerkerbenennungen im Französischen. Kiel 1902.
KÖPKE, J., Altnordische Personennamen bei den Angelsachsen I. Berlin 1909.
LANGENFELT, G., Toponymics or Derivations from Local Names in English. Uppsala 1920.
LARCHEY, L., Dictionnaire des Noms. Paris 1880.
Lib. Alb. = Liber Albus; v. Munimenta Gildhallæ Londoniensis.
Lib. Cust. = Liber Custumarum; v. Munimenta Gildhallæ Londoniensis.

LIND, E. H., Norsk-isländska personbinamn från medeltiden. Uppsala 1920
—21.
LITTRÉ, É., Dictionnaire de la langue française. Paris 1863—72.
LUICK, K., Historische Grammatik der englischen Sprache. B. 1. Abt. 1.
Leipzig 1914—21.
MAHNKEN, G., Die Hamburgischen niederdeutschen Personennamen des 13.
Jahrhunderts. Dortmund 1925.
MARTIN, C. T., The Record Interpreter. London 1910.
MAWER, A., Problems of Place-Name Study. Cambridge 1929.
—, Some Unworked Sources for English Lexicography. In A Grammatical
Miscellany Offered to Otto Jespersen on his Seventieth Birthday. Copenhagen 1930.
MICHAËLSSON, K., Études sur les noms de personne français d'après les rôles
de taille parisiens. Uppsala 1927.
Munimenta Gildhallæ Londoniensis; Liber Albus, Liber Custumarum, et Liber
Horn. Ed. H. T. Riley. London 1859—62.
NED = The Oxford English Dictionary, Being a Corrected Re-Issue ... of
A New English Dictionary. Ed. J. A. H. Murray, H. Bradley, W. A.
Craigie, C. T. Onions. Oxford 1933.
NÜSKE, H., Die Greifswalder Familiennamen des 13. und 14. Jahrhunderts
(1250—1400). Greifswald 1929.
PACHNIO, R., Die Beinamen der Pariser Steuerrolle von 1292 unter Heranziehung der Steuerrolle von 1313 und zahlreicher Urkunden. Königsberg
1909.
Pl. Soc. De (etc.) = The Publications of the English Place-Name Society.
Devonshire (etc.).
Prompt. P. = The Promptorium Parvulorum. EETS Extra Ser. 102 (1908).
Camden Soc. 1843—65.
REDIN, M., Studies on Uncompounded Personal Names in Old English.
Uppsala 1919.
REIMPELL, A., Die Lübecker Personennamen unter besonderer Berücksichtigung der Familiennamenbildung bis zur Mitte des 14. Jahrhunderts.
Hamburg 1928.
RITTER, E., Les noms de famille. Collection philologique 5. Paris 1875.
SALZMAN, L. F., English Industries of the Middle Ages. Oxford 1923.
—, English Trade in the Middle Ages. Oxford 1931.
SEARLE, W. G., Onomasticon Anglo-Saxonicum. Cambridge 1897.
SOCIN, A., Mittelhochdeutsches Namenbuch. Basel 1903.
SR 1292 (Paris), v. Géraud.
TOBLER, A. — LOMMATZSCH, E., Altfranzösisches Wörterbuch A—D. Berlin
1925 ff.
VERWIJS, E. en VERDAM, J., Middelnederlandsch Woordenboek. 's-Gravenhage
1885—1929.
VH Ha (etc.) = The Victoria History of the Counties of England. Hampshire
(etc.).
VISING, J., Franska språket i England. Göteborg 1900—2.

WEBER, H., Die Personennamen in Rodez (Aveyron) um die Mitte des XIV. Jahrhunderts. Jena und Leipzig 1934.
WEEKLEY, E., Surnames. London 1927.
—, The Romance of Names. London 1928.
—, Words and Names. London 1932.
WESSÉN, E., Nordiska namnstudier. Uppsala universitets årsskrift. 1927.
WRIGHT, J., The English Dialect Dictionary. London 1898—1905.
YONGE, C. M., History of Christian Names. London 1884.
York Pl. = York Plays. Ed. L. Toulmin Smith. Oxford 1885.
ZACHRISSON, R. E., A Contribution to the Study of Anglo-Norman Influence on English Place-Names. Lund 1909.

Abbreviations.

a (as a1300) = ante
AF = Anglo French
Berks = Berkshire
Bk = Buckinghamshire
Ca = Cambridgeshire
c (as c1300) = circa
Ch = Cheshire
Cu = Cumberland
Db = Derbyshire
De = Devonshire
der. = derivative
Du = Durham
Ess = Essex
F = French
fem. = feminine
Gl = Gloucestershire
Ha = Hampshire
Hu = Huntingdonshire
Ke = Kent
L = Latin
La = Lancashire
Le = Leicestershire
Li = Lincolnshire
Lo = London
masc. = masculine
MDu = Middle Dutch
ME = Middle English
med. L = medieval Latin
MFlem = Middle Flemish
MG = Middle German

MHG = Middle High German
MLG = Middle Low German
MSw = Middle Swedish
Nb = Northumberland
NE = New English
Nf = Norfolk
Np = Northamptonshire
Nt = Nottinghamshire
OE = Old English
OF = Old French
ON = Old Norse
ONF = Old Northern French
Oxf = Oxfordshire
pl. = plural
pl. n. = place-name
Sal = Shropshire
sb = substantive
Sf = Suffolk
sg = singular
So = Somersetshire
Sr = Surrey
St = Staffordshire
Sx = Sussex
vb = verb
Wa = Warwickshire
Wi = Wiltshire
WMl = West Midland
Wo = Worcestershire
WS = West Saxon
Y = Yorkshire

INTRODUCTION.

A. Scope and Aim. Explanatory Notes.

The present treatise does not comprise all surnames [1] of occupation; it turned out during the work that a limitation was necessary. The most interesting part of them has been chosen, namely the surnames denoting *artisans* and *dealers*. These two groups cannot be separated, as those who made an article usually also sold it. There may be some difference of opinion as to what surnames should be included in the first group, artisans; I have not followed any rigorous definition, but instead taken all the surnames that have any connection with the manufacture of articles.

The surnames dealt with belong to the period 1100—1350. The beginning coincides with that of the Middle English period, which is the time when material for surnames begins to become fairly frequent; from the OE period practically no names of the kind treated in this volume have been delivered to us. Because the material found was very abundant, it proved to be quite sufficient to finish with the year 1350. In this way many valuable subsidy rolls from the beginning of the 14th century have been included. After 1350, however, the surnames become less interesting, the article is often dropped, and in most cases people have not those occupations that their surnames denote, as these become more and more hereditary. The period thus formed is the most interesting in the history of English surnames; it is now that they are formed. It is true that new surnames have been added in later times, e. g. those borrowed from other countries, but on the whole most modern surnames go back to this period, although they have often been much changed in spelling and pronunciation.

---

[1] I take *surname* in the wide sense of *second name*, whether hereditary or not. This has been most convenient, because it is generally impossible to decide, if a surname is a family name or only belongs to one person.

There is also another limitation that has been necessary; the case is that it proved to be too much to take material from all counties, and a selection has therefore been made including counties that represent different parts and dialects of England. In many counties, however, there was not enough material, so that I had to choose among the others, and this hampered, in some way, my selection. The counties dealt with are ten: Essex, Sussex, Hampshire, Somersetshire, Worcestershire, Staffordshire, Lancashire, Yorkshire, Lincolnshire, and Norfolk.

For the sake of comparison, rolls from other counties have also often been examined, and if valuable instances have been found of surnames scantily evidenced in the other ten counties, they have been included among the others; such instances have sometimes been taken also from the time *after* 1350. If entirely new surnames have been found in the »outside» counties, they have been omitted, except if they throw new light on the explanation of the other names; in this case they have only been mentioned in a note under those names. — Some surnames, however, are so rare that only one or two examples have been found. Such forms may, of course, be due to mistakes made by the scribe or the publisher, and if this has been suspected, these names have not been included.

Besides surnames of occupation, I have also collected material for another group of names, which I have called TOPONYMICAL SURNAMES. These names, which have been dealt with in an excursus, have been included, because no serious attention has hitherto been paid to them, and because they are often so like surnames of occupation that they may easily be confused with them.

The material has been taken from those sources — published or unpublished — that are mentioned in the bibliography. The most valuable of these are the subsidy rolls, which only consist of long lists of names. But the assize rolls and court rolls have also supplied abundant contributions. The rolls that are published are often not very reliable with regard to the surnames, which may have been misread in the originals. Great care has therefore been necessary, and doubtful spellings have — when it has been possible to me — been checked at the Public Record Office.

The etymologies and significations have, as a rule, been taken from NED, if the names are found there. My early and often numerous instances, however, have often made either a slight improvement or a complete change of both etymology and signification necessary. When dealing with French names I have used Godefroy's dictionary. Besides Scandinavian names, which are usually recorded in NED, there seldom occur any other foreign names at this early period. — In this connection it might be pointed out how great difficulties an investigator of Middle English surnames has to cope with when trying to explain the often entirely new words that he meets. Many difficult names must be left unexplained; these were — in the majority of cases — only of a temporary character, and most of them certainly belonged to nicknames.

A systematical investigation into Middle English surnames has not yet been made; all that exists is more or less popular books on modern surnames. Of these Bardsley's and Harrison's dictionaries, which contain many suggestions as to the interpretation of surnames, have been of value to me. Neither of them, however, is reliable, and this is also the case with several other works on modern English surnames. They have all in common that they start from modern names, which they try to explain, but for this purpose a comprehensive collection of Middle English surnames is necessary, and such a one is still lacking. Not until the Middle English material has been worked up, can modern surnames receive a satisfactory explanation.

The value of an investigation such as the present one is manifold. Besides explaining modern surnames, as has already been mentioned, it gives us many new words not previously found and furthermore early and often numerous instances of other common or rare words. By means of these early examples new light is not seldom thrown on the etymology, and the signification may sometimes be altered. In contradistinction to the literature of this period, the time and the place of the occurrence of each instance of a surname are well fixed, and thus the material gives a contribution to Middle English phonology. This material has hitherto not been used by linguists, but it is of the greatest value for the determination of the extension of the different dialects, as the same word can be followed in the different parts of England; there is hardly any other material that can be compared with that of surnames in this respect. —

The distribution is also shown not only of surnames, but also of the various names that a trade may have; the case is that a trade often had different names in different parts of England.[1] Last, but not least, the civilization of this period is elucidated; we are informed what trades existed, how common they were in relation to each other, in what parts of England they flourished, and how specialized they were.

The surnames in this treatise have been arranged according to the occupations that they imply; this has primarily been done with regard to the material (cloth, wood, metal, etc.) that was the object of working. It has often been difficult, however, to carry through this, and for practical reasons exceptions have sometimes been made in order to get trades that belong closely together at the same place; *those who make bows and arrows* (who work both in wood and metal), for instance, have been put together with *the manufacturers of metal weapons* (under »Metal Workers»). — *Those who deal in special articles* have been included among *those who manufacture them*; only *the dealers who do not sell any specified articles* have been put under a special heading.

If many instances have been found of a surname, all these have generally not been included, except when they are of particular interest; a selection of different spellings from different times and rolls has therefore been made. When such a surname is of little interest, only a small portion of the examples has been included, and the frequency is mentioned in a note.

The instances of each surname have been arranged by counties, which have always been placed in the same order; within a county the arrangement is chronological. When two or more instances belonging to one person occur (if this has been possible to decide), they have been put together. The figure that follows after the name of a roll (e. g. 1255 Ass *18*) denotes the *page* in this, if printed, and the *membrane,* if unprinted. The year of the earliest example in NED — when the surname is recorded there — has also been given for the sake of comparison; the year has been put within round brackets when the significations differ essentially. The date

---

[1] Cf surnames like. MILNER, MULEWARD; BAKERE, BAKESTERE; BREWERE, BREWSTERE; WEBBE, WEBBESTER; DEYER, LITESTER; FULLERE, WALKERE, TOUKERE; etc.

of my earliest example is given after the heading of each surname.

Common Christian names have been abbreviated, which is generally also the case in the unprinted originals, e. g. Will. = Willelmus, William; Joh. = Johannes; Henr. = Henricus, etc. In order to avoid confusion, however, female names have usually not been abridged.

The etymologies and significations have, as a rule, been made as short as possible, especially when they do not differ from those in NED. At the end of a surname some notes have sometimes been made on things that are particularly worth being observed. For the sake of space no exhaustive treatment has been made of the cultural side of the subject; it is left to the reader to make his own conclusions on this point.

B. A Short Survey of Middle English Surnames.

1. The Rise of Surnames.

In Old English times people generally had only one name, the Christian name, and there were a great many such names. But already during this period the need of a second name began to be felt, and a number of such names have been delivered to us (v. Kemble). How common these by-names were, is impossible to decide, as we have not sufficient material for this. What we especially want are rolls or books containing the names of the lower people. It is possible, therefore, that by-names were in fairly common use at the end of the Old English period. In the Charters, however, people usually appear without any second names throughout the period.

In Domesday Book there are many instances of second names, but most persons still appear with a Christian name only. In the beginning of the Middle English period the development advances rapidly, and in the documents from this time second names become more and more common; in the 13th century one rarely finds a person mentioned only by his Christian name.[1]

---

[1] This change was more rapidly brought about in England than in Germany, where second names, in certain parts of the country (e. g. Bremen, Hamburg), were rare as late as the 14th century (v. Bähnisch p. 110).

The reason why the need of second names became stronger after the conquest is that Christian names were completely changed. Most of those that existed in Old English died out, and instead the Christian names of the Normans came into common use, but these were not so numerous. Thus there were only about 25 male names that were common; it is true that others existed, but they rarely occurred. Within the same village, therefore, one very often meets with persons who have the same Christian name.[1] Owing to this an extra name was required to distinguish such persons; the next stage was to give other persons, too, a second name.

The Normans had second names when they came to England, and these were added to those that already existed, thus accelerating the development.

During the whole period, however, the Christian name was the most important, and it was retained throughout a person's life. But this was not the case with the second name; this could be changed, which often happened. A person could also have two or more surnames at the same time, of which sometimes one, sometimes the other was used. This was probably more common than appears from the rolls. I have found not a few instances, however, of persons having more than one surname, and I here mention some of them:

Joh. de Brake & Bakestere 1275 RH 511 (Nf). — Dionisia de Bechefeld 1279 Ass 369, D. de Ba ib. 350 (Nb). — Ric. le King, R. le Kydiere 1280 3.Hal 65 (Wo). — Henry de Walsham le cunreur 1290 CDN 32, H. Kyng le Cunreur 1298 ib. 64 (Nf). — John le Coroner, J. de Vintry, J. Clerk of the Vintry 1309 CLB (D) 15 (Lo). — John le Mazeliner, J. Lambyn 1312 CLB (D) 21 (Lo). — Rob. le Convers, R. le Orfevre 1321 CLB (D) 184 (Lo). — John le Tipper, J. the Parson 1326 9.Ass 113 (St). — Will. Faber in the Walles 1295 BBA 29, W. Faber filius sacerdotis (undated) ib. 24, W. in la Walle 1315 ib. 55 (So). — Joh. de Rudstane, barker, le frere 1367 Free Y 65. — Ralph Halstede, late woolmonger, R. Nunthey de Halstede 1378 CLB (H) 111 (Lo). — Adam Chaungeour, A. de St. Ive 1392 CLB (H) 386 (Lo). — Matthew Spicer, otherwise called »Tyce», »goldbeter» 1414 CLB (I) 124 (Lo). — Thom. Stanall al(ia)s Browdster, drapour 1444 Free Y 164 (Y). — Joh. Skryvener alias Fletcher, tapiter 1533 Free Y 253 (Y).

---

[1] In a village taken at random (*Falgham* SR 1296 Sx p. 79) there occur the following Christian names: Willelmus 7 times, Robertus 5, Johannes 3, Ricardus 3, Radulphus 3, Adam 3, Petrus 3, Simon 2, Lucas 2, Henricus 2, Rogerus 1, Nicolaus 1, Reginaldus 1, Stephanus 1, Alicia 1, Emma 1.

In the subsidy rolls for Paris Michaëlsson (p. 75) has found a number of instances in which a person is mentioned only by his surname, although the Christian name is of most importance there, too. This not seldom occurred also in Old Norse, and a person was therefore often known only by a nickname; this was particularly the case with slaves and servants (v. Kahle p. 145). To judge from the rolls this custom does not seem to have been common in England. All that I have found of that sort is a number of instances of the following kind: Walt. filius *Thecker* 1199 3.Ass 35 (St). Rog. filius *Kydier'* 1275 RH 369 (Li). John fyz *le Messer* of Eston' 1278 (So). Will. son of *Lewaynrith* 1246 Ass 89 (La). Relicta *atte Pyrie* 1327 SR 154 (Sx). Alic' Relicta *le Stepere* ib. 114.

There may be different opinions as to how much belongs to a person's surname; it has also been suggested that surnames might be invented by the scribe. The following »surnames» may be taken into consideration: Rob. filius Jalf patris Muriellis uxoris Roberti filii Roberti 1219 Ass 119 (Li). — Sim. pater Sabine uxoris Nicholai de Radestan et Alicie sororis ipsius Sabine 1221 Ass 620 (Wo). — Descriptions of this kind, which are common in early assize rolls, are of course not surnames. The persons in question probably had no satisfactory surnames that distinguished them from other persons, and the scribe therefore put down their personal relations in order to avoid misunderstandings. — The following surnames, however, seem to have been borne, in spite of their length: Nich. Bourwardesleyesman 1344 *Ass* 14 (So). Rad. le Priourespalfreyman 1328 *Ass* 8 (Li). Ad. le Brothermeysterman 1292 *1.Ass* 17 (La). Rob. le Yungehusebonde 1298 7.Ass 49 (St).

The surname sometimes seems to have been insufficient to distinguish a person, and his place of residence is therefore added, e. g.: Joh. del Grene, *de Donyngton* 1293 Free Y 5. Thom. de Selby, *de Stayngat* 1305 ib. 11. Will. de Dalle, *de Ripon*, pelter 1336 ib. 31. Will. de Bramlay *de Lincoln* Parmenter 1340 *Ass* 22 (Li). — These additions are generally no surnames, but they may sometimes adopt this function, and in this case the person has two surnames: Rob. *de Malteby*, Ferour 1340 FF 97, R. le Ferour *of Malteby* 1341 ib. 101 (Sx). — Rob. *de Chedle* Suour 1333 11.Ass 49, R. Suour, *of Chedle* 1334 ib. 50 (St). — A trade-name may also be added and is usually no surname: Adam Dauber, *carpenter* 1326 Free Y 23.

With the exception of such additions, second names were certainly looked upon as real names and probably used as often as was necessary for the sake of clearness. Cf the following quotations: »*Rich. le Cutiler* stated he was called *Rich. le Quylter* and not *Rich. le Cutiler*» 1300 7.Ass 69 (St). — »*Rose the regratere* was hir rihte name» 1377 (Langland: Piers Plowman 226).

Another thing which shows that surnames had reached a certain stage of permanency is that in assize rolls there sometimes occur suits in which the plaintiff has made a slight mistake when giving the name of the defendant and therefore been sentenced to withdraw his action.[1]

The *names of women* generally differ from the names of men; in the majority of cases the former only consist of more or less loose descriptions of the following kind: Agnes uxor Philippi 1301 SR 106 Y; Relicta le Flesmongere 1333 *SR* 4 Ha; Emma que fuit uxor Roberti sumetarii 1200 P 216 Sr; Alicia mater Ricardi clerici 1275 SR 81 Wo; Johanna soror uxoris Sewhali f. Henrici 1200 P 20 Db. These »names» very rarely appear as surnames in *English:* Anota Sergauntmanwif 1332 SR 69 Cu; Margaret Wilkesdogthter ib. — Sometimes, however, women have ordinary surnames of the same kind as those of men; this is of course regularly the case after surnames had become hereditary. In the rare cases when a married woman appears with a real surname, this is generally different from her husband's: Will. Camerarius, Muriellis de Busseto (his wife) 1219 Ass 147 Li; Nic. Webbe, Angnes Palmer (his wife) 1366 BBA 153 So; but sometimes identical: Alicia la Wymplere relicta quondam Henrici le Wympler 1284 Lo (NED s. v. *wimpler*). — In the Middle Ages women often performed the same kind of work as men — even the hard work of smiths, masons, miners, etc. (v. Salzman: Med. Ind. 55 et passim); in such cases, of course, they may have the corresponding occupative surnames.

2. Surnames in Latin and French.

The medieval rolls were written in Latin, and Christian names and surnames were also, when practicable, often translated into Latin. This was especially the case in the early Middle Ages (12—

---

[1] v. for instance Selden Society vol. 39 (1922) p. 102 ff.

13th cent.), and surnames in English are therefore rarely met with so early. The surnames that appear in Latin are chiefly those names that are in common use, e. g. Carpentarius, Cissor, Cocus, Faber, Fullo, Marescallus, Medicus, Mercator, Molendinarius, Pelliparius, Pistor, Sutor, Tannator, Textor, Tinctor. The surnames, however, that were rare and difficult to translate, e. g. Wirdragher, Chesewright, Heyberare, Geldehirde, generally occur in English, even in early rolls.

In the 14th century these translations gradually pass out of use, and the native or French form becomes predominant. Thus, for instance, there is a considerable difference between SR 1275 and SR 1327 (Wo); in the former there are a large number of names in Latin, but in the latter there are hardly any translations at all.

These surnames in Latin seem to have had some influence on the later development; the case is that some of them still exist as surnames, e. g. *Faber, Pistor, Sutor.*

Besides in English, surnames also occur very frequently in French; I have made a calculation and found that one third of the surnames of occupation treated in this book is of French origin. The reason for this is to be found in the predominating position that the French language had during this period. French was spoken by all educated people, and English by the lower classes. Those who spoke French had, of course, surnames in French, and probably also used the French forms of English names when speaking with each other. It is possible, too, that those people who spoke English were influenced by this and used the French forms of their names, which, of course, were finer. During this period a large number of French names came into the language, and a great many of these have survived to the present day, whereas the corresponding substantives have often died out.

There is also another reason, however, for the frequent occurrence of French names; the case is that the scribe often translated English names into French, especially in early rolls. These translations, which are most common in assize rolls, are principally due to the fact that the court proceedings were generally held in French. I have found some instances in which both the English and French forms occur of the same person's surname, e. g.:

Humfrey le *Syur* 1270 Ass 144, H. le Sawyere ib. 139 (So). — Ric. le Charpentir 1327 SR 211, R. le Wryth 1332 SR 96 (St).

Surnames of occupation and nicknames are usually preceded by the definite article, *le* (masc.) or *la* (fem.); the two forms are regularly kept apart in the earlier rolls, but in the 14th century they are often confused. Those names in this book that are preceded by *the* have all been taken from rolls translated into English, and *the* has been inserted by the editor instead of *le* or *la*. The case is that *the* hardly ever occurs in the manuscripts; cf the following instances, which show the custom in reality: Rose *the* regratere 1377 (Langland: Piers Plowman 226). Lucia *ye* Aukereswoman 1275 1.RH 413 (L. *la* Aukereswomman ib. 426).

Sometimes *de* occurs instead of *le;* this is due to an error made either by the scribe or the editor. The case is that *de* has an extensive use in local surnames, e. g. Thom. *de* Selby. Other prepositions (*in, atte, of* etc.) are not so common, especially not in early rolls.

The article, however, is often left out; this is rare in the 12th and 13th centuries, but becomes common in the middle of the 14th century. There is an obvious difference between different parts of England: in the South the article precedes the surname almost regularly during the present period, while in the North it is very often omitted. The final disappearance of *le* takes place in the latter half of the 14th century; in most counties one rarely finds it after c1375, but in some cases, e. g. in Lancashire, *le* occurs fairly often as late as c1400. *De* is often retained some 50 years longer than *le:* in York it disappears in the early 15th century, in Lancashire it sometimes occurs c1450, while in the South it is regularly dropped at the end of the 14th century.

3. Classification of Surnames.

A brief account of the different types of Middle English surnames will be given in the following. These are naturally divided into four groups, just as modern names:

a. LOCAL SURNAMES. This is by far the largest group, and probably comprises as many names as the others put together. Local surnames generally consist of the French preposition *de* +

the name of a country, county, town, village, etc.: Will. de Irelond, Galfr. de Dorsete, Joh. de Bristoll, Thom. de Selby. The name denotes the place from where the person comes, or sometimes — if the place is small — his residence. Cf Thom. de Appelby, manens in Bouthum 1334 Free Y 30; Joh. de Popilton, de Heslyngton 1335 ib. 30. — Another group of local surnames, which is also very common, is formed from topographical elements preceded by *atte, del, de la, in the, uppe, binethe,* etc.; they denote the residence of a person: Joh. atte Forde; Agnes atte More; Joh. del Grene; Rich. in le Lone; Adam Binetheweie; Rob. Uppehulle; Thom. Bithebroke. There is a group of surnames closely connected with these names which also belongs here, viz. *the toponymical surnames;* these have been treated specially at the end of this volume.

A small group of local surnames consists of adjectives: Will. le Frensch 1327 SR 203 So; Ric. Kentissh 1332 SR 260 Sx; Galfr. le Devenysse 1327 SR 208 So.

b. SURNAMES OF RELATIONSHIP. These names, which are also very common, denote a person's relationship — whose son, daughter, etc. a person was; in early rolls they are generally latinized: Walt. filius Haldein; Will. filius Gilberti frater Ricardi; Agnes filia Willelmi filii Herewardi; Thom. fil. Willelmi filii Beatricis; Emma relicta Johannis. In later sources they appear in the English form: Walt. Malkynesone (1332 SR 261 Sx); Thom. Adamsone (1376 Free Y 74); Walt. Henreson (1384 ib. 82); Will. Raynaldmagh[1] (1332 SR 26 Cu). These surnames generally contain the father's (rarely the mother's) *Christian name,* but sometimes his *surname:* Thom. filius fabri 1327 SR 213 St (Thom' le Smythsone 1332 SR 97); Adam le Clerkessone 1327 SR 205 St; Adam le Barkersone 1327 *SR* 3 La; Henr. Le Stiwardesone 1305 *Ass* 1 Li. The surnames ending in *-son* (generally latinized) are most common in the North of England, which seems to be due to Scandinavian influence. Instead of *filius* (etc.) there can be another word, *serviens:* Ric. serviens Hugonis; in English: Adam Henriman; Joh. le Smytheman.[2]

---

[1] *maugh* 'brother-in-law or son-in-law' (NED).

[2] Servants sometimes adopted the surnames of their masters: Will. Payne, serv. Joh. Payne 1323 Free Y 22. Ric. Redhode, draper, serviens Willelmi Redhode 1386 ib. 85.

The last element of the surnames mentioned is not seldom left out, and the new type of names thus formed ends in *-es:* Editha *Roberdes* 1327 SR 212 St (Edith *Roberti* 1332 SR 98); Emma Walteres 1327 SR 220 So; Rog. le Persones 1324 10.Ass 57 St; Margery La Mazones 1310 CR 4 Ess.

Christian names without *-es* also occur as surnames: Rad. Robert 1296 SR 52 Sx; Joh. Godefrey 1327 SR 203 So; Ric. Johan 1332 SR 262 Sx; Thom. Michel 1332 SR 273 Sx. The general explanation is that *-es* has been dropped in these names, but this is not probable, as the type without *-es* occurs earlier, e. g. Henr. Joseph 1190 P 137; Gilb. David 1230 P 23. In Paris there was a habit to take as one's surname the Christian name of one's father or some famous personage or else from the Bible (v. Michaëlsson 82 ff.). In Scandinavia, too, it often occurred that the same name was used both as a Christian name and a surname (v. Björkman: Nord. Pers. in Eng. 187 ff.). These customs apparently existed also in England, and names from the Bible were fairly common: Nich. Abraham 1342 Free Y 37; Joh. Daniel 1301 SR 111 Y.

c. SURNAMES OF OCCUPATION. The name of a person's occupation or trade was also frequently used as a surname. This was a convenient way of distinguishing different persons, as there were generally only a few who had the same trade at one place. Of these names very few instances have been found in OE (e. g. Stephanus *se īrensmiþ* Dial. Greg. 318, v. Klump 99; Æthelstan *Churchward*, Searle), but this does not necessarily mean that they were rare or later than others; in fact, we know very little about the second names of the lower classes in OE. — The surnames of occupation are undoubtedly the most interesting names, and they have therefore been made the object of the present treatise, but as only about half of them have been dealt with, a short survey of the others may be in its place here.

The first group comprises *dignitaries and officers:* 1. *Sheriff, mayor, judge, clerk,* etc.: Adam le Schirreve 1275 SR 30 Wo; Joh. le Maire 1297 SR 121 Y; Henr. Le Chauncelr' 1327 SR 37 Wo; Adam le Jugge 1309 Inq 34 Wo; Ric. le Gaylor 1275 SR 61 Wo. — 2. *Military officers:* Rad. le Comaunder 1332 SR 19 Wo; Will. le Conestable 1297 SR 135 Y; Jord. le Horsmon 1275 SR 108 Wo. — 3. *Ecclesiastical officers:* Nich. Le Parson 1327 SR 3 Wo; Rob. le Chapeleyn 1301 SR 5 Y; Will. le Priour 1332 SR 14 Wo; Will. le Chirchewart 1275 SR 90 Wo; Henr. le Scolmaister 1332 SR 25 Wo.

The second group comprises *occupations belonging to the country:*
1. *Agricultural occupations:* John Plouman 1316 3.Wake 106 Y; Joh. le Mawer 1297 SR 9 Y; Rog. le Heyberare 1306 Reg 155 Wo; Henr. le Thresschere 1294 Hal 296 Wo. — 2. *Pastoral occupations:* Thom. le Hyrde 1301 SR 49 Y; Will. le Horshird 1309 2.Wake 192 Y; Nich. le noutehird 1296 Free Y 7; Joh. le Calvehirde 1297 SR 8 Y; Rob. Le Shepherde 1327 SR 7 Wo; Joh. le Wetherhirde 1297 SR 6 Y; Will. le Swynemon 1278 Hal 106 Wo. — 3. *Forestal and venary occupations:* Maude la Forester 1251 Ass 56 Y; Ric. le Wodeward 1275 1.Wake 51 Y; Phil. le Hunte 1244 Inq 1 Wo; Will. le Venur 1269 Epi 11 Wo; Adam le Oterhunter 1246 Ass 89 La; Thom. le Fyscher 1304 Hal 477 Wo.

The third group, which is at least as large as the other two put together, comprises *those who manufacture or sell different articles,* and coincides with the surnames that are treated in this volume.

d. NICKNAMES. These names, which are also of great interest, though they form the smallest group, are very old; they occur frequently already in OE, which is probably due to the fact that many of them came from Scandinavia, where nicknames were extremely common (v. Björkman: Z. Eng. Namenk. 3—4). It is noteworthy to see the large number of nicknames — pleasant or unpleasant — that were in vogue among high and low in the Middle Ages. They were not taken by the bearer, but they were given to him by other people, and finally clung to him and even became hereditary. Nicknames could be taken from almost any domain, but a few typical examples must suffice here:

1. *From appearance, size, age:* Will. le Blake 1296 SR 69 Sx. Joh. le Rede ib. 72. Agnes la White 1327 SR 204 So. Ad. Whitberd 1332 SR 260 Sx. Rich. Balleheved 1327 SR 206 So. Rad. le Lange ib. 202. Thom. le Large ib. 209. Will. le Smale 1301 SR 84 Y. Joh. le Yong 1327 SR 202 So. — 2. *From manners, disposition:* Thom' Curtays 1296 SR 72 Sx. Henr. Gladewyne 1332 SR 6 Wo. Will. Wynsum 1275 SR 43 Wo. Rob. Bolde 1327 SR 207 So. Will. Prude 1301 SR 74 Y. Ad. le Wylde 1332 SR 260 Sx. Alic. le Schrewe 1286 *Ass* 135 Nf. — 3. *From animals and plants:* Rob. le Bule 1296 SR 70 Sx. Galfr. Lambe 1301 SR 73 Y. Joh. le Wolf 1327 SR 205 So. Joh. le Camule 1332 SR 266 Sx. Henr. Chauntecler 1327 SR 71 Wo. Henr. le Kyngesfissher 1327 *3.SR* 2 Li. Rob. le Fisch 1327 SR 205 So. Agnes Lyly 1301 SR 78 Y. — 4. *Various nicknames:* Thom' le Frend 1296 SR 69 Sx. Rob. Wisdom 1327 SR 206 So. Adam Puddyng ib. Will. Honylikker' 1333 *SR* 35 So. Lucia le Budesloue 1332 SR 265 Sx. Will. Midewynter 1327 SR 204 So. Rob. Frydey 1296 SR 12 Sx. — 5. *The »Shakespeare» type* (verb + object): Al. Schakspeye 1281 *1.Ass* 40 Li. Rad. Brekespere 1296 SR 71 Sx. Adam Louegold 1329 *SR* 31 Nf. Thom. Waggestaffe 1301 SR 2 Y. — 6. *Pageant names* (these originate from the miracle plays, in which common people acted on the stage as popes, kings, cardinals, martyrs, etc.):

Thom. le Emperur 1255 *Ass* 36 Wo. Will. Kyng 1296 SR 70 Sx. Will. Prynce 1301 SR 73 Y. Rob. le Pope 1275 SR 105 Wo. Thom. Cardinal 1199 P 45 Y. Joh. Bisshop 1327 SR 203 So.

C. **Surnames of Occupation.**

1. **Surname and Trade. A Comparison.**

When dealing with Middle English surnames of occupation one meets with the question, whether a person really had the occupation that his surname imports, or if this was only the case during a certain time or under certain circumstances. To decide this in a fully satisfactory way, is probably not possible, because the real trade can only be found out in exceptional cases. I have noted a number of instances, however, in which it appears from the context that the persons really have the same trades as their surnames imply, and from these some conclusions can be made. I here give a few of these instances from different times:

Theobaldus Cementarius 1171 P 34 (Ha). Gilb. the miller 1243 Ass 288 (So). Thom. abbas de Begeham 1262 FF 51 (Sx). Nich. the Fuller 1269 2.VH 479 (Ha). Rog. the Fuller ib. Rich. le Neyler 1274 1.Wake 96 (Y). Piers le Graver 1290 Salzman Med. Ind. 7. Nich. le Ropere 1301 CLB (C) 96 (Lo). Will. le Smyth ib. 97. Geoffrey le Sauser 1307 7.Ass 176 (St). Hugh le Seler 1333 Salzman: Med. Ind. 132 (Y). Abraham the tinner 1357 ib. 79.

From such examples one gets the impression that people generally had surnames in conformity with their trades. This is probably the case before 1300 and in the beginning of the 14th century, but towards 1350 this is less common, and in the latter half of the century it is very rare.

It is possible — and sometimes also probable — that a person had a surname of occupation as a nickname, e. g. because he had been seen performing something that belonged to the trade in question; one who mended his own boots, for instance, might be called 'the shoemaker'; one who spoke like a priest might be nicknamed accordingly. In case of surnames denoting trades, however, one should probably be careful not to exaggerate the frequency of such nicknames; they may often have their natural explanation. A clergyman, for instance, could have a common trade beside his proper calling (cf York Pl. Intr. 39), and consequently the following surnames may be »genuine»: Pet. le *Semester* vicarius ecclesie Linc' 1275 RH 318 (Li). Joh. le *Vesseler* persona ecclesie de Chitehurst 1305 FF 184 (Sx). John le *Ferrur* of N. S., chaplain 1310 FF 7 (Sx).

2. Specialized Trades.

A circumstance concerning Middle English surnames of occupation that immediately attracts one's attention is the great specialization of trades and the many names of trades that one finds within a group. Whatever group of trade-names one looks up in this book, one will find persons who have surnames of occupation that comprise such a small part of a common trade that it is surprising that they could live by this. It is unnecessary to mention any such names, they are to be found on every page.

Specialization seems to have been greatest within *the cloth industry*; there are 165 surnames belonging to this group. *The weavers* are particularly common, but also *the dyers of cloth*, which group alone comprises 25 surnames. The last group in that chapter (»Maker or seller of hats, caps, hoods, plumes») is also interesting; there are 18 different surnames in it. *The metal industry* is also very specialized: it contains 108 names. *Those who make or sell provisions* are numerous, too, and have supplied 107 surnames.

The specialization of trades that existed during this period has not advanced in later times, but the development seems rather to have gone in the opposite direction. Here may be referred to a comparison made by Bücher (Die Berufsnamen p. 16); he has collected medieval trade-names from Frankfort-on-the-Main and compared these with those trades he found in the same town from the year 1886. He came to the result that the trades in the Middle Ages were five times as numerous as those in 1886.[1] This comparison, however, is probably not quite satisfactory, because in the former case the material comprises a period of 200 years,

---

[1] This specialization of trades in the Middle German period has also been mentioned by Bähnisch: »Bei den Handwerksbezeichnungen der alten Zeit fällt oft eine ins einzelne gehende Zerteilung der Gewerbe auf» (p. 88). Cf also Nüske (p. 34), Carstens (p. 80), Mahnken (p. 40).

while in the latter case it is taken from one year only. In spite of this, however, I think that it points in the right direction, and that we can say that — with the exception of modern factories — specialization of trades was considerably greater in the Middle Ages than in modern times.

How is this early specialization to be explained? Bücher mentions one reason, in which there seems to be some truth, i. e. the inconsiderable development of medieval technique. In the keen competition people wanted to improve their productions, but this could only be obtained by means of specialization. — There are certainly other reasons, too. It should first be noticed that several names mean the same thing; a French name often occurs by the side of a synonymous native one. A great number of names of occupation came into the language after the Norman conquest, and doublets became common. In later times one of these has generally disappeared, but during this early period they existed side by side.

Another thing to which attention might be called in this connection is that an artisan often did not make only the article that the name of his trade suggests. A trade-name could be taken from that of the articles manufactured which was most important. Thus the *girdler* made not only girdles, but also small articles in metal work; the *pinner* made, besides pins, also wire articles, etc. — Sometimes a person may have had an incidental occupation by the side of his ordinary trade, and he may have taken his surname from this, since he would be better distinguished from his fellow-craftsmen in this way. This is probably the right explanation of surnames like BLODLETER, VERSHEWERE, etc.

Did this specialization exist before the Middle English period? The trade-names that are recorded in the Old English literature have been collected by Klump (Die altengl. Handwerkernamen). It is noteworthy that these are comparatively few in number; they are chiefly general names of trades, usually not specialized. A great number of the names in the present treatise are not represented there. To infer from this that all these did not exist in OE, is of course premature. The case is that we have no documents from that time in which trade-names are common. Much speaks in favour of the opinion, however, that many names of occupation did not come into existence until after the Norman conquest.

As regards *surnames* of occupation we can notice that they become less specialized towards the end of the period, and if we examine rolls after 1350, we shall be surprised at the rarity of specialized names as compared with the earlier period. The reason for this has nothing to do with what has been said above about *trades*; it is connected with the heredity of surnames, which now begins to become prevalent. The specialized surname of occupation coincided with the trade of a person and, as a rule, does not seem to have been hereditary, which is probably due to its length and to the fact that it very easily calls to mind the trade itself. The surnames that became hereditary were usually short and denoted common trades, e. g. *Smith, Cook, Tailor, Turner,* etc.; it is almost exclusively names of this kind that one finds in later rolls. It is true that there are surnames of the specialized type that have survived to modern times, e. g. *Arrowsmith, Cheesewright,* but they are probably very rare; they owe their existence to the fact that the corresponding trade has died out or that the corresponding substantive has become extinct and its signification been forgotten, e. g. *Billiter* (= ME *Belleyetere*), *Jenner* (= ME *Gynour*), etc.

3. Names not Found in NED. Antedating.

A great many of the surnames of occupation in this book are not recorded in NED; this has been specially indicated for each surname, and it is therefore unnecessary to give any list of them here. The number of them is 252. This figure shows better than anything else how much new material Middle English surnames contain. Of these 252 names, 91 are of French origin, and the others are native or Scandinavian names — with only a few exceptions from other languages.

As regards the other group of names — those that are evidenced in NED — my first instances are, in the majority of cases, earlier than NED's first quotations. It is either a question of a short period or of hundreds of years. Thus I have found 32 surnames the earliest instances of which are 300—400 years before those of NED; further: 9 surnames 400—500 years earlier; and 15 surnames more than 500 years earlier. Another thing worth noting is that the names found in NED have often only one or two quotations there, while my instances may be numerous and contain spellings and forms not found in NED.

In this connection it may be appropriate to say something about the frequency of the surnames dealt with in this book. Some of them are so rare that only one or two instances have been found, while hundreds of examples have been met with in other cases. Nothing need be mentioned here about the first category, because all instances of them have been included. But it may be of interest to know which of the others are most common. I have therefore selected the 25 surnames of which I have found most instances, and I here give a list of them. They have been arranged so that the most common come first and the least common last, but of all I have found more than 100 examples, of many of them several hundred:

Taillour, Chapman, Mareschal, Carpenter, Mason, Smyth, Coke, Coupere, Tannere, Fullere, Turnour, Milner, Muleward, Keu, Mouner, Bakere, Barber, Ferrour, Pottere, Coliere, Mercer, Feuere, Skynnere, Deyer, Leche.

D. **The Heredity of Surnames.**

There has not yet been made any satisfactory examination of the question when and under what conditions surnames became hereditary in England. Statements concerning this are not lacking, but they are very divergent and founded on suppositions or on unsatisfactory grounds; the fact is that it is very easy to make erroneous conclusions. I have therefore considered it appropriate to enter into this question more in detail than in other cases and give the results that can be obtained from the material that has been examined.

It must at once be emphasized that there is no definite time when surnames became fixed. This happened very slowly, and during a period of more than a hundred years there existed hereditary names by the side of non-hereditary in the same class of society; if we include the surnames of the Normans, this period will extend over 300 years. The case is that the French noblemen who came over with William the Conqueror had surnames which often descended to their sons, and thus became hereditary. In the Introduction to Domesday Book several such persons are mentioned, who have become the ancestors of aristocratic families bearing their surnames, e. g. Rob. *Dispensator* (Ellis p. 404), Henr. *de Ferieres* (p. 418), Rob. *de Stadford* (p. 487), Albericus *de Ver* (p. 498), etc. — Similar hereditary surnames of French origin often occur in early rolls:

Rob. *de Ferrariis* filius Roberti *de Ferrariis* 1201 3.Ass 73 (St). — Rob. *le Blund;* Rob. *le Blund,* his father 1246 Ass 14 (La). — Rob. *de Gurnay;* Hawise *de Gurnay,* his grandmother; Maelus *de Gurnay* her kinsman, Pet. *de Gurnay* 1243 Ass 173—4 (So). — Phil. *Marmiun;* Rob. *Marmiun,* his father 1248 4.Ass 105 (St). — Will. *Maunsell;* Walt. *Maunsell,* his father 1248 4.Ass 105 (St). — Rob. *Purcel;* Henry *Purcel,* his son 1247 4.Ass 107 (St). — Rob. *Durand* the elder; Rob. *Durand* the younger; Eleanor *Durand;* Rich. *Durand* (their father) 1268 Ass 32 (So). — Juliana Mauger filia Claricie Mauger 1268 BBA 14 So. — Rog. *Louel* father of Rob. *Louel* 1277 Ass 103 (So). — Walt. *Mustard,* father of Will. Mustard and Cristina Mustard ib. 119—20. — Nich. *la Warre,* father of Thom. *la Warre* ib. 126.

It should not be inferred from this that surnames were regularly hereditary in France during the present period; the case is that hereditary surnames began to appear there at about the same time as in England. An examination of this question has been made by Michaëlsson (p. 142 ff.) with regard to the surnames in Paris about 1300. He comes to the result that there are a fairly large number of names that are hereditary, but that many are still only individual.

I now pass over to an inquiry into the heredity among common people in England. It is not easy to find suitable material for this, as it only occurs in exceptional cases that two persons' surnames and relationship are mentioned. I have noted those cases I have come across when collecting my material. I first give examples of hereditary surnames and then of such names as are not hereditary.

The earliest instances of heredity are: Reg. de Steinwath pater Ade de Steinwath 1218 Ass 56 Li. Sarra de Burum, Ran. de Burum filius suus 1219 Ass 137 Li. Warin le Pestur, Will. le Pestur, his father 1246 Ass 11 La. Rob. le Cyrur pater Johannis le Cyrur 1263 *Ass* 14 Sx. These are not certain, however, since father and son might take their surnames from the same place-name, and since the son often had the same trade as his father. — The following examples, however, are beyond doubt: John le Wylde, Laurence

Wylde (his father) 1275 Ass 17 So. Rich. le Kat, Adam le Kat (his son) ib. 22. These are, then, the earliest certain instances that I have found. — I now give a selection of later instances; most of the local surnames, which occur frequently, have been excluded:

Maud le Cygur, Will. le Cygur, her father 1276 Ass 52 So. Rob. de Dockeseye, Hugh de Dockeseye (brothers) 1276 6.Ass 81 St. Rich. del Mes, father of Rich. son of Rich. del Mes ib. 78. Ralf le Vylur of Westwode, uncle of Will. le Vylur of Westwode 1279 Ass 211 So. Joh. le Tauerner fil. Reginaldi le Tauerner 1280 *Ass* 70 Ha. Nich. son of Nich. le Archer, Will. le Archer, the great grandfather (proavum) of Nich. 1284 ib. 133. Rob. son of Thomas le Hount, Will. le Hount, his uncle 1285 Ass 212 La. Will., the son of Peter le Pundermaker 1286 CDN 7 Nf, Will. le Pundermakere (same person) 1303 ib. 97. Steph. de Bagenholte, Rob. de Bagenholte, John de Bagenholte (three brothers) 1293 6.Ass 284 St. Will. le Siour called le Gos, Alan Gos (his brother) ib. 269. Matilda la Brune the mother of Phil. le Brune; Rob. son of Rob. le Brune 1301 7.Ass 88 St. Thom. le Screvayn of Newcastle, John Screveyn of Newcastle (brothers) 1306 ib. 154—5. Will. le Flemyng, Adam le Flemyng (brothers) ib. 166. Peter de Broke le Mustarder, Will. le Mustader (his son) 1313 CDN 43 Nf.

The following examples have all been taken from BBA (So):

Ric. de Godyvelande filius Roberti de Godyvelande 1245 p. 4. Will. Bat filius Willelmi Bat 1296 p. 31. Thom. de Langebrok filius Walteri de Langebrok 1299 p. 36. Will. Cori filius et heres Johannis Cori 1315 p. 55. Joh. Halewey filius Johannis Halewey 1322 p. 70. Joh. Cabbel filius Thome Cabbel 1326 p. 78. Will. Wrench filius Roberti Wrench 1328 p. 80. Matheus Kelyng filius Stephani Kelyng 1333 p. 85. Johanna Godwyne relicta Johannis Godwyne 1343 p. 96. Walt. Bat filius Gilberti Bat 1343 p. 98. Joh. Busschel filius Galfridi Busschel 1344 p. 99. Joh. Saladyn fil. et heres quondam Johannis Saladyn iunioris 1345 p. 102. Will. Hatherych filius Johannis Hatherych 1347 p. 106. Thom. Goldsmyth fil. et heres Thome le Goldsmyth 1349 p. 110. Joh. Donman filius Johannis Donman 1366 p. 152. Alicia Herker, quondam uxor Johannis Herker; Jacobus Herker (son of Alicia H.) 1376 p. 230.

From Free Y (instances have been included up to 1390; after this year they become very numerous):

Joh. de Catton, frater Ran. de Catton 1311 p. 14. Gilb. de Carliolo, fil. Andreæ de Carliolo, carnifex 1327 p. 24. Ric. le sauser, pelter, filius Johannis le sauser 1331 p. 26. Hen. de Amias, fil. Rog. de Amyas 1332 p. 27. Rob. de Pountfracto, frater Adæ de Pontfracto, taillour 1334 p. 30. Will. le couper, fil. Adæ le couper, de Neuton 1335 p. 31. Gerwinus Giffard, de Gaunt, tixtor; Levekyn Giffard, frater ejus 1356 p. 51. Joh. Britte, fil. Thomæ Britte 1380 p. 78. Ric. Marshall, filius Rogeri Marshall, de Bilburgh 1381 p. 79. Rad. Cooke, filius Roberti Cooke 1383 p. 80. Thomas del Gare, filius Willelmi del Gare, mercer 1384 p. 81. Will. Beaumond, filius Thomæ

Beaumond ib. Joh. Marreys, mercer, filius Johannis Marreys 1386 p. 85.
Rob. Fulbaron, fil. Rogeri Fulbaron 1389 p. 89.

The above instances, in which the relationship is expressly mentioned, are not the only cases from which hereditary surnames can be inferred. A few other ways have also been tried. Thus it not seldom occurs that two persons bearing the same surname and Christian name are styled *senior* and *junior;* in most cases these certainly denote father and son:

Joh. Bosse Junior', Joh. Bosse Senior' 1296 SR 35 Sx. Joh. Rolf Senior', Joh. Rolf Junior' SR 1327 175 Sx. Joh. Gotewyk senior, Joh. Gotewyk Junior' 1332 SR 270 Sx. Joh. Wyot senior', Joh. Wyot junior' ib. 287. Joh. le Walsh junior', Joh. le Walsh senior' ib. 306. Rich. le Fest the elder, Rich. le Fest the younger 1340 FF 97 Sx. Thom. Ython, jun(io)r, mariner, Thom. Ython, senior, mariner 1401 Free Y 105.

Another more far-reaching way of establishing heredity is afforded by the subsidy rolls; the case is that in these, where the surnames are arranged by villages, there often occur two or more persons bearing the same surname in the same village. If this surname is local, which is the most common case, this is no definite proof of its heredity, nor if it is occupative; but if the same *nickname* occurs two or more times in the same village (among 25 persons or thereabouts), I think we are justified in assuming that it is hereditary. The four following persons: Rob. Buffary, Will. Buffary, Thom. Buffary, Joh. Buffary (1327 SR 253 St) appear in the same village, where only 12 persons are mentioned. Cf also Will. Kyng, Augustinus Kyng, Rob. Kyng (1296 SR 5 Sx) in the same village (among 22 persons). Such instances can hardly be explained as due to a mere coincidence, they must belong to the same family.

As has already been mentioned, local surnames are most frequently met with; in most subsidy rolls one finds such examples (two or more of the same name in one village) on almost every page. They may very well be hereditary, but I have not taken much account of them, and only a few instances will be mentioned here:

Reg. de Wynham, Galfr. de Wynham, Beniamin' de Wynham, Joh. de Wynham, Walt. de Wynham 1296 SR 9 Sx. — Will. de Posterne, Agn. atte Posterne, Petrus de Posterne, Will. de Posterne, Andr. de Posterne, Henr' de Posterne 1332 SR 322 Sx. — Rog. de Leghe, Rob. de Leghe, Adam de Leghe, Gilb. de Leghe 1327 SR 162 So.

It is not only local surnames that occur frequently in this way, other types of names are also found in abundance. I must therefore confine myself to giving only a few instances from each subsidy roll:

SR 1332 Sr: Rob. Koc, Joh. Koc, Sim. Koc 34. Rob. le Limer, Pet. Limer' 45. Steph. Hereward, Will. Hereward 45. Rob. Godyng', Brice Godyng' 50. — SR 1296 Sx: Will. Lump, Hereward le Lump 32. Nic. Henry, Rad. Henry 33. Petr' Monek, Will. Monek 34. Ric. Hayne, Martin' Hayne 38. — SR 1327 Sx: Thom' Arnold, Joh. Arnold, Will. Arnold 187. Will. Sloman, Joh. Sloman 189. Joh. Eueny(ng), Walt. Euenyng, Thom. Euenyng 191. Rob. le Felagh, Dionis' le Felagh 193. Rob. Dauy, Agn' Dauy 195, Ad' Daui 196. — SR 1332 Sx: Symon le Wroghte 298, Will. le Wroghte, Hugo le Wreghte 299. Joh. Knoller, Walt. Knoller 300. Joh. Elyot, Joh. Elyot, Rob. Elyot 302. Joceus Partrych, Rob. Partrych, Matild' Partrych 304, Joh. Partrych 305. Walt. Adelwald, Joh. Adelwald 306. — SR 1327 So: Rog. Lude, Nich. Lude 184. Rob. le White, Will. le White 188. Adam Bolle, Thom. Bolle 190. Joh. Melkesop, Will. Melkesop 190. Will. Geffray, Joh. Geffray 192. — SR 1275 Wo: Adam le Surreys, Thom. le Surreys, Joh. le Surreys 80. Joh. Coc, Ric. Coc, Walt. Coc 80. Will. Travers, Adam Travers, Joh. Travers 82. Joh. Savage, Gregorius Savage, Will. Savage, Walt. Savage 77. — SR 1327 Wo: Juliana Robates, Joh. Robates 23. Joh. Baldwyne, Henr. Baldwyne, Rob. Baldwyne, Joh. Baldwyne 23. Isolda Le Large, Alicia Le Large, Walt. Le Large 24. Will. Broun, Ric. Broun 25. — SR 1332 Wo: Ric. Palmar, Will. Palmar 19. Will. Henry, Joh. Henry 21. Galfr. Martyn, Joh. Martyn, Crystiana Martyn 24. Ric. Bonevyll, Joh. Bonevyll 11, Thom. Bonevyll 12. Henr. Gladewyne, Petr. Gladewyne 6. — SR 1327 St: Rob. Byssop, Steph. Byssop 213. Thom. Wytecoke, Henr' Wytecok 215. Alicia le Rede, Joh. le Rede 243. Joh. Lovekyn, Benedictus Lovekyn 245. — SR 1332 St: Will. Wylymot, Will. Wylymot 108. Joh. Gamel, Hug' Gamel 111. Joh. Devyle, Will. Devyle 113. Sim. Fox, Elias Fox 113. — SR 1332 La: Ric. le Harpour', Thom. le Harpour, Rob. le Harpour 71. — SR 1297 Y: Will. Bard', Margar' Bard' 135. Ernisius Stersman, Henr. Steresman 137. Steph. Frauncays, Nich. Frauncis, Ric. Frankis 125. Alan. Hogge, Rad. Hogge 125. — SR 1301 Y: Beatric' le Bret', Nich. le Bret' 74. Rad. le Barne, Hugo Barne 77. Juliana Norays, Thom. Norays, Agnes Norays 77. Adam Byschop, Rob. Bischop 82.

It is not easy to ascertain the heredity of *surnames of occupation,* but there is one type of names that is generally believed to be proving, namely that followed by a trade-name, e. g. Henr. Chaundeler, fruiter 1332 SR 82 Lo. Joh. le hatter, parcheminer 1305 Free Y 11. Much speaks in favour of this opinion, though it must be admitted that a person probably could have two trades at the same time if these were insignificant,[1] and that the surname

---

[1] Cf Adam de Ireland, *cotoler vel haberdasscher* 1344 Free Y 30; such instances are rare so early.

may sometimes be explained as a nickname. Of this kind of names, which are rare in early rolls but grow more and more common in the 14th century, I have recorded more than a hundred instances, but only a few will be mentioned here:

Joh. Pistor, »peleter» 1281 CLB (B) 8 Lo. Walt. le Seinturer, »coureer» ib. 10. Joh. le Nettere, paternostrer 1298 ib. 69. Rich. le Plomer, chaplain 1305 CDN 106 Nf. Joh. le Combestere, piscenarius ib. 107. Will. le Mustardman, fishman 1332 ib. 176. Hugo le Tayllor, brewer 1332 SR 65 Lo. Walt. le Mareschal, Bocher ib. 74. John le Clerk, hodere ib. 82.

From Free Y: Rob. le parchemyner, pistor 1296 p. 6. Hugo le biller, pelter ib. Joh. le carpenter, de Thresk, cordwaner 1309 p. 12. Thomas le mouner, portur 1312 p. 14. Thom. Launder, mariner 1330 p. 26. Rob. le cue, de Acum, tannator 1335 p. 31. Thomas Couper, cordwaner 1344 p. 38. Joh. le graver, de Beverle, pulter 1350 p. 44. Joh. le sauscer, teghlemaker 1352 p. 47. Joh. le clerk, nailer 1360 p. 55.

I now proceed to give instances of surnames that are *not* hereditary:

Walt. le Swein pater Willelmi le Paumer 1221 Ass 482 Wo. Rob. le Sawyere, John Golde of Pederton (brothers) 1270 Ass 139 So. Rob. clericus filius Roberti le Sopere 1275 *1.Ass* 8 Wo. Rob. le Turner, Will. le Pestur, his father 1285 Ass 210 La. Pet. le Chaucer son of John le Tundur 1287 CDN 15 Nf. Beatrix le Clubber, daughter of Will. le Verer 1302 ib. 91. Adam le Dun, Laurence le Keu (his father) 1292 6.Ass 204 St. Ad. Le Skynnere fil. Ade Le Potter' 1305 *Ass* 9 So. Will. Marchant fil. Gilb. le Tannere 1320 *Ass* 19 So.

In BBA (So) the examples of non-heredity are much less common than those of heredity; after 1318 I have only found two instances of the former kind (whereas hereditary surnames have been found in abundance):

Alicia Tumpere relicta Galfridi Fronckeleyn, undated (c1290) 25. Will. de Wemedone fil. Danielis de Edinestone, undated (c1298) 32. Joh. le Tayllur filius Henrici le Tuker, undated (c1307) 44. Walt. Pocok et Johanna de Kerdesbery uxor sua 1311 p. 51. Rog. Capellanus filius Willelmi Textoris 1318 p. 64. Joh. Benet fil. et heres Benedicti Cloteworthy 1358 p. 128. Nic. Webbe de Brugewater et Angnes Palmer (his wife) 1366 p. 153.

From Free Y: Will. de Kent, fil. Isabelle Burdon 1315 p. 16. Nich. Keller, fil. Jurdani le scrivayner 1317 p. 17. Will. de Ripon, filius Thoma· de Skelton 1320 p. 19. Thom. le seler, fil. Johannis le couraur 1327 p. 24. Will. de Brigg, fil. Johannis le taillour 1332 p. 27. Thom. le parchemyner, filius Johannis le hatter 1334 p. 30. Joh. de Esingwold, filius Roberti de Hoby 1340 p. 35. Joh. de Kyrkeby, fil. Willelmi del Bakhouse 1367 p. 65. Rob. de Ellerton, mercer, filius Rogeri Alcok 1379 p. 78. Joh. de Moreton, fil. Willelmi de Dalby 1391 p. 91.

The relationship is frequently mentioned in Free Y — except in the beginning — and this roll is therefore valuable for the present purpose. My examination of it has shown that before 1350 there are 14 instances of hereditary surnames and 30 of non-hereditary names. The corresponding figures for 1350—75 are 8 and 10; for 1375—1400: 55 and 8. We thus see how rapidly the first group (hereditary surnames) increases at the end of the century. During the period 1400—25 there occur more than 200 instances of heredity, but only 11 of non-heredity. Even after this time surnames of the latter type are found now and then, but the percentage is very small; the last instance I have found is from 1468.

After having thus supplied the essential part of my material, I will now give the conclusions that I have arrived at. It should first be pointed out that the various types of names did not become fixed at the same time. *Local surnames,* especially those that denote a person's dwelling-place (generally preceded by *atte*), were probably the first names to adopt this function. This is natural since such names automatically became the same for father and son. *Nicknames* were also hereditary very early, and it is easy to establish when these were fixed or not. It is sometimes alleged that *surnames of occupation* became hereditary early, because the same trade often passed over from father to son. This has not been borne out by my material; at any rate, I have not found many instances of this kind. In my opinion it is quite to the contrary; I think it took a long time before *a baker* called himself *Smith* etc.; these surnames probably became fixed fairly late. There is another kind of names, however, that became hereditary still later, viz. the type Thomas *Adamsone,* and this needs no explanation. Even as late as 1450 one can find an instance of the following kind: Thomas *Johnson,* baker, fil. *Johannis* Henrison, baker 1450 Free Y 171. Such examples are certainly exceptional so late; anyhow, instances of heredity occur earlier, e. g. Petrus Williamson, plasterer, fil. Nicholai Williamson, plasterer 1419 Free Y 129.

It is probable that surnames did not become fixed definitively at the same time in the whole of England. A large material would be required to solve this question, however, but to judge from my own, it seems as if this took place some fifty years earlier in the South than in the North. In York surnames were generally hereditary by the end of the 14th century; the occasional instances of non-heredity that occur later should not be taken much account of. Even though a person had a hereditary surname, there was nothing that prevented him from adopting a new one, just as people do nowadays. This was, of course, easier during this time when the same importance was not attached to the surname as now. Moreover, it still happened that a person had two surnames; in this case the son could choose one of these, and thus father and son might appear with different surnames. I have noted a few instances of this kind, e. g. Rob. *Bowland,* fysshmanger, fil. Rogeri *Floyter* al(ia)s *Bowland* 1415 Free Y 124. Will. *Gayt,* cordewaner, fil. Willelmi *Gayt* al(ia)s *Stylyngton,* cordewaner 1420 ib. 131. In the following example the son (John) has sometimes one, sometimes the other of his father's names: Matthew *Spicer,* otherwise called »*Tyce*», »goldbeter» 1414 CLB (I) 124 (Lo); John *Spicer* ib.; John *Tyce* »goldbeter» 1416 ib. 153; John *Spicer,* otherwise called »*Tyce*», son of Matthew *Tyce,* late goldbeater 1416 ib. 127. — Even in the 16th century a person may have two surnames: Hen. *Walmesley* al(ia)s *Maltman,* fissher 1517 Free Y 240. Joh. *Skryvener* alias *Fletcher,* tapiter 1533 ib. 253.

In summing up we may say that hereditary surnames existed among the Norman noblemen already in the early 12th century. Among people in general they began to come into use in the following century, and by the end of this they were fairly frequent (esp. local surnames and nicknames). This custom increased rapidly in the course of the fourteenth century, and by the end of it practically all people were provided with hereditary surnames.

Why did surnames become hereditary? The reasons for this are several. In the first place we may mention the imitation of the nobility. It is usual — in many respects — for the lower classes to imitate those who stand higher than themselves. The surnames of the nobility seem to have become fixed owing to the fact that their fees were hereditary (cf Michaëlsson 174, Dauzat 78). — One might also think that a need was felt to unite the members of a family by means of a common surname. In Old English times this need had been satisfied by the alliteration of the Christian names within a family, but as this was not possible in the Middle English period, another way had to be found out. — The place where a family lived was generally the same through several generations, and as local surnames are extremely common, this type of names has probably to a great extent contributed to the fixing of surnames. As surnames of this kind were most common in the country, I think that they began to become hereditary there (the nobility also lived in the country). The general opinion (in France and Germany; v. Michaëlsson 166), however, is that this procedure began in towns, but I cannot find any reasons that support this view. My material from the subsidy rolls shows that hereditary surnames were very common in the country, even as early as the end of the 13th century.

E. **Two Suffixes of Obscure History.**

1. **The Ending -ESTER.**

Sufficient material from the early Middle Ages has hitherto been lacking to elucidate the problems that are connected with the occurrence of the endings *-ester* and *-ier*. As the surnames treated in this volume contain much valuable material of this kind, it may be appropriate to give a short account of the results that can be obtained from this.

The ending *-ester* occurs very frequently; I have found 42 surnames containing it, which are as follows:

Bakestere	Deyster	Scherestere
Blacchester	Dreyster	Semester
Blakestere	Fullester	Sewstere
Bleykestere	Girdelester	Sheppestere
Blextere	Heustere	Sopestere
Bredmongestere	Huckestere	Tannestere
Brewstere	Litester	Thakestere
Kallemakestere	Lokyestere	Touestre
Capiestere	Madster	Upholdestere
Cardestere	Maltestere	Wadester
Kembestere	Mongestere	Webbester
Combestere	Quernestere	Whelster
Corklittster	Ridelestere	Wyggester
Cuppestere	Ropestere	Wollestere

Some of these surnames are very common, e. g. *Bakestere, Brewstere, Litester, Webbester,* while in some cases only one or two instances have been found.

It is true that the surnames in *-ester* occur in the whole of England, but with regard to their frequency there is a distinct difference. The case is that they chiefly belong to the Anglian counties; most instances have been found in *Nf* (over 100 inst.), *Li, Y, La,* and *St,* but many also in *Wo* and *Ess.* In the WS counties *(Sx, Ha, So)* these surnames occur very seldom; thus I have only found 3 inst. in *So,* 5 in *Ha,* and 11 in *Sx.*

We now come to the difficult question whether the suffix *-ester* is a feminine ending or not. There has been no difference of opinion about this until recently, when Jespersen propounded an entirely new theory (Linguistica 420—429). According to the general view, *-ester* was originally a special feminine ending, which, however, was later applied to men as well as to women. This transition from fem. to masc. is usually explained through the supposition that the work that was at first done only by women, was later performed by men, too, and that the fem. denominations were transferred on men at the same time.

Jespersen believes this theory to be »entirely false», and he tries to prove »that the ending from the very first was used for both sexes». »The transition of a special feminine ending to one used of men also is, so far as I can see, totally unexampled in all languages. Words denoting both sexes may in course of time be specialized so as to be used of one sex only, but not the other way. ... Family names, too, would hardly be taken from names denoting women doing certain kinds of work: yet this is assumed for family names like *Baxter, Brewster, Webster;*[1] their use as personal names is only natural under the supposition that they mean exactly the same as *Baker, Brewer, Weaver* or *Web,* i. e., some one whose business or occupation it is to bake, brew or weave.»

In the following Jespersen points out »that from the very first words formed with this ending were very frequently applied to males, some even exclusively so. It is true that some are found with the feminine meaning only, but these are chiefly formations created on the spur of the moment by glossarists who wanted a translation of a Latin feminine. Most, if not all, of the words belonging to actual living speech were evidently two-sex

---

[1] I have not seen any suggestion of this kind. The case is, however, that surnames became hereditary much later, than Jespersen seems to think, and the names mentioned were, of course, often used also of men at that time.

words from the first, and like most two-sex words denoted occupations chiefly followed by men.»[1]

The material, however, that Jespersen has used is scanty, especially that in Middle English. In this respect — as in many others — valuable information can be obtained from the surnames; an examination of the above-mentioned names has given the following result.

Of the 42 surnames in *-ester* 16 are used only of women, and 12 only of men; the remaining 14 are used both of men and women.

I have made a calculation of all the instances of these surnames that I have found in order to establish how many (different) persons of either sex they denote; the figures are: 77 women and 242 men. These figures, however, do not show the actual relation between males and females, because the names of women do not occur as often as the names of men in medieval rolls. I have therefore examined 2000 instances of my other surnames in this respect and come to the result that the names of men are 12 times as common as those of women. We shall therefore have to multiply the number of female surnames (77) by 12 (= 924). The final result will thus be: 79 % female names and 21 % male names. I think that these figures show the percentage of the surnames in *-ester* that would have occurred in Middle English rolls, if the names of women had been as common as those of men.

Another thing revealed by the above-mentioned examination is that there is a distinct difference between the Saxon and Anglian counties. In the former the names in *-ester* are almost regularly used of women only, but in the latter they are very often applied to men. Thus. of the 11 (different) persons who have been found bearing such names in *Sx*, 10 are women and 1 is a man; further: in *Ha* 5 women (no men); in *So:* 2 women, 1 man. *Ess* has apparently been influenced by the Anglian counties: 16 women, 7 men, and *Wo* still more: 8 women, 15 men. In the Anglian counties the names of men are predominant: in *Nf:* 9 women,

---

[1] Cf NED: »In OE. the suffix may be said to have retained its original function, for the few instances in which it is used as a masculine are renderings of Latin designations of men exercising functions which among the English were peculiar to women, as *byrdistræ* embroiderer (gl. *blaciarius, primicularius*), *bæcestre* baker (gl. *pistor*), *séamestre* tailor (gl. *sartor*), *wæscestre* washer (gl. *fullo*)».

66 men; in *Li:* 9 women, 55 men; in *Y:* 6 women, 41 men; in *La:* 6 women, 30 men; in *St:* 26 men and no women at all. Besides these instances there are a few in »outside» counties (*Lo* 3, *Sr* 1, *Oxf* 1, *Hu* 1) all referring to women. — Cf NED -STER.

From what has been said, we may conclude that during the present period the suffix *-ester* was generally felt to be a feminine ending. This was at least the case in the South of England,[1] but even in the Anglian counties there is — if we take into consideration the relation between male and female surnames in general — preponderance for the names of women.

With regard to the nature of the suffix *-ester* some elucidation can be obtained from the significations of the present surnames, especially of those that occur most frequently. The most common of them are the following (ranged after frequency; the figure denotes the number of persons that have been found bearing the surname): Bakestere 63, Litester 60, Webbester 47, Brewstere 33, Huckestere 10, Heustere 9, Blextere 8, Kembestere 7, Deyster 7, Sheppestere 7, Bleykestere 6, Thakestere 5, Combestere 5, Dreyster 5. All the trades denoted by these names — with the only exception of *Thakestere* — are of such a character that they can very well be supposed to have originally been carried out only (or almost only) by women.[2] I think, therefore, that we are entitled to conclude that the words in *-ester* were at first used only of women, and that the old and general theory holds true. This ending, however, was also applied to men in OE, but that this happened so often as it really did, may be due to the fact that women do not appear as frequently as men in the OE sources.

The most common of the words in *-ester* probably early lost their feminine character in some degree, whereas this was retained in the rare words. The case is that the surnames of which only a few instances have been found, generally refer to women, while the three most common names are very often used of men (*Bakestere* 7 women, 56 men; *Litester* 6 women, 54 men; *Webbester* 3 women, 44 men). That the names in *-ester* are not used more often of women than is really the case, is to a certain extent due to this

---

[1] This may, in some measure, explain why the surnames in *-ester* occur less frequently in the South.

[2] This is also the case with the remaining less common surnames, but these are perhaps later or temporary formations.

last-mentioned circumstance; this particularly refers to the Anglian counties, to which the three names belong.

It has not been my intention to say that the results that my material seems to give, would be in any way conclusive, but only to indicate what I think might be inferred from it.

2. The Ending -IER.

The material afforded by the present surnames with regard to the suffix *-ier,* which is still more obscure than that dealt with above, is earlier and more instructive than that given by NED (s. v. -IER) for the explanation of this ending. The surnames containing *-ier* regularly — or almost regularly — are the following (the year of the earliest instance spelt *-ier* is also given):

Bachiere 1280	Glasyer 1316	Siuyere 1275
Bowyer 1255	Heliere 1280	Solier 1279
Brasier 1327	Hosiere 1197	Sporiere 1288
Capiere 1275	Lokyere 1280	Tawyere 1280
Kydiere 1275	Lotyer 1296	Whittawyere 1280
Coliere 1172	Meriere 1320	
Gatier 1332	Sawyere 1270	

Besides these surnames one instance in *-ier* has been found of each of the following surnames (together with other more numerous instances in *-er*): Aruwemakere (-makiere 1305), Blacker (Blakiere 1332), Borere (Boriere 1318, 2 inst.), Bowemakere (-makiere 1309), Fleshhewere (Fleshewyer' 1323), Holere (Holyer' 1319, 3 inst.), Lakere (Lakyare 1391), Lyther (Lythyer' 1332), Netmaker (-makyer' 1288), Oylemaker (Hulimakiere 1221), Paniermaker (-makier' 1310), Skynnere (Skiniere 1280), Spadere (Spadier' 1332), Towere (Towyere 1280, 2 inst.), Tunnere (Tuniere 1280), Wirdragher (-drawiere 1320), Whittowere (Wyttowier 1281).[1]

There is also another group of surnames, viz. those of French origin, that must be taken into consideration. In OF these end in *-ier,* but this ending normally becomes *-er* in AF. In the surnames,

---

[1] I have also found two instances in which *-i-* occurs in the fem. ending *-ester: Capiestere* 1280 (Ha), *Lokyestere* 1288 (Sx); these are exceptional.

however, there sometimes occur forms in *-ier*, but though the French names are extremely numerous, there are none that have this suffix regularly; there only occur occasional instances, especially of those names that are very frequent. Thus, of each of the following surnames I have generally found only one or two inst. in *-ier*, but often 50—100 inst. (sometimes more) in *-er:*

Aguiller, Botoner, Bucher, Caneuacer, Carpenter, Cordewaner, Cuver, Draper, Feutrer, Furmager, Furner, Lyneter, Lorimer, Mercer, Parmenter, Rower, Sachere, Sauser, Seinter, Teynturer, Teler, Wayder, Wanter.

According to NED, the suffix *-ier* »is of obscure and app. of diverse origin. Among the earliest examples are *cottier* (*cotier*), *tilier,* and *bowyer:* the first is a. OF. *cotier* = med. L. *cotārius,* and its retention of *-ier* is remarkable, because OF. *-ier* normally became *-er* in AFr. and Eng., as in *butler, draper, farmer; tiliere* (1250—1400), 'tiller, cultivator', appears to be an analogical formation on OE. *tilia,* early ME. *tilie,* on the analogy of such pairs as OE. *hunta,* ME. *huntere,* since the etymological formation would have been *tilere;* for *bowyer* (1297 *bowiare,* a1450 *bowȝere, bowyere*), the suggestion has been made that the *i, y,* represents the ȝ of ME. *boȝe,* Bow; but this is doubtful. Other examples are *collier* (15th c. *koliere, cholier, colyer,* etc.), *lawyer* 1362 (but also, a1400, *lawer*), *lockyer* (1407 *lokier*), *brazier* (1400—50 *brasier, brasyere*), *hellier, hillyer* (15th c. *helier, helyer, hillyer*), *spurrier* a1450, *halyer* 1479 (*haulyer* 1577), *grazier* c1500.» (NED).

It is remarkable how late the words are that NED quotes; only two of them are evidenced before the end of my period.

The chief origin, then, of this ending is, according to NED, the assimilation to words from French in *-ier,* and this is the only explanation given under separate words like *collier, glazier, hellier, sawyer,* etc. As I have already pointed out, however, the French forms in *-ier* were very rare, and can hardly have had such great influence.[1] Other reasons for this will be given later. I shall try to prove that the suffix is of native origin — from a source, which, curiously enough, has not (so far as I know) been mentioned before.

If we examine the surnames in *-ier,* we shall find that there are two types:

---

[1] A thing passed by in silence by NED is that the first instance of *cottier* (*cotier*), which seems to have been considered as a very important word for the origin of *-ier,* is as late as 1386. In my opinion *cottier* is a native word (fr. OE *cot* or *cote*), and the *-i-* is quite regular.

1. This type is formed from OE verbs in *-ian* with *short* stems: *Brasier* fr. OE *brasian*; *Heliere* fr. OE *helian*; *Tawyere* and *Whittawyere* fr. OE *tawian*; *Hulimakiere, Netmakyer', Aruwemakiere, Bowemakiere, Paniermakier'* fr. OE *macian*; *Boriere* fr. OE *borian*. In the names of this kind the *-i-* is certainly regular, though NED is of the opposite opinion (cf what is said above about *tiliere*, which comes fr. OE *tilian*; cf also *brazier, hellier*, etc. in NED). It is quite as regular in this case, as it is in the corresponding ME verbs, e. g. *borien, makien*, etc.;[1] the geographical distribution of the endings *-ier* and *-ien* is also the same (v. below). This type in *-ier* occurs already in OE: *wudigere (wudiere)* 'wood-man, wood-carrier' (NED a1100) fr. *wudian* 'to cut wood'. — The derivatives of other kinds of verbs have regularly *-er*; the occasional exceptions (Fleshewyer; Towyere, Wyttowier; Wirdrawiere) are analogous formations.

2. The second type of names in *-ier* is formed from OE substantives with *short* stems; the OE substantive has one or two syllables: *Bowyer* fr. OE *boga*; *Coliere* fr. OE *col*; *Glasyer* fr. OE *glæs*; *Hosiere* fr. OE *hosa*; *Lokyere* fr. OE *loc*; *Sawyere* fr. OE **sagu, saga; Siuyere* fr. OE *sife; Sporiere* fr. OE *spora;* further one instance of each of the following surnames: *Bachiere* fr. OE *bœce*; *Blakiere* fr. OE *blæc*; *Gatier* fr. OE *geat*; *Holyer'* fr. OE *hol*; *Lakyare* fr. OE *lacu*; *Lythyer'* fr. OE *hlip*; *Lotyer* fr. OE *hlot*; *Meriere* fr. OE *mere; Solier* fr. OE *sol; Spadier'* fr. OE *spadu*.[2] — There are remarkably few exceptions to this type of names; though there are a large number of surnames with *long* stems (e. g. Crockere, Feltere, Glouere, Hornere, etc.), there is — besides the two occasional instances *Skiniere* and *Tuniere* — only one surname that has the ending *-ier*, viz. *Capiere* (spelt with one *-p-*) fr. OE *cœppe*. Some words with long stems have later been reformed on the analogy of those with short stems, e. g. *Clothier* fr. OE *clāþ* (I have only found the form *Clothere*).

---

[1] It is true that the *-i-* later disappeared in these verbs, but this is due to the fact that the whole ending was lost, which did not take place in the substantives.

[2] This occurrence of *-ier*, which does not seem to have been observed before, has sometimes helped me to settle uncertain etymologies: *Meriere* fr. OE *mere*, not *gemǣre*; *Blakiere* fr. OE *blæc*, not *blācian*, etc.

The *-i-* of the second type (*Coliere*) is not so easy to explain as that of the first type (*Brasier*). It can hardly be due to a regular development, and must therefore be formed on the analogy of similar words with *-i-*. I think these must be the first type, *Brasier*, the stem of which is also short. It is true that the words of this kind are not very common, but this possibility is, at any rate, more probable than the influence from the French words. These may have facilitated the development, but the fact is that among the 23 instances of the French surnames in *-ier* (v. above) there are only two or three with short stems. Moreover, these names occur regularly in the whole of England, and not only in the South (cf below).

In general, the words in *-ier* probably arose before the lengthening of vowels in open syllables, which took place in the first half of the 13th century — in the North in the 12th cent. (Jordan). The earliest instances of the surnames are: *Coliere* 1172; *Hosiere* 1197; *Hulimakiere* 1221; *Bowyer* 1255. As has already been mentioned, *wudiere* occurs in OE.

The surnames in *-ier* do not occur regularly in the whole of England; most of them are confined to the Saxon counties. There is one surname, however, that occurs regularly and frequently in all parts of England, i. e. *Coliere*; this is probably a very early word. Besides this, there occur stray instances in the Anglian counties of the following names: *Bowyer, Kydiere, Hosiere* (Y 5 inst., Nf 4), *Lokyere, Siuyere*. In other cases the instances found in these counties end in *-er*. This is sometimes the case also in the South of England; v. BOWYER, LOKYERE, SAWYERE. These circumstances may have some connection with the different times for the lengthening of vowels in open syllables. Some words in *-ier* probably arose after this process had taken place; this may have been the case with *Hattere* (fr. OE *hæt*), of which no forms in *-ier* have been found.

MIDDLE ENGLISH
SURNAMES OF OCCUPATION

CHAPTER I.

DEALERS, TRADERS.[1]

A. Merchant, Dealer.

Marchaunt. 1219. NED: c1290.

Ess: Galfr. le marchaund 1230 P 154. Thom. le Markaunt 1255 *Ass* 32. Ric. Le Marchaunt 1300 *2. GDR* 10. — *Sx:* Hugo Le Marchant 1249 *Ass* 39. Joh. le Marchaund 1279 *Ass* 35. Nich. Marchaunt 1332 SR 249. — *Ha:* Henr. le Marchaund 1280 *2. Ass* 15. Will. Marchant 1333 *SR* 6. — *So:* Adam le Marchant 1235 FF 98. Thom. le Markaund 1274 RH 118. Will. le Marchaunt 1320 *Ass* 20. — *Wo:* Joh. le Marschand 1275 SR 82. — *St:* Geoffrey le Marchant 1227 4.Ass 48. Joh. le Marchant' 1332 SR 119. — *La:* Edw. le Marchaunt 1332 SR 2. — *Y:* Ric. le Marschaunt 1268 *Ass* 31. Alan. Markaund' 1297 SR 119. — *Li:* Warinus le marchant 1219 Ass 182. Ric. le Marchand 1245 *Ass* 28. Will. Markand 1327 *2.SR* 18. Agnes Marchaunt' 1327 *1.SR* 5. — *Nf:* Jord. le Marchant 1250 *Ass* 2. Odo le Marchaunt 1287 CDN 9. Rob. Merchaunt 1332 *SR* 52.

OF *marchand, marchëant.* — *Merchant, trader.* This surname is particularly common in *Ess, Nf,* and *Li.*

Chapman. 1202. NED: c890.

Ess: Rog. Chapman 1285 *Ass* 45. Henr. le Chapman 1319 *SR* 7. Will. le Chapman 1332 *SR* 1. — *Sx:* Rob. Chepman 1202 FF 14. Pet. le Chapman 1249 *Ass* 39. Rob. Chepman 1279 *Ass* 1. Walt. le Chapman 1288 *Ass* 40. Virgilius Chepman 1296 SR 9. Thom. le Chepman 1327 SR 127. Rad. le Chepman 1332 SR 233. Matild relicta Chupman 1332 SR 271. — *Ha:* Rob. Chapman 1272 *Ass* 2. Alan. le Chepman 1280 *1. Ass* 67. Alvred' le Chapman 1287 *Ass* 1. Matill' le Chapman 1327 *SR* 9. Henr. le Chupman 1327 *SR* 10. Sim. le Chupman ib. 9. Adam le Chepman 1333 *SR* 3. Walt. Chuppman ib. 4. Mauricius le Chapman 1340 *SR* 7. — *So:* Osmund Chapman 1227 FF 57. Joh. Le Chepman 1305 *Ass* 13. Nich. le Chipman 1320 *Ass* 19. Walt. le Chapman ib. 22. Will. Chipman 1327 SR 198. Joh. le Chepman ib. 249. Joh. Kyng Chipman 1344 *Ass* 15 (Joh. Chapman ib. 13). — *Wo:* Walt. le Chapman 1255 *Ass* 1. Rog. le Chapmon 1294 Hal 274. Steph. Le Chepman

---

[1] In this chapter have been included only those general names of dealers that are not related to the other groups. Specified dealers have been put together with the manufacturers of the respective articles.

1307 *Ass* 3. Thom. Le Chapmon 1327 SR 37. — *St:* Thom. le Chapman 1266 4. Ass 162. Hugo le Chapmon 1327 SR 203. Will. le Chapmon 1332 SR 89. — *La:* Alex. le Chapman 1292 *1. Ass* 8. Will. Chapmon 1332 SR 10. — *Y:* Will. le Schapman 1286 1.Wake 225. Clemens Chapman 1301 SR 47. Adam le Chapman c1346 *SR* 5. — *Li:* Walt. Chapman 1275 RH 306. Rad. le Chapman 1281 *1. Ass* 43. Agnes Chappeman 1327 *2. SR* 17. Walt. le Schapman 1332 *2. SR* 1. Alan. le Chapman ib. 4. — *Nf:* Ric. Le Chapman 1286 *Ass* 42. Cecilia le Schapman 1299 CDN 73. Thom. le Chapman 1329 *SR* 32. Nich. chapman 1332 *SR* 11.

OE *cēapmann, cȳp(e)mann, cēpemann*. — As is seen above, there are four distinct spellings of this surname, viz. Ch*a*pman, Ch*e*pman, Ch*u*pman, and Ch*i*pman (the last two of which are not recorded in NED after the OE period), and it is interesting to note the distribution of these in the different parts of England. This is as follows:

Ess: only Chapman. *Sx:* Chepman 42 inst., Chapman 14, Chupman 1. *Ha:* Chepman 21, Chapman 10, Chupman 10. *So:* Chepman 22, Chapman 10, Chipman 4. *Wo:* Chapman 14, Chepman 2. In the Anglian counties (*St, La, Y, Li, Nf*) there is only one form, Chapman. It is consequently only in the WS counties that the forms with -*e*-, -*u*-, -*i*- occur, and here these are predominant, except in *Wo,* which county, however, partly belongs to West Midland.

Signification: *Merchant, trader, dealer*. — *Chapman* is a very common surname during this period.

Grocer. 1350. NED: [1321].
Ess: John and Isabella Grocer 1350 CR 216 (John Grocer and Isabella, his wife ib. 217).

OF *grossier* 'marchand en gros' (Godefroy). — *Wholesale dealer*.

Mangere. 1275. NED: a975.
So: Ric. le Manngere 1327 *SR* 39. Rob. le Manger ib. Will. Manger 1333 *SR* 31. — *Wo:* Ric. le Manger 1275 SR 25. Nich. Manger ib. 87. Hugo le Mongur 1278 3.Hal. 49. — *Y:* Rob. Monger 1316 4.Wake 143.

OE *mangere*. — *Monger, dealer, trader*. — This surname is rare, except in compounds.

I have found a few instances of the corresponding fem. form, *Mongestere,* in other counties, e. g. Mabilla la *Mongastr'* 1332 SR 28 (Sr). Sara la *Bredmongestere* 1311 CLB (D) 265 (Lo) 'seller of bread'. OE had *smeorumangestre* 'butter-woman'.

Vendur. 1277.   NED: 1594.
Wo: Henr. le Ventur 1277 Hal 78. — *Y:* Will. Vendur 1301 SR 119. Will. le Vendour ib. 121. — *Li:* Will. le Vendur 1305 *Ass* 17. Hugo Le vendour' 1327 *2. SR* 24. Will. vender' ib. 23. Marg. le Vendour 1332 *3. SR* 26.

AF *vendour*, OF *vendeor, venteour*, perh. also **vendier*. NED has three words: vendor 1594, vender 1596, venter 1620. — *Vendor, seller, dealer.*

Regrater. 1219.   NED: [1301].
Li: Gaufridus le Regrater 1219 Ass 170. Phil. le regrater 1230 P 303.

AF *regrater*, OF *regratier*. — *One who regrates victuals or other commodities, a retailer* (NED).

B. Pedlar, Hawker, Barterer.

Peddere. 1166.   NED: a1225.
Ess: Walt. le Peddere 1255 *Ass* 34. Mich. le Peddere 1285 *Ass* 11. Thom. le Pedder' 1303 *2. GDR* 13. Phil. Le Pedder 1310 CR 4. Sim. le Pedder 1337 ib. 165. — *Ha:* Ric. le Peddere 1327 *SR* 11. — *St:* Pet. le Peddere 1306 7. Ass. 129 — *La:* Rich. le Peddere 1258 Ass 121. John le Peddere 1262 FF 138. Alex. le Peddere 1292 *1. Ass* 41. Ad. le Peddere 1292 *3. Ass* 109. — *Y:* Will. le Peddere 1166 P 45. Thom. Peddere 1212 FF 166. Dauid le Peddere 1293 *Ass* 58. Pet. le Peddere 1297 1.Wake 304. Geraudus Pedur 1301 SR 57. Will. Pedur ib. — *Li:* Joh. le Pedder 1305 *Ass* 15. Hugo Pedder 1327 *2. SR* 9. Walt. pedder ib. 18. Rad. le Pedder 1332 *3. SR* 18. — *Nf:* Martinus le Peddere 1275 RH 444. Galfr. le Peddere 1312 *GDR* 13. Hugo Le peddere 1329 *SR* 6. Joh. le Pedder' 1332 *SR* 57.

A der. of ME *pedde* 'a pannier' (of unknown origin). — *One who carries about goods for sale, a pedlar* (NED).

Pedelare. 1307.   NED: 1377.
Wo: Will. Le Pedelare 1307 *Ass* 2.

Origin obscure. — *Pedlar, hawker.*

Huckestere. 1281.   NED: c1200.
Ess: Walt. le Hokestere 1285 *Ass* 48. Isolda la Hokkestre 1299 *2. GDR* 8. Agnes la Hukkester 1310 CR 6. Annabel la Hukkestere 1311 ib. 19. Isabella la Hukkestere 1312 ib. 74. — *Wo:* Matill' la Hockester' 1305 *Ass* 1 (le Hocstare ib. 3). — *Li:* Anota le Hokester 1281 *1. Ass* 38. Juliana Hogester 1327 *1. SR* 10 (Hokester 1332 *2. SR* 13).

The fem. form of HUCKERE. — *Retailer of small goods, pedlar, hawker* (NED).

Huckere. 1307. NED: 14..
So: Joh. Le Hukker' 1307 *Ass* 4. Nich. le Hukker 1327 SR 240. Rob. le Hukkere 1333 *SR* 2. Joh. le Hucker' ib. 14. Rog. le Hucker' ib. 35. — *Wo:* Rob. Le Hockar 1327 SR 60.

A der. of ME *hucke* 'to bargain' (of uncertain origin). — *Petty dealer.*

Pakeman. 1317. NED: a1625.
Ess: Ric. Pakeman 1319 *SR* 16. Roys' Pakeman 1327 *SR* 14. Sim. Pakeman 1337 CR 150. Will. Pakeman 1332 *SR* 18. — *La:* Thom. le Pakmon(?) 1324 CR 129. — *Y:* John Pakmon 1317 4.Wake 178.

ME *pake, pak, packe* 'a pack, bundle' (v. NED *pack*) + *man.* — *Hawker, pedlar.*

Panierman. 1301. NED: 1482—3.
Y: Thom. le Paynerman 1301 SR 37.

ME *panier* 'a basket' (OF *paniere*) + *man.* — *A hawker who carries fish or other provisions in a pannier to his customers.* — Cf Thom. Webster, de Sywardby, *fissher alias panyarman* 1473 Free Y 194.

Kydiere. 1233. NED: 1551—2.
Sx: Gilb. le Keddere 1279 *Ass* 10. — *Wo:* Ric. le Kydiere 1280 3.Hal 61, 73. — *La:* Rog. Kidere 1233 FF 146. Will. Kyder 1292 *3.Ass* 109. — *Y:* Till' le Kider' 1279 *Ass* 14. Joh. le Kyder 1293 *Ass* 76. Pet. le Kedere ib. 33. Thom. le Kidere 1301 SR 105. — *Li:* Rog. fil. Kydier' 1275 RH 369. Walt. Kyder 1327 *2. SR* 10. Cecilia Kydiere 1328 *Ass* 6. — *Nf:* Will. le Keder 1286 *Ass* 116. Will. Kyder 1313 *GDR* 18.

Origin obscure (NED). Cf MDu *keder* 'one who announces or proclaims'. — *Kiddier, hawker, badger.*

Brokur. 1260. NED: 1377.
Ha: Isaak le Brokur 1280 *3. Ass* 44. Rob. le Brokur ib. 25. — *Y:* Steph. le Brokur 1260 Ass 122. Will. Brocour 1297 SR 132. — *Li:* Hugo le Brokur 1281 *1. Ass* 5.

AF *brocour* = ONF *brokeor.* — *Broker, retailer, pedlar.*

Brogour. 1334. NED: [1386]
Y: Thom. le brogour 1334 Free Y 29.

AF *broggour,* a corruption of *brocour.* — *Agent, jobber, broker.*

Trauenter. 1292. NED: [1233].
Ess: Hugo le Trauenter 1292 *2. GDR* 3.

Med. L *travetarius*, v. NED *tranter*. — *Carrier, hawker, huckster*.

Trucker. 1281. NED: 1598.
Wo: Will. Le Trocher' 1327 SR 44. — *Li:* Thom. Truker' 1281 *1. Ass* 8 (Trucker 1281 *2. Ass* 10).

A der. of ME *trukke* 'to barter' (F *troquer* 'to truck, barter', Norman-Picard form of OF **trocher*, which is the source of the *Wo* form). — *One who trucks, a barterer*.

Chappere. 1327. NED: —
Ha: Will. le Chappere 1327 *SR* 17.

A der. of ME *chapien* (fr. OE *cēapian* 'to bargain, trade'); v. NED *chap* vb (a1225). — *One who buys and sells, a barterer*.

Cosere. 1294. NED: 14..
Ess: Rad. le Kosser' 1299 *2. GDR* 9. Will. Le Cosere 1316 *3. GDR* 36 (le Cosere 1317 *2. GDR* 41). — *Lo:* Hugh le Cussere 1294 CLB (A) 199.

A der. of *coss* vb (of uncertain derivation). — *Dealer, broker, 'horse-corser'*.

Corser. 1227. NED: c1380.
St: Anketill le Corser 1227 4.Ass 54.

A der. of *corse* vb (of uncertain origin). — *Jobber, horse-dealer*.

Horsmongere. 1272. NED: a1400.
Ha: Reg. le Horsmongore 1272 *Ass* 21. — *Ca:* Leo le Horsmongere 1279 RH 362.

OE *hors* + *mangere*. — *Dealer in horses*.

Drovere. 1327. NED: c1425.
St: Henr' le·Drovere 1327 SR 238.

A der. of OE *drāf* 'drove'. — *Drover, dealer in cattle* (NED). Cf the following instance fr. London, in which this word occurs as the name of a trade: Joh. Hank, *Drovere* 1332 SR 76.

Heymongere. 1230. NED: —
Lo: Reg. le Heymongere 1291 CLB (C) 190. — *Li:* Henr. Heimongere 1230 P 302.

OE *hēg* 'hay' + *mangere*. — *Seller of hay*.

CHAPTER II.

MANUFACTURERS OR SELLERS OF PROVISIONS.

A. Miller, Sifter.

Milner. 1275. NED: 1362.

Ess: Joh. le Melner' 1316 *3. GDR* 31. Ric. le Meller' 1319 *SR* 3. Agnes le Meller' 1327 *SR* 3. Joh. Milnere ib. 22. Steph. le Meluner ib. 23. Galfr. le Mellere 1332 *SR* 16. Adam le Mellere 1341 *Ass* 7. — *Sx:* Rad. Muller 1296 SR 41. Reg. Miller 1327 SR 173. Thom' le Mullar 1332 SR 250. — *Ha:* Galfr. le Mullere 1333 *SR* 1. — *So:* Joh. Mullere 1333 *SR* 30. — *Wo:* Joh. le Mulnare 1275 SR 16. — *La:* Henr. Le Milner 1292 *1. Ass* 40. John le Melner 1324 CR 18. Hug. le Milner 1332 SR 44. Will. le Milner 1333 *Ass* 15. — *Y:* Rob. le Milner 1297 SR 118. Will. le Milnere 1297 1.Wake 284. Jord. the Milner 1297 2.Wake 1. Galfr. le Melner 1301 SR 29. Sim. le Milner 1332 *SR* 14. Emma Mulner c1346 *SR* 13. — *Li:* Rob. le Milnere 1281 *1.Ass* 37 (le Millere 1281 2.*Ass* 33). Rog. Mylner 1317 *Ass* 12. Ric. Milner 1327 *2.SR* 1. Nich. le Milner 1327 *3.SR* 3. Hugo Meller 1327 *2.SR* 17. Will. Mulner 1328 *Ass* 11. Joh. le Milner 1332 *2. SR* 1. Rob. Muller ib. 5. Adam Muller ib. Rob. le Milner 1340 *Ass* 12. — *Nf:* Thom. le Mullere 1286 *Ass* 33. Matill' le Mellere ib. 56. Elyas le Milnere 1308 *GDR* 2. Rad. le Millere 1329 *SR* 19. Sim. le Miller' 1332 *SR* 6. Joh. Milnere ib. 47. Thom. Le Meller' ib. 76.

Perhaps fr. an OE **mylnere* or a der. of ME *mylne* (OE *mylen*) 'mill'. The frequent occurrence of this surname in the North and East of England (v. below), however, seems to show that, partly at least, it may be derived fr. ON *mylnari* 'miller'. For the spelling with *-ll-, -ln-,* v. KYLNER. — Signification: *Miller.*

This surname should be compared with *Muleward*, because these two names belong to different parts of England. *Muleward* is very common in southern and western counties (*Sx, Ha, So, Wo,* and *St*), whereas *Milner* is very rare there (I have only found seven instances in these counties). In the remaining parts of England (*Ess, Nf, Li, Y,* and *La*) *Milner* is very common, while *Muleward* does not occur there at all, except in *Ess,* where I have found three instances.

Mylnari also occurred as a surname in ON (v. Kahle p. 192).

Muleward. 1280. NED: c1000.

Ess: Joh. Melward' 1304 2. *GDR* 14. Alic' Meleward 1319 *SR* 6. Will. Le Melleward 1327 *SR* 1. — *Sx:* Rob. le Muleward 1296 SR 64. Walt. Meleward ib. 45. Rob. le Meleward 1314 *1. GDR* 11. Ric. le Meleward 1327 SR 140. Rad. le Muleward ib. 175. Henr' le Muleward 1332 SR 231. Pet. Mulleward 1348 FF 124. — *Ha:* Rob. le Meleward 1280 *3. Ass* 5. Henr. Le Muleward 1306 *Ass* 2. Joh. le Mulleward 1323 *Ass* 8. Nich. le Muleward 1327 *SR* 9. Agnes la Muleward 1333 *SR* 1. Alex. Meleward ib. 8. Will. le Muleward 1340 *SR* 5. Adam le Moleward ib. 7. — *So:* Hugo Le Mileward 1305 *Ass* 2. Ric. Le Muleward 1320 *Ass* 8. Thom. le Meleward ib. 19. Joh. le Moleward 1327 SR 87. Nich. le Milleward ib. 122. Hugo le Muleward 1333 *SR* 8. Rad. le Molward ib. 9. Rob. le Mulleward 1344 *Ass* 7. — *Wo:* Rob. le Muleward 1316 Inq 95. Will. le Mileward 1322 Inq 112. Will. Le Muleward 1327 SR 6. Steph. Le Muleward ib. 13. Alicia Le Muleward ib. 31. Joh. le Muleward 1332 SR 6. — *St:* Ric. le Meleward 1327 SR 223. Rob. le Meleward ib. 225. Thom' le Muleward 1332 SR 114. Sim. le Muleward ib. 129. John le Mulleward 1344 12. Ass 30.

OE *myle(n)weard* 'the keeper of a mill'. As this surname occurs frequently, I here give a survey of the spellings of all the instances found:

Ess: only Meleward. *Sx:* Muleward 45 inst., Mele- 19. *Ha:* Muleward 75, Mele- 4, Mole- 2. *So:* Muleward 39, Mile- 6, Mele- 1, Mole- 2. *Wo:* Muleward 17, Mile- 2. *St:* Muleward 14, Mele- 3. — Note that this surname does not occur in *La, Y, Li,* and *Nf.* Cf MILNER.

Signification: *Miller.*

Mouner. 1200. NED: —

Ess: Ric. le Mouner 1274 RH 160. Joh. le Muner 1285 *Ass* 15. Alex. le Mouner 1319 *SR* 18. — *Sx:* Joh. le Mouner 1249 *Ass* 5. Rad. le Mouner 1263 *Ass* 27. Ad. le Mouner 1279 *Ass* 10. Joh. le Moner 1327 SR 120. — *Ha:* Rad. le molnier 1200 P 266. Steph. le Mouner 1272 *Ass* 1. Laur. Le Mouner 1306 *Ass* 2. — *So:* Edw. le *mudiner* 1243 Ass 192. John le *mudner* ib. Will. le Muner 1270 Ass 128. Bened. Le Mouner 1307 *Ass* 9. Pet. le Mouner 1333 *SR* 30. — *Wo:* Hen le Muner 1255 *Ass* 7. Joh. le Mouner 1294 *Ass* 5. Adam Le Mowner 1327 SR 25. — *St:* Rob. le Muner 1242 4.Ass 95. Nich. le Mouner 1280 6. Ass 112. Rich. le Muner 1305 7. Ass 139. — *La:* Henr. le Muner 1246 Ass 50. Bymme le Mouner 1277 Ass 151. Rog. le Mouner 1338 *Ass* 5. — *Y:* Alex. le Mouner 1268 *Ass* 24. Pet. le Mouner 1296 1.Wake 236. Henr. le Mouner 1332 *SR* 5. — *Li:* Geoffrey Le Mouner 1246 FF 35. Sim. le Muner 1287 *Ass* 6. Henr. le Mouner 1327 *2. SR* 3. Sabina la Mouner 1332 *2. SR* 4. — *Nf:* Rad. le mouner 1250 *Ass* 2. Phil. le Muner 1315 *GDR* 24. Pet. le Mauner 1330 CDN 156 (le Maner 1339 ib. 216). Rob. Le Mouner 1332 *SR* 19.

OF *molnier, mousnier, moonier, muner, monier, maunier, mannier* 'meunier' (Godefroy). The form *Mud(i)ner So* corresponds to OF *mousnier; s > d* before *n* in AF (v. Jordan § 261). — *Miller.* This surname is frequent, especially in early rolls.

Moliner. 1279.   NED: —

Ess: Rob. Le Moliner 1312 *4.GDR* 4. — *Sx:* Rob. le Moliner 1279 *Ass* 29. — *Ha:* Rob. le Molenir 1327 *SR* 4 (le Molener 1333 *SR* 3). — *So:* Will. *Molindiner* 1327 SR 230. — *St:* Thom. le Molyner 1332 SR 91. — *La:* Henr. le Molyner 1323 *Ass* 26. Alan. le Moliner 1327 *SR* 3. — *Y:* Rich. le Moliner 1297 1.Wake 297.

OF *molinier* 'meunier' (Godefroy). *Molindiner So* is an extended form, influenced by the Latin equivalent, *Molendinarius*. — *Miller.*

Melemakere. 1274.   NED: a1400.

Ess: Ric. le Melemakere 1323 *3. GDR* 29. Roysya la Melemaker' 1323 *2. GDR* 32. — *La:* Rog. le Melmakere 1292 *1. Ass* 43 (le Melemakere ib. 29). Adam le Melemakere 1292 *3. Ass* 15. — *Y:* Adam le Melemakere 1274 1. Wake 16. Rob. le Melemaker 1275 ib. 26. Rich. le Melemaker 1297 ib. 300. Cicely Melemaker 1317 4.Wake 181. Rad. Melmaker 1332 *SR* 13.

OE *melo* 'meal' + a der. of *macian*. — *Miller.*

Another possibility would be to derive the first element from OE *mēle* 'a tub'. This does not appear probable, however, for in York Pl. (Intr. p. 40) there is a regulation for *melemakers*, from which it is clearly seen that they were *millers*. This is also borne out by the following trade-names in Free Y: Will. Barnard, *otemelemaker* 1454 p. 175. Will. Malson, *haver-melmaker* 1490 p. 216 'maker of oatmeal'.

Cf also the following synonymous surname, of which I have only found one instance: Rob. le *fflourmakere* 1332 SR 63 (Lo) 'one who makes flour'.

Gryndere. 1230.   NED: 1483.

Ess: Thos. Gryndere 1346 CR 206. — *So:* Will. le grindere 1230 P 43. — *St:* Henry le Grynder 1347 FF 161. — *Li:* Rob. Grynder 1332 *3. SR* 25. — *Nf:* Steph. Le Gryndere 1286 *Ass* 41.

OE *grindere* 'molitor'. — *One who grinds corn, etc., a miller.*

Broyer. 1301.   NED: —

Y: Walt. le Broyer 1301 SR 105.

OF *broier*, only recorded in the sense 'mortar'; cf *broyeur* 'celui qui broie' or 'instrument servant à broyer' (Godefroy). — Signification: = GRYNDERE.

Quernestere. 1333.   NED: —
Ha: Juliana la Quernestre 1333 *SR* 6.

A fem. der. of OE *cweorn* 'a quern'. — *One who grinds corn, etc., in a hand-mill.* — The following trade-name is probably synonymous: Ralph de Assindone, »*quernbetere*«(?) 1277 CLB (B) 271 (Lo).

Boltere. 1272.   NED: c1440.
Ess: Joh. le Boltere 1299 *2. GDR* 9. Ric. le Boltere 1316 ib. 47. Matill' la Boltere 1317 *3. GDR* 39. — *Sx:* Joh. le Boltere 1296 SR 66 (le Bultar 1332 SR 227). Rob. Bolter 1332 SR 332. — *Ha:* Rob. le Bultere 1272 *Ass* 22. Joh. le boltere 1280 *2. Ass* 65. Walt. le Boltere ib. 69. Henr. Le Bolter' 1305 *Ass* 12. Galfr. le Bultere 1327 *SR* 1. Johanna la Boltere 1333 *SR* 9. Hugo le Bultare ib. 6. — *So:* Joh. *Boltor* 1327 SR 159 (Boltare 1333 *SR* 6). — *Wo:* John le Boleter 1308 Inq 27. — *Nf:* Ric. le Boltere 1275 RH 435. Ric. le Boltere 1286 *Ass* 29 (le Bultere ib. 116).

OF *buleteor* 'one who sifts meal'; perhaps also **buletier*, or (rather) fr. ME *bulte* 'to bolt' (OF *buleter*). — *One who sifts meal, etc.* — The form *Boltere* may also be = BOLTSMITH, q. v.

This name, which is most common in *Ha*, has not been found in *St, La, Y*, and *Li*.

Ridelere. 1230.   NED: 1603.
Ess: Hardyngus le Rideler 1302 *2. GDR* 12. — *Sx:* Steph. le Rydelere 1296 SR 66. Will. le Rideler ib. 68. Thom. Ridelar 1332 SR 299. — *Ha:* Walt. le Ridelere 1272 *Ass* 7. — *So:* Galfr. le ridelere 1230 P 44. Walt. le Ridelare 1327 SR 232. Thom. le Rydelare 1333 *SR* 16.

A der. of ME *rid(e)len* 'to sift' (fr. OE *hriddel* 'a sieve') — *Sifter of corn, etc.*

Ridelestere. 1255.   NED: —
Ess: Brunnan la Ridelestere 1255 *Ass* 3. — *Wo:* Will. le Rydelester' 1255 *Ass* 24 (Le Ridelester' ib.).

The fem. form of RIDELERE. — Signification: = RIDELERE.

Criblur. 1236.   NED: —
Sx: Adam le Criblur 1236 FF 87.

OF *cribleur* 'celui qui passe au crible' (Godefroy). — *Sifter*.

B. Corn-Monger, Meal-Monger.

Cornmongere. 1177. NED: c1515.
Ess: Ædw. le Cormangere 1177 P 148. Pet. le cormangere 1190 P 107. Ran. le Cornmangere 1255 *Ass* 33. — *Sx:* Will. le Cornmanier 1249 *Ass* 20. Rad. Le Cornmonger 1279 *Ass* 2. Rob. le Cornmonger' 1288 *Ass* 31. Steph. le Cornmongere 1296 SR 83. Ad' le Cornmonger' ib. 100. Will. le Cornmongare 1323 *Ass* 24. Ph. le Cornmongar' 1332 SR 232. — *Ha:* Barth. Cornmongere 1333 *SR* 9. Thom. le Cornmongere ib. 5. — *So:* Golfridus Cornmanger 1327 SR 100.

OE *corn* + *mangere*. — *One who deals in corn.*

Otmongere. 1300. NED: 1327.
Ess: Thom. Le Otmongere 1300 2.*GDR* 11. Joh. Otmonger 1319 *SR* 7. — *Sx:* Maur' Le Otmongere 1314 *1.GDR* 8. — *So:* Thom. le Otemangere 1327 SR 128.

OE *āte* 'oats' + *mangere*. — *Dealer in oats.*

Hauerman. 1332. NED: —
Li: Sim. Hauerman (4 times) 1332 *1. SR* 16.

ME *haver* 'oats' (fr. ON *hafre*) + ME *man*. — *Dealer in oats.*

Melemongere. 1288. NED: 1766.
Sx: Gilb. Le Mellemongere 1288 *Ass* 28 (le Melemongere 1296 SR 83). — *So:* Alicia la Melemongeres 1320 *Ass* 13. — *Li:* Rog. Melmanger 1327 *2. SR* 21.

OE *melo* 'meal' + *mangere*. — *Seller of meal.*

Meleman. 1275. NED: 1552.
So: Walt. Melmane 1327 SR 167. Adam Melmane ib. — *Wo:* Rog. le Meleman 1275 2. *Ass* 19. — *Nf.* Joh. Melleman 1329 *SR* 31. Joh. Melman 1332 *SR* 18. Will. Le Melleman ib. 48.

OE *melo* 'meal' + *mann*. — *One who deals in meal.*

Fariner. 1305. NED: —
Li: Thom. Le Fariner 1305 *Ass* 14. Agnes La Fariner 1327 *1. SR* 6. Ric. Le Fariner ib. 1 (le Fariner 1332 *2. SR* 1).

OF *farinier* 'marchand de farine' (Godefroy). — *One who deals in meal.*

C. Baker, Maker or Seller of Bread.

Bakere. 1177.   NED: a1000.
Ess: Jord. le Baker' 1255 *Ass* 18. Alex. le Bakere 1285 *Ass* 33. Steph. le Bakere 1332 *SR* 26. Nich. le Bakere 1341 *Ass* 6. — *Sx:* Will. le Bakere 1263 *Ass* 44. Ric. le Bakere 1296 SR 46. Reg. le Baccare ib. 85. Walt. le Baker 1332 SR 268. — *Ha:* Ric. le Baker' 1272 *Ass* 17. Walt. le Backere 1280 *3. Ass* 22. Ric. le Bakere 1327 *SR* 2. Joh. le Bakere 1333 *SR* 3. — *So:* andr. Le Baker 1305 *Ass* 11. Ric. le Bakere 1320 *Ass* 14. Agnes le Baker' 1333 *SR* 6. — *Wo:* Rob. le Bakare 1275 SR 31. Joh. le Backer 1305 Hal 510. Ric. Le Baker 1327 SR 8. — *St:* Will. le Baker 1306 7.Ass 153. Joh. le Bakere 1327 SR 223. — *La:* Rob. Bakere 1246 Ass 34. Adam le Baker 1332 SR 76. — *Y:* Galfr. le Bakere 1293 *Ass* 100. Joh. le Baker 1332 *SR* 10. — *Li:* Ric. le Bakere 1281 *1. Ass* 1. Rob. Le Baker 1327 *2. SR* 2. Oliuerus Le Baker 1327 *1. SR* 9. Alicia le Baker 1332 *2. SR* 3. — *Nf:* Will. le Bakere 1177 P 137. Rog. Le Bakere 1286 *Ass* 111. Rad. Bakere 1332 *SR* 19.

OE *bæcere*. — *Baker*. This surname is very common in the South and East of England, but it is rare in the other parts. Cf BAKESTERE.

Bakestere. 1275.   NED: c1000.
Ess: Hugo le Baxstere 1317 *2. GDR* 39. Isabella la Baxstere ib. 19. — *Sx:* Jul' la Bakestr' 1310 *2. GDR* 6. Muriel le Bakestr' 1332 SR 262. — *Wo:* Rad. le Baxter 1300 Hal 403. Emmot la Baxster 1307 Hal 565. Henr. Le Baxster' 1327 SR 16. — *St:* Nich. le Bacster 1306 7.Ass 160. Joh. le Bacstere 1327 SR 198. Elias le Baxter 1332 SR 89. Henr' le Baxtere ib. 99. — *La:* Ad. le Bacster 1327 *SR* 16. Rob. le Baxster 1332 *Ass* 13. Henr. le Baxster 1333 *Ass* 16. — *Y:* Galfr. le Bakester 1297 SR 118. Will. le Bakstere 1301 SR 120. Rob. le Bakester c1346 *SR* 4. — *Li:* Rob. le Bakester 1321 *Ass* 40. Joh. Bakester 1327 *2. SR* 19. Rad. Le Bakkester 1328 *Ass* 49. Thom. Bakyster 1332 *1. SR* 3. Elias Bakester 1340 *Ass* 7. — *Nf:* John de Brake & Bakestere 1275 RH 511. Beatrix la Baxstere 1295 *GDR* 9. Rad. le Baxtere 1313 *GDR* 17. Thom. le Bakister' 1332 *SR* 42. Hugo Bakestere ib. 52. Pet. Baxtere 1337 *SR* 2.

OE *bæcestre*, fem. of *bæcere*. — *Baker*. — *Bakestere* belongs chiefly to the Anglian counties, where it is common. Only a few instances have been found in the South (in *Ha* and *So* none at all).

Pestur. 1239.   NED: [1607].
Ess: Rob. le Pestur 1255 *Ass* 33. Eustach. le Pestur 1285 *Ass* 21. Galfr. le Pestour 1302 *2. GDR* 12. — *Sx:* Dauid le pestur 1249 *Ass* 34. Will. le Pestur 1279 *Ass* 28. Henr. le Pestur 1296 SR 84. — *Ha:* Thom. le Pestur 1272 *Ass* 10. Adam le Pestur 1280 *2. Ass* 92. Agatha Pestor 1333 *SR* 2. —

So: Rob. le Pestur 1243 Ass 316. Walt. le Pestur 1278 Ass 130. Gilb. le Pestour 1333 *SR* 27. — *Wo:* David le Pestur 1271 Inq 12. Steph. Lepestur 1275 *1. Ass* 21. Walt. le Pestur 1293 Inq 47. — *St:* Rog. le Pestur 1269 4. Ass 177. Will. le Pestour 1302 *GDR* 1. John le Pistour 1307 7.Ass 187. — *La:* Warin le Pestur 1246 Ass 11. Will. le Pestur 1285 Ass 210. Henr. Le Pestur 1292 *3. Ass* 32. — *Y:* Joh. le Pestur 1268 *Ass* 19. Ric. le Pestour 1293 *Ass* 5. Gilb. le Pestour 1301 SR 120. — *Li:* Will. Le Pestur 1239 FF 303. Joceus le Pestur 1288 *Ass* 14. Thom. le Pestour 1328 *Ass* 13. — *Nf:* Ph. le pestur 1250 *Ass* 21. Walt. le Pestur 1299 CDN 72. Iuo le Pestur 1332 *SR* 46.

AF *pistour, pestour* = OF *pestor, -eur.* — Baker.

Furner. 1208.   NED: a1483.
Ess: Springoldus le Furner 1312 CR 61. Sim. le Fourner' 1332 *SR* 24. Will. Fournyr ib. 6. — *Sx:* Will. le Fornir 1279 *Ass* 28. Osb. le Furnere 1296 SR 52. — *Ha:* Rob. le Fournir 1327 *SR* 3. — *Wo:* Henr. le Furner 1275 SR 3. Will. Le Forner 1327 SR 55. — *La:* Joh. Le Furner 1292 2. *Ass* 6 (Joh. Le Furnur ib.). — *Y:* Will. le Furner 1208 Cur 266. Sim. Furner 1212 ib. 336. Will. le fourner 1331 Free Y 27. — *Li:* Reg. le Forner 1275 RH 385. Joh. Fornier 1319 *Ass* 26. — *Nf:* Ric. le Furnier 1286 *Ass* 135.

OF *fornier, fur-, four-* 'boulanger, pâtissier' (Godefroy). — *Furner, baker.*

Bolenger. 1180.   NED:—
Sx: Terricus le Bulenger 1180 P 32. Alex. le Bolinger 1278 FF 102. Will. Bolonger 1327 SR 171 (Bolenger 1332 SR 286). — *Ha:* Joh. Bolynger 1333 *SR* 3.

OF *bolengier, bolonger, boulengier.* — Baker.

Knedere. 1280.   NED: c1440.
Sx: Joh. Kneder 1296 SR 8. — *Ha:* Rob. le Knedere 1280 *3. Ass* 42. — *Li:* Will. Cnedar 1327 *2. SR* 18.

A der. of OE *cnedan* 'to knead'. — *One who kneads, a baker.* — Cf Prompt. P.: Knedar, or pastare: pistor.

Doghere. 1332.   NED: 1483.
Sx: Ric. le Douar' 1332 SR 261. Joh. le Douar' ib. 262. — *So:* Will. le Doghere 1333 *SR* 25. — *Sr:* Joh. le Dogher' 1332 SR 11.

A der. of OE *dāh* (gen. *dāges*) 'dough'. — *A maker of dough, a baker.*

Payndemeynere. 1337.   NED:—
Ess: Matilda le Payndemeynere 1337 CR 155.

A der. of ME *paindemeine* 'white bread' (fr. AF *pain demeine*, med. L *panis dominicus*). — *One who makes or sells white bread.*

Wasteler. 1327.   NED: —
Li: Joh. Wasteler' 1327 *1. SR* 2. Ric. Wasteler 1332 *1. SR* 17.
OF *gastelier, wastelier* 'pâtissier, faiseur ou marchand de gâteaux' (Godefroy). — *Maker or seller of wastels* (bread made of the finest flour).

Wygger. 1332.   NED: —
Ess: Will. le Wygger 1332 *SR* 26.
A der. of ME *wygge* (= MLG, MDu *wigge* 'wedge, wedge-shaped cake'). — *Maker or seller of 'wigs'* (a kind of bun or cake).

Wyggester. 1296.   NED: —
Sx: Matild' la Wyggestr' 1296 SR 54.
The fem. form of WYGGER. — Signification: = WYGGER.

Waferer. 1255.   NED: 1362.
Ess: Rad. le Wafrer 1255 *Ass* 26 (le Wafror ib. 13). Joh. le Waffrour 1316 *3. GDR* 49 (le Wafrour 1316 *2. GDR* 46). — *Sx:* Will. Le Wafrur 1279 *Ass* 14. — *St:* Rog. Wafrer 1327 SR 236. — *Y:* Joh. le Waferer 1293 *Ass* 25. — *Li:* Joh. Waferer 1332 *3. SR* 12. Sim. Waffrer ib. — *Nf:* John le Wafrer 1301 Free L 4. Adam le Wafrer 1312 CDN 38. Mich. le Wafrour 1336 ib. 197.

AF *wafrer* fr. *wafre* 'wafer' (NED). There seems also to have been an AF **wafrour*. Godefroy has only *waufrier* (1455) 'marchand de gaufres'. — *Maker or seller of wafers or thin cakes.*

D. **Cook, Sauce-Maker.**

Coke. 1269.   NED: c1000.
Ess: Will. le Cok' 1285 *Ass* 33. Sewallus le Cok' 1319 *SR* 15. Johanna Le Cok' 1327 *SR* 7. — *Sx:* Rad. le Cook 1296 SR 62. Joh. le Couk' 1321 *Ass* 33. Hugo le Couk 1327 SR 116. Rob. le Cook 1332 SR 309. — *Ha:* Joh. le Cok' 1280 *2. Ass* 44. Elias Le Cook' 1305 *Ass* 6. Cecilia la Couk' 1327 *SR* 2. Galfr. le Coke 1333 *SR* 4. — *So:* Henry Coke 1279 Ass 230. Joh. Le Couk' 1307 *Ass* 3. Pet. le Cook 1333 *SR* 16. — *Wo:* Ric. le Coc 1270 Hal 20. Will. Le Cok' 1305 *Ass* 3. Joh. le Kook 1332 SR 14. — *St:* Rich. Cok 1269 4. Ass 175. Joh. le Coke 1327 SR 204. Ric. le Coke 1332 SR 92. — *La:* Adam Cok' 1292 *1.Ass* 5. Galfr. le Coke 1332 SR 40. — *Y:* Pet. Cok' 1297 SR 118. Thom. le Coke c1346 *SR* 12. — *Li:* Rob. le Cok' 1321 *Ass* 45. Rob. Cook'

1327 *1. SR* 8. — *Nf:* Hugo le Cok' 1286 *Ass* 16. Alex. le Coke 1327 CDN 137. Sim. Le Cok' 1332 *SR* 15.

OE *cōc* 'cook'. — *One who prepares food for a great household; a tradesman who prepares and sells cooked food* (NED). — Coke is a very common surname.

Keu. 1243. NED: —

Ess: Rad. le Keu 1255 *Ass* 32. Pet. le Ceu 1285 *Ass* 30. Reg. le keu 1332 *SR* 19. — *Sx:* Joh. le Cu 1249 *Ass* 21. Barth. le Keu 1259 FF 34. Joh. le Keu 1296 SR 57. — *Ha:* Will. le Keu 1272 *Ass* 19. Joh. le Co 1327 *SR* 11. Andr. le Keu 1333 *SR* 8. — *So:* Walt. le Keu 1243 Ass 296. Rich. le Ku 1279 Ass 193. Rossel le Keu 1344 *Ass* 16. — *Wo:* Walt. le Keu 1264 Inq 8. Will. le Kou 1275 SR 42. Phil. Le Keu 1327 SR 50. — *St:* Ralph le Keu 1282 6.Ass 125. Henry le Ku 1303 7.Ass 110. Adam le Keu 1327 SR 245 (le Cu 1332 SR 120). — *La:* Hugh le Kew 1246 Ass 48. Joh. le Keu 1341 *SR* 4. — *Y:* Rog. le Keu 1268 *Ass* 27. Alex. le Keu 1297 SR 63. Will. le cue, pestour 1335 Free Y 31. — *Li:* Normannus le Keu 1245 *Ass* 20. Will. le Keu 1281 *2. Ass* 58. Hugo Le Keue 1327 *2. SR* 5. Rog. le Cu 1332 *2. SR* 3. — *Nf:* Will. le Keu 1286 *Ass* 136. Rich. le Cu 1294 CDN 51. Ran. Le koo 1332 *SR* 64.

OF *queu, keu, kieu, cou, cu,* etc. 'cuisinier' (Godefroy). — Signification: = COKE. — This surname occurs frequently in all counties.

Cusyner. 1327. NED: 1533.

Ess: Thom. Le Cusyner 1327 *SR* 1.

OF *cuisinier, cosinier* (Godefroy). — *Cook.*

Hasteler. 1190. NED: [?c1175].

Ha: Henr. le hasteler 1190 P 134. Joh. le Hastelyr 1280 *3.Ass* 40. Joh. le Hastelyr 1333 *SR* 9. Joh. Hastelir Junior 1340 *SR* 7. Joh. Hastelir Senior ib. — *Wo:* Ric. Le Hastiller 1307 *Ass* 3. — *Li:* Galfr. Hasteler 1332 *3. SR* 25.

AF **hasteler,* fr. **hastele,* diminutive of *haste,* F *hâte* 'spit' (NED). — *One who roasts meat.*

Potager. 1327. NED: 1377.

Ha: Rog. le Potagere 1340 *SR* 7. — *So:* Joh. le Potager 1327 SR 272. — *Li:* Joh. Potager 1327 *1. SR* 9.

OF *potagier* 'cuisinier qui s'occupe des légumes' (Godefroy). — *Maker of pottage; one who cooks vegetables* (NED).

Flaoner. 1211. NED: —

Ess: Ran. le Flaoner 1329 CR 91. — *Lo:* Thom. le Flauner 1280 CLB

(A) 31. — *Le:* Ric. le Flauner 1211 RBL 23. — *Y:* Adam le flaoner, cocus 1318 Free Y 18.

OF *flaonnier, flaunier* 'celui qui fait des flans' (Godefroy). NED has *flawn* c1300. — Maker or seller of flawns (a kind of custard or cheese-cake).

Sauser. 1202.   NED: —
Ess: Joh. Sauser 1316 *2.GDR* 44. Agnes Saucer 1319 *SR* 13. Will. Sauser 1332 *SR* 11. — *Sx:* Adam le Sauser 1263 *Ass* 42. Will. le Sauser 1279 *Ass* 28. Thom. le Saucer 1296 SR 92. Will. Saussir 1327 SR 119. Joh. le Saucyr 1332 SR 230. — *Ha:* Reg. le Sauser 1280 2. *Ass* 31. Thom. Saucier 1323 *Ass* 6. Alex. le Sauser 1340 *SR* 3. — *So:* Rob. le Sauser 1243 Ass 287. Rob. le Sauser 1260 FF 186. Joh. le Sauser 1320 *Ass* 22. — *Wo:* Walt. Sauser 1275 SR 56. — *St:* Alured le Sauser 1220 4. Ass 13. Geoffrey le Sauser 1307 7. Ass 176. — *Y:* Pet. le Sauser 1202 FF 41. Will. le Sauser 1277 1. Wake 159. Thom. Sauser 1301 SR 32. Warinus le sauser 1318 Free Y 18. — *Li:* Gilb. Sauser 1248 FF 48. Henr. le Sauser 1327 *3.SR* 3. — *Nf:* Walt. le Scauser 1275 RH 468. Will. le Sausar 1298 CDN 69. Henry Sausur 1306 ib. 110.

OF *saussier, saulcier; saussieur* 'saucier' (Godefroy). — *One who makes or sells sauces, mustard, etc.* The 'sauser' may also have been in charge of the saucery in large households. — Cf the *'salsemakercrafte'* NED a1410 s. v. *sauce-maker*.

Cf the following synonymous surname: Rog. *Saucemaker* 1353 FF 43 (Y).

Mustarder. 1281.   NED: 1805.
Ess: Ernaldus le Mustarder 1285 *Ass* 43. Henr. le Mustarder 1341 *Ass* 5. — *Sx:* Rob. Le Mustarder 1319 *2. GDR* 30. — *Ha:* Isolda la Mostardere 1327 *SR* 17. — *Li:* Rog. le Mostarder' 1281 *1. Ass* 3. Stilo le Mustarder 1288 *Ass* 19. Will. Mustarder' 1327 *1. SR* 1. Joh. Mustarder 1328 *Ass* 27. Sim. Mustarder' 1332 *1. SR* 10. Lota le Mustarder' 1332 *2. SR* 1. — *Nf:* Ric. Le Mustarder 1286 *Ass* 67. Pet. le Mustarder 1312 CDN 41. Will. le Mustarder ib. 43.

OF *mostardier, mous-* 'celui qui fabrique, qui vend de la moutarde' (Godefroy). — *Maker or seller of mustard.*

Mustardman. 1275.   NED: —
Nf: Pet. le Mustardman 1275 RH 531. Rob. le Mustardman 1286 *Ass* 82. Benedict le Mustardman 1318 CDN 86. Will. le Mustardman 1329 ib. 149.

ME *mustard* (OF *moustarde*) + ME *man*. — Signification: = MUSTARDER.

E. Maker or Seller of Cheese or Butter.

Cheseman. 1263. NED: —

Ess: Joh. Chisman 1319 *SR* 20 (Cheseman 1323 *2. GDR* 32). — *Sx:* Pet. Le Cheseman 1263 *Ass* 18. John le Chesman 1317 FF 30. Thom. Cheseman 1324 *Ass* 17. Thom' le Chusman 1327 SR 140. Will. Chesman 1327 SR 186. Galfr. le Chesman 1332 SR 257. Joh. Chusman 1332 SR 261. — *Ha:* Henr. Chusman 1327 *SR* 17, 1333 *SR* 8. Joh. le Chusman 1333 *SR* 5. — *So:* Adam le Chisman 1327 SR 181. Alicia Chisman ib. Joh. Chusman 1327 SR 195. Cristina Chysman 1335 FF 175. — *Nf:* Rob. Chesman 1302 Free L 5. Rad. Cheseman 1329 *SR* 64.

OE *cēse*, *cīese, *cȳse 'cheese' + *mann*. — *Maker or seller of cheese.*

Cheser. 1332. NED: —

Wo: Rad. le Chesar 1332 SR 15. John le Chesar 1350 OCW 27.

A der. of OE *cēse* 'cheese'. — *Cheese maker or seller.* — Cheser is a trade-name in the following instance: Joh. de Hugat, *cheser* 1316 Free Y 17. Cf BUTERER.

Chesemakere. 1275. NED: —

Y: Thom. Kesemakere 1279 *Ass* 55. — *Li:* Rob. le Chesemaker 1275 RH 350 (le Jesemaker ib.)

OE *cēse* 'cheese' + a der. of *macian*. The form *Kesemakere* owes its *K*- to Scandinavian influence. — *Maker of cheese.*

Chesewright. 1293. NED: —

Y: Augustinus le Chesewryghte 1293 *Ass* 83.

BT has *cȳswyrhte*, fem. '(female) cheese-maker'. There may also have been an OE *cēsewyrhta. — *Maker of cheese.* — Curiously enough, this surname, of which I have only found one instance, has survived to the present day.

Chesemonger. 1186. NED: c1510.

Ess: Will. le Chesmonger' 1327 *SR* 20, 1332 *SR* 19. — *Ke:* Baldewinus le Chesemangere 1186 P 191. — *Nb:* Aungerus le Chesemongere 1269 Ass 212. — *Li:* Alan. Chesemanger 1327 *2. SR* 15. Adam Chesemonger 1327 *4. SR* 7 (Chesemanger 1332 *1. SR* 19).

OE *cēse* 'cheese' + *mangere*. — *One who sells cheese.*

Furmager. 1198. NED:—

Ess: Joh. le Furmager 1319 *SR* 19. — *Ke:* Henr. Furmagier 1198 P 208. — *Li:* Rob. Formagier 1275 RH 325. — *Nf:* Ran. le Furmager 1295 CDN 56. Will. Le Furmager 1301 *GDR* 22.

OF *fromagier, formagier* 'celui qui fait ou vend des fromages' (Godefroy). — *Maker or seller of cheese.*

Chesewryngere. 1281. NED:—

Li: Ric. le Chesewryngere 1281 *1. Ass* 2.

OE *cēse* 'cheese' + a der. of *wringan* 'to wring, squeeze'. — *One who wrings or presses cheese.*

Wringer. 1327. NED: a1300.

Sx: Ric. le Wringar 1327 SR 143.

A der. of OE *wringan* 'to wring, squeeze'. — *One who wrings something;* perhaps = CHESEWRYNGERE.

Deye. 1269. NED: a1000.

Ess: Marger. la Daye 1317 *2. GDR* 43. Gilb. le Daye 1332 *SR* 18. — *Ha:* Rog. le Daye 1327 *SR* 3. Ric. le Deye 1333 *SR* 5. — *So:* Walt. le Daye 1269 Ass 72. Gilb. le Deye 1327 SR 113. Rob. le Deye 1333 *SR* 6. Will. le Deye 1344 *Ass* 13. — *Wo:* Ric. le Deye 1305 *Ass* 1. Alicia Le Deye 1327 SR 22. — *St:* Rich. le Daye 1277 6. Ass 83. Thom. le Deye 1327 SR 210. Rob. le Deye 1332 SR 114. — *La:* Rob. le Daye 1292 *1.Ass.* 44. Joh. le Deye 1332 SR 9. Alic. la Dey 1339 *Ass* 17. — *Y:* Agnes le Daye 1301 SR 33. Joh. le Dey c1346 *SR* 5. — *Li:* Eborardus le Deye 1287 *Ass* 12. Matild. Le Daye 1327 *1.SR* 6. Thom. le Deye 1332 *2.SR* 3. — *Nf:* Emma la Daye 1286 *Ass* 73. Rob. le Deye 1300 *GDR* 21. Joh. le deye 1332 *SR* 12.

OE *dǣge* fem. 'maker of bread, baker'. — *One who has charge of a dairy, a maker of cheese and butter.* — *Deye* was originally only used of women, but was later transferred on men; the first quotation referring to men in NED is from 1351. It was certainly used in this latter sense much earlier; the case is that among all the instances that I have found, there are only a few referring to women.

Butterman. 1301. NED: 1802.

Y: Thom. Butterman 1301 SR 51. — *Li:* Joh. Butterman 1327 *2. SR* 8. Henr. Butterman 1332 *3. SR* 22.

OE *butere* + *mann*. — *Maker or seller of butter.*

Buterer. 1327. NED: —

Sx: Will. le Buterar' 1327 SR 116, 1332 SR 239.

A der. of OE *butere*. — *Butterman*.

Smeremongere. 1286. NED: 1297.

Ess: Galfr. Smeremongere 1326 *3. GDR* 10. — *Sx:* Will. Smermongere 1296 SR 82. — *Y:* Walt. Smermanger 1305 *Ass* 12. — *Nf:* Rob. le Smeremongere 1286 *Ass* 111. Phil. le Smeremongere 1296 *GDR* 1.

OE *smeoru* 'fat, lard' + *mangere*. The fem. form, *smeorumangestre* 'butterwoman', is evidenced in OE. — One who sells fat, lard, or butter.

Smereman. 1255. NED: —

Ess: Rob. Smereman 1255 *Ass* 27. Will. Smerman 1319 *SR* 18. Ric. Smereman 1332 *SR* 23. — *Y:* Rob. Smerman 1301 SR 32. — *Li:* Agnes le Smereman 1287 *Ass* 5. — *Nf:* Phil. le Smereman 1307 *GDR* 1.

OE *smeoru* 'fat, lard' + *mann*. — Maker or seller of fat, lard, or butter.

Smerekernere. 1326. NED: —

Ess: Galfr. Smerekernere 1326 *3. GDR* 9.

ME *smere* (OE *smeoru*) + ME **kernere* (fr. ME *cherne* 'to churn', NED c1440; cf MG *kirnen, kernen* 'to churn'). The *k-* is prob. due to Scandinavian influence. NED has *smear* only in the sense of 'fat, lard'. — One who churns butter. — Cf the following surname containing only the last element: ... el le *Kerner* 1332 SR 85 (Lo).

F. Maker or Seller of Spices, Garlics, Oil.

Spicer, Especer. 1184. NED: 1297.

Ess: Ric. le espicer 1285 *Ass* 48. Gilb. le Speser 1302 *2. GDR* 12. Joh. le Spicer' 1319 *SR* 1. Samannus Le Spiser 1327 *SR* 6. Juliana la Spicer' 1332 *SR* 26. — *Ke:* Will. le Espicier 1184 P 151. — *Sx:* Will. le Espicer 1272 FF 86. Walt. le Spycer 1296 SR 82. Rob. le Spicer 1327 SR 183. Nich. Spisour 1332 SR 308. — *Ha:* Bertram le Specier 1200 P 199. Will. le Especier 1280 *2. Ass* 31. Isabella la Spicer 1327 *SR* 17. Joh. le Spicer 1333 *SR* 2. — *So:* Rob. le Spicer 1201 Ass 15. Rob. Le Espicer' 1305 *Ass* 3. Rich. le Spycer 1327 SR 254. Will. le Spicer 1333 *SR* 8. — *Wo:* Phil. le Spicer 1275 SR 5. Will. le Especier 1275 *2. Ass* 25. Adam le Espicer 1292 Epi 416. Henry le Spicer 1303 Reg 39. — *St:* Will. Specer 1199 3. Ass 39. Adam le Especer 1293 6. Ass 271. Thom. le Spyser 1332 SR 83. — *La:* Hugh le Spicer 1204

FF 22. Adam le Especer 1292 *1. Ass* 17. Rob. le Spiser 1332 SR 52. Rob. le Specer 1338 *Ass* 8. — *Y:* Henry le Spicer 1260 Ass 138. Elias le Spicer 1301 SR 118. Walt. the Specer 1317 4. Wake 169. Alan. le Specer c1346 *SR* 5. — *Li:* Ad. lespicer 1245 *Ass* 45. Joh. le Spicer 1281 *1.Ass* 44. Remund. Le Spicer' 1327 *1.SR* 1. Bened. lespicer 1332 *3.SR* 25. — *Nf:* Joh. le Especer 1286 *Ass* 73. Adam le Specer 1298 CDN 63. Gerard le Spicer 1309 ib. 12. Thom. spicer 1329 *SR* 33. Phil. Le Spicer 1332 *SR* 14.

OF *espicier, especier* 'celui qui tient un commerce d'épicerie' (Godefroy). The initial *E*- has generally been dropped, especially in later rolls. — *A dealer in spices; an apothecary or druggist* (NED). — This surname occurs very frequently in all counties.

Honyman. 1275. NED: 1552.
Sx: Sim. Hunyman 1296 SR 17. Joh. Honyman ib. 66. — *Wo:* Juliana Honemon 1275 SR 26. Nich. Honymon 1327 SR 33.

OE *hunig* 'honey' + *mann*. — *One who sells honey.*

Garlekmongere. 1280. NED: 1393.
Ess: Rog. le Garlekmonger' 1318 *3.GDR* 46 (le Garlekmongere 1318 2. GDR 37). — *Ha:* Thom. le Garlekmongare 1280 *2.Ass* 64 (le Garlecmongere 1280 *3. Ass* 13).

OE *gārlēac* 'garlic' + *mangere*. — *Dealer in garlics.*
I have found two instances of another surname of the same signification: Thom. *Garleker*, taillour 1387 Free Y 86 (*Garlyker*, tailor 1400 YMB 247 Y).

Lekman. 1319. NED: —
Nf: Hugh le Lekman 1319 CDN 89. Thom. Lekman 1332 *SR* 39.

OE *lēac* 'leek' + *mann*. — *Dealer in leeks.*

Leker. 1279. NED: —
Y: Adam lekere 1279 *Ass* 3. Will. le Leker 1293 *Ass* 104. Alan. le Leker ib. 53. Henry le Leker 1336 FF 101. Rob. Leker c1346 *SR* 7. Galfr. Leker ib.

A der. of OE *lēac* 'leek'. — Signification: = LEKMAN. Cf GARLEKER (same county).

Porer. 1285. NED: —
Ess: Will. le Porer 1285 *Ass* 50.

OF *porier* 'marchand de porreaux, de légumes' (Godefroy). — *Seller of leeks and vegetables.*

Fruter. 1203. NED: a1483.

Ess: Martin. le Fruyter 1327 *3.GDR* 6. — *Sx:* Joh. le Friter **1288** FF 146. Henr' Fryter 1296 SR 26. — *St:* Rob. le Fruter 1203 3. Ass 88. **Rich.** le Fruter 1227 4. Ass 57. — *Y:* Gerard le fruter 1322 Free Y 21. Phil. le fruter 1336 ib. 32. — *Nf:* John Fruytr 1286 CDN 5. Thom. le Fruter 1312 ib. 36 (Fruyter 1323 ib. 125).

OF *fruitier, frutier, fritier* (Godefroy). — *One who deals in fruit;* perhaps also *a fruit-grower.*

Elymaker. 1344. NED: —

So: Rog. le Elymaker 1344 *Ass* 15, 12. Reg. Elymaker 1372 BBA 193.

OE *œle* 'oil' + a der. of *macian.* — *Maker of oil.* — As the name of a trade: Nic. de Anlep *elymakere* 1345 RBL 63 (Le). — The following is another compound of the same signification: Tho. *Elyman* 1377 RBL 157 (Le).

Oylemaker. 1221. NED: —

Wo: Aluredus Vli maker' 1221 Ass 460 (Hulimakiere ib. 642). — *Le:* Hug. le Oillemakere 1307 RBL 255. — *Li:* Will. Oylemaker 1332 *3. SR* 2.

ME *oli, oyle, uile,* 'oil' (fr. OF *oile, oille, uille*) + ME *maker.* — *Maker of oil.*

Oyler. 1281. NED: 1552.

Le: Reg. le Oyler 1286 RBL 209. — *Li:* Ric. le Oyller' 1281 *1. Ass* 11. Will. le Oyellere 1281 *2. Ass* 30 (le Oyller ib.). Will. Oyller 1328 *Ass* 57 (Oyler ib. 54). Alic. Oyler 1332 *3. SR* 15.

OF *olier, uillier, huilier* 'fabricant ou marchand d'huile' (Godefroy). — *Maker or seller of oil.*

Oilman. 1275. NED: c1440.

Wo: Joh. le Ulemon 1275 SR 74. Joh. Hulemon ib. 96. — *Y:* Ric. Olman 1297 SR 62.

ME *oli* etc. (v. OYLEMAKER) + ME *man.* — *One who makes or sells oil.*

G. Maker or Seller of Salt, Soap, Candles, Wax.

Saltere. 1243. NED: a1000.

Ess: Rad. le saltere 1255 *Ass* 22. Walt. le Salter 1303 *2. GDR* 13. Ric. le Salter' 1319 *SR* 18. Milo le Salter' 1327 *SR* 24. — *Sx:* Rog. le saltere 1249 *Ass* 22. Rad. le Saltere 1288 *Ass* 32. Thom. le Selter' 1296 *SR* 33. Will. Selter

1327 SR 198. Ric. Saltare 1332 SR 246. — *Ha:* Will. le Saltere 1272 *Ass* 10. Rob. le Saltere 1280 *2. Ass* 80. Alicia la Saltere 1327 *SR* 14. Galfr. le Saltere ib. Joh. le Saltere 1333 *SR* 3. — *So:* Rob. le Saltere 1243 Ass 264. Adam le Saltere 1305 *Ass* 9. Will. le Saltere 1327 SR 164. Jord. le Saltere ib. 242. — *Wo:* Will. le Salter 1272 Hal 39. Hugo le Saltere 1275 SR 110. Pet. Le Salter' 1307 *Ass* 3. Rob. Le Saltere 1327 SR 36. — *St:* Rich. le Saltere 1306 7.Ass 153. — *La:* Adam le Saltere 1292 *1.Ass* 5. Will. le Salter' ib. 11. Mich. le Salter 1324 CR 4. Gilb. le Salter 1333 *Ass* 14. Henr. le Salter 1338 *Ass* 8. — *Y:* Rob. le Salter 1260 Ass 139. Rog. le Salter 1301 SR 27. Adam Salter 1315 3.Wake 78. Nich. Salter 1332 *SR* 18. — *Li:* Walt. le Saltere 1275 RH 275. Rog. le Saltere 1281 *2. Ass* 53. Hugo Salter 1320 *Ass* 30. Joh. le Salter 1332 *2. SR* 9. Rosa Salter 1340 *Ass* 16. — *Nf:* Thom. le Saltere 1286 *Ass* 117. Henr. Le Saltere 1329 *SR* 6. Will. Le Saltere 1332 *SR* 81.

OE *sealtere*. — *Maker or seller of salt*. — This surname occurs frequently, especially in *Ha, Wo, La,* and *Y*.

Saltman. 1306.   NED: —
Nf: Will. Saltman 1306 CDN 113. Henr. Saltman 1329 *SR* 1. Will. Saltman 1332 *SR* 36.

OE *sealt* 'salt' + *mann*. — *Maker or seller of salt*.

Wellere. 1272.   NED: 1388.
Sx: Ric. le Weller 1272 FF 83. Aunfr. le Willere 1323 *Ass* 22 (le Wellere 1324 *Ass* 19). Will. le Weller 1327 SR 136. Will. le Willer ib. 142. Rob. le Wyliar 1332 SR 236. — *Ha:* Joh. le Wylyare 1327 *SR* 5. Will. le Wyliere 1333 *SR* 1 (le Weller 1340 *SR* 7). — *Li:* Will. Weller 1332 *3. SR* 17.

A der. of OE *wiellan, wællan, wellan* 'to boil'. — Prob. *a saltboiler*.

Cf the OE pl. n. *'wylleres seaðon'* 995, containing *wyllere* 'saltboiler' and *sēaþ* 'a pit' (Ekwall: Trades in Eng. Pl. N.). — The interpretation of this surname, however, is not very easy; it may also mean 'one who casts metal', v. NED. Besides this, its forms entirely coincide with a toponymical surname, WELLERE, q. v.

Sopere. 1195.   NED: c1225.
Ess: Rob. le sopere 1255 *Ass* 22. Bricius le Sopper' 1327 *SR* 1. Joh. le Sopper 1332 *SR* 23. — *Sx:* Mart. le Sopere 1263 *Ass* 36. Nich. Le Sopere 1279 *Ass* 14. Will. le Sopere 1296 SR 43. Ric. le Sopere 1327 SR 139. Steph. le Soper 1332 SR 274. — *Ha:* Pet. le Sopere 1272 *Ass* 24. Agnes la Sopere 1327 *SR* 8. Rob. le Sopare 1327 *SR* 5. Will. le Sopere 1333 *SR* 4. Ric. le Sopere 1340 *SR* 6. — *So:* Walt. le Soper 1243 Ass 312. Will. le Sopere 1307 *Ass* 8. Adam le Sopare 1315 FF 55. Galfr. le Sopere 1327 SR 182. Ric. le Sopere 1333 *SR* 21. — *Gl:* Will. le Sopere 1195 P 180. — *Wo:* Rob. le Sopere 1275

1. Ass 8. Margeria Soper 1332 SR 3. — *Y:* Ric. le Sopere 1293 *Ass* 81. Emma la Sapere 1301 SR 120. Will. Saper 1332 *SR* 17. — *Li:* Nich. le Sopere 1281 *2. Ass* 54. — *Nf:* Walt. Le Sopere 1286 *Ass* 84. Rog. le Soper 1305 Free L 6. John Sopere the Hattere 1322 CDN 108. Alan. Sopere 1337 *SR* 5.

A der. of OE *sāpe* 'soap'. — *Maker or seller of soap.* — Most instances of this surname have been found in *Sx* and *So*. In the former county there also occurs another form, *Sapiere,* which seems to belong here: Rob. le Sapiere 1324 *Ass* 19 (le Sapiar 1332 SR 257). The same form occurs seven times, but it probably refers to the same person.

OE **sāpere* is found in *Sapperton Gl* (*Saperetún* 969); v. Ekwall: Trades in Engl. Pl. N.

Sopestere. 1285.   NED: —
Ess: Amya le Sopestere 1285 *Ass* 45.

The fem. form of SOPERE. — Signification: = SOPERE.

Sauoner. 1225.   NED: —
Sx: Joh. le Sauenir 1288 *Ass* 23. — *Ha:* Rob. le Sauoner 1280 *2. Ass* 51. Nich. le Sauoner 1280 *3. Ass* 35. — *So:* Rich. le Savoner 1225 Ass 96. Godstan le Savoner ib. 74. — *Y:* John le Sauoner 1231 FF 161 (the Sawuner 1251 ib. 62).

OF *savonnier* 'celui qui fabrique du savon' (Godefroy). — *Maker or seller of soap.*

Chaundeler, Candeler. 1285.   NED: 1389.
Ess: Will. le Chaundeler 1285 *Ass* 34. Rad. le Chaundeler 1319 *SR* 1. Alex. Le Chaundeler 1327 *SR* 14. Joh. le Chaundeler 1332 *SR* 6. Elias Chaundeler 1341 *Ass* 22. — *Sx:* Jord. Le Chaundeler 1288 *Ass* 27. Will. le Chaundeler 1323 *Ass* 22. Rob. Chaundelir 1327 SR 120. Juliana le Chaundelir 1332 SR 230. Ad' le Chaundelir ib. 265. — *Ha:* Rad. le Chaundeler 1287 *Ass* 11. Rob. le Chaundeler 1327 SR 7. Henr. le Chaundelir 1333 *SR* 8. Ph. le Chaundeler 1340 *SR* 6. — *So:* Will. le Chaundeler' 1333 *SR* 30. — *Wo:* Will. le Chaundeler 1316 Inq 72. Ric. Le Chaundeler 1327 SR 35. David Le Chaundelr' ib. 8. — *St:* Henr' le Chaundeler 1327 SR 223. Thom' le Chandeler 1332 SR 107. — *La:* Will. le Condeler 1332 SR 57. Joh. le Condeler ib. Will. le Candeler 1338 *Ass* 8. — *Y:* Rog. le Chaundeler 1293 *Ass* 83. Joh. le Candelor 1301 SR 92. Nich. le Candelere ib. 120. Will. le candeler 1321 Free Y 20. — *Li:* Theophilus le Chaundeler 1328 *Ass* 54. Will. Candeler 1332 *1. SR* 5. Thom. Candeler 1332 *3. SR* 7. — *Nf:* Thom. Le chaundeler 1286 *Ass* 91. Will. le Chaundeler 1298 CDN 68. Joh. Chandeler 1332 *SR* 48. Walt. Shaundeler ib. 53. Thom. Chaundeler 1340 CDN 219.

OF *chandelier, candelier*. Note the forms *Candeler, Condeler*, the latter of which has been influenced by OE *condel* 'candle'. These two forms only occur in Anglian counties. — *Maker or seller of candles of different kinds*. The chandler also made small wax images for ecclesiastical offerings (1. YMB Intr. p. 45).

Candelmaker. 1289.   NED: 1611.
Li: Alan. le Candelmakere 1289 *Ass* 37. Theophilus Candelmaker 1327 *3.SR* 2. Joh. Candelmaker ib. 1. — *Nf:* Rog. le Candelmaker 1316 CDN 66. Will. le Candilmaker 1328 ib. 141.

OE *candel* + a der. of *macian*. — *Maker of candles*. — A synonymous trade-name, *candle-wright*, is found in the name of a London street: *Candelwryttestrete* 1230 P 106.

Candelman. 1332.   NED: —
Nf: Rob. Candelman 1332 *SR* 39.

OE *candel* + *mann*. — *Maker of or dealer in candles*.

Cyrer. 1230.   NED: —
Lo: Rob. le Cyrger 1277 CLB (A) 16. — *Sx:* Rob. le Cyrur 1263 *Ass* 14. Joh. le Cyrur ib. — *Nf:* Rob. le Cirer 1230 P 91. Adam le Cyrer 1286 CDN 7.

OF *cirier* 'fabricant, marchand de cierges, de bougies' (Godefroy); prob. also OF **cirour*. — *Maker or seller of candles*.

Waxmongere. 1310.   NED: —
Nf: Rob. le Waxmongere 1310 CDN 19, 1321 ib. 101.

OE *weax* 'wax' + *mangere*. — *One who sells wax*.

Waxman. 1185.   NED: —
Wo: Adam Wexman 1185 P 123. Adam Waxmon 1322 Inq 111.

OE *weax* 'wax' + *mann*. — Signification: = Waxmongere.

H. **Butcher, Poulterer.**

Bucher. 1184.   NED: [1292].
Ess: Joh. le Buchere 1285 *Ass* 33. Rog. le Bochier 1332 *SR* 29. Edm. le Boucher 1334 CR 124. — *Lo:* Ailwardus le Bochere 1184 P 141. — *Sx:* Thom. le Butcher 1249 *Ass* 38. Sim. Le Bocher' 1288 *Ass* 7. Alex' le Bucher 1296 SR 91. Walt. le Bocher 1327 SR 139. Joh. Buchier 1332 SR 308. — *Ha:* Will. le Bochere 1280 2. *Ass* 56. Thom. le Bochere 1280 3. *Ass* 33. Joh. le Bocher

1327 *SR* 12. — *So:* Will. le Bocher 1243 Ass 247. Joh. le Bucher' 1320 *Ass* 20. Joseph. le Bouchere 1333 *SR* 2. — *Wo:* Adam le Bucher 1275 SR 48. Milo Le Bocher 1307 *Ass* 3. — *Y:* John the Bocher 1314 3. Wake 52. John Boucher 1343 FF 170. — *Li:* Henr. le Bucher' 1281 *1. Ass* 22. Sim. le Bocher 1328 *Ass* 5. Pet. le Bocher 1332 *Ass* 8. — *Nf:* Sim. le Bucher 1275 RH 483. Thom. le Bucher 1310 *GDR* 11. Joh. Le Bucher 1332 *SR* 1. Henr. Bocher ib. 53.

AF *bocher, boucher,* OF *bochier, bouchier.* — *Butcher.* — It is not improbable that in some cases this surname might come from OF *buschier, bucher* 'marchand de bois' (Godefroy).

Fleshhewere. 1268. NED: 1335.
Sx: Ric. Le Fleshewere 1314 *1.GDR* 8. — *Ha:* Will. le Fleshewyer' 1323 *Ass* 8. — *Wo:* Pet. Le Fleshewar' 1327 SR 39. Phil. Le Flesshewar ib. 54 (le Fleysheware 1332 SR 16). — *St:* Pet. le Flesshewere 1331 11. Ass 23. Rich. le Flechhewere 1344 12. Ass 33. — *La:* Rob. Flesshewer 1338 *Ass* 5. — *Y:* Ric. le Fleshewere 1268 *Ass* 14. Adam le Flessehewere 1293 *Ass* 83. Rog. le Flesshewer 1340 FF 147. — *Li:* Will. Fleshewer 1327 *1. SR* 4. Ric. Fleshewer 1328 *Ass* 32. — *Nf:* Isabella la Flesshewere 1315 *GDR* 31. Joh. le Fleshewere 1332 *SR* 39. Rob. le Flesshewere ib. 40.

OE *flǣsc* 'flesh' + a der. of *hēawan.* — *Butcher.* — The same surname occurs in MG: *fleysschawer* 1355 (Bücher).

Fleshmongere. 1279. NED: c1000.
Ess: Joh. le Fleschmonger' 1324 *4.GDR* 8. — *Ha:* Matheus le Flesmongere 1280 *2. Ass* 23. Gilb. Le Fleysmonger' 1305 *Ass* 15. Joh. le Fleschmangere 1327 *SR* 2. Rad. le Fleschmongere ib. 18. Rob. Flesshmongere 1333 *SR* 4. Steph. le Flehsmongere ib. 7. — *Y:* Luc. Fleysmanger 1279 *Ass* 76.

OE *flǣscmangere.* — *One who sells flesh, a butcher.*

Ketmongere. 1275. NED: —
Nf: Adam Ketmongere 1275 RH 470.

ON **kiǫtmangari,* Old Swed. *kiötmangare* 'fleshmonger'. This trade-name is found in the name of a street in York: *Chetmangeregate* 1175, *Ketmangeregate* 1194 (v. Lindkvist: A Study on Early Medieval York, Anglia 50, p. 370). — Signification: = FLESHMONGERE.

Stikkere. 1279. NED: a1585.
Sx: Joh. Le Stikere 1279 *Ass* 5, 32. — *So:* Joh. le Stikkere 1327 SR 190.

A der. of OE *stician* 'to stick, stab'. — *One who kills swine, a butcher.*

Macecrer, Macegre. 1235.   NED: —
Ha: Henr. le Mazerer 1280 *3. Ass* 35 (le Maserer 1280 *2. Ass* 87). — *So:* Rog. le Macecrer 1243 Ass 178. — *Wo:* Syremon le Macekre 1275 SR 9. — *Y:* Will. the Massecrer 1235 FF 33. Henry le Macegre 1260 Ass 118.

OF *maceclier, macecrier, maserier* 'boucher, charcutier'. The shorter forms apparently come fr. OF *macegref* »forme altérée de *maceclier*» (Godefroy). — *Butcher*. There is a regulation for the craft of the »macecriers» (or »bochiers») of Reading in Gross: Gild M. vol. 2, p. 205

Bukmongere. 1275.   NED: —
La: Adam de Bukemonger 1314 FF 15. — *Nf:* Hugo Bucmonger 1275 RH 470. Will. le Bukmongere 1286 *Ass* 56. Hugo le Bukmongere 1288 CDN 20. Joh. le Bucmongere 1295 *GDR* 14. Gregor. le Bugmongger' 1332 *SR* 73.

OE *buc, bucca* 'buck' + *mangere*. — *Dealer in bucks, venison*.

Bukmarter. 1275.   NED: —
Nf: Hugo le Bugmarter 1275 RH 539.

OE *buc* 'buck' + a der. of *mart* vb 'to bargain, to traffic in' (NED 1553), fr. *mart* sb (fr. Du *markt*). For the spelling *Bug-*, cf BUKMONGERE (*Bug-*). — Signification: = BUKMONGERE. — Hugo le *Bugmarter* is the same person as Hugo *Bucmonger* mentioned under the preceding surname.

Budiner. 1327.   NED: —
Ha: Will. le Budiner 1327 *SR* 9 (le Budenere 1333 *SR* 6).

OF *boudinier* 'marchand de boudin' (Godefroy). — *Maker or seller of sausages*.

Puleter. 1230.   NED: a1400.
Ess: Sym. le Poleter 1283 *1. GDR* 9. Gilb. Le Poletter 1304 *2. GDR* 14. Walt. le Polyter 1319 *SR* 15. Thom. le Pulter 1332 *SR* 7. Rob. Pulter 1341 *Ass* 15. — *Sx:* Alex. le Poleter 1288 *Ass* 35. Laur. Le Puleter ib. 21. Walt. le Puleter 1296 SR 58. Joh. le Poleter ib. 82. Ric. le Poleter 1327 SR 183. — *Ha:* Adam le Politer 1306 *Ass* 2. Rob. le Poleter 1325 *Ass* 2. Nich. le Poletir 1327 *SR* 6. Joh. le poulleter 1340 *SR* 6. Will. le Poulleter ib. — *Wo:* Rob. le Pultere 1275 *1. Ass.* 4. Rob. le Poleter 1275 SR 8. Thom. le Poleter 1316 OCW 88. — *Sal:* Osbertus le puleter 1230 P 226. — *La:* John le Pulter 1325 CR 112. Will. le Pulter 1326 ib. 76. — *Y:* Galfr. le pulter 1277 Free Y 3. Henr. le pulter 1315 ib. 16. Ric. le Pulter c1346 *SR* 6. — *Li:* Will. le Puleter 1281 *1. Ass* 28. Pet. Le Pulter 1305 *Ass* 16. Rog. le Pulter 1327 *3. SR* 3. Joh. Pulter 1340 *Ass* 7. — *Nf:* Ric. le Pulleter 1286 *Ass* 135. Walt. le Pultir 1324 CDN 129. Edw. pulter 1329 *SR* 18. Reynerus Pulter 1332 *SR* 8.

OF *pouletier, poulletier, poletier* (Godefroy). — *Dealer in poultry.* — In London (about 1300) the poulterer sold rabbits, game, eggs, and poultry (Lib. Alb. Intr. 83).

Henmongere. 1263.   NED: —
  Sx: Adam Le Henmongere 1263 *Ass* 44. — *So:* Adam Le Henmanger' 1305 *Ass* 7. — *Nf:* Katerine la Hennemongere 1291 CDN 40. Thom. le Hennemonggere 1310 *GDR* 11 (le Hennemongere 1312 CDN 34).

  OE *henn* 'hen' + *mangere*. — *Dealer in hens, poulterer.*

Gelyner. 1242.   NED: —
  Le: Ric. le Geliner 1242 RBL 62. — *Nf:* Joh. Le Gelyner 1286 *Ass* 91 (le Geliner 1286 CDN 6). Henr. Geliner 1295 *GDR* 16.

  OF *gelinier* 'poulailler' (Godefroy). Cf NED *geline* (1430) 'hen'. —*Poulterer.*

Gosmanger. 1344.   NED: —
  So: Joh. le Gosmanger 1344 *Ass* 12.

  OE *gōs* 'goose' + *mangere*. — *A dealer in geese, a poulterer.*

Gosere. 1327.   NED: —
  So: Joh. le Gozer 1327 SR 219 (le Gosere 1333 *SR* 21). Ric. le Gosiar' 1327 *SR* 32.

  A der. of OE *gōs* 'goose'. — Signification: = Gosmanger. — The first person (Joh. le G.) is probably the same as the one quoted under Gosmanger.

I. Seller of Fish.

Pessoner. 1208.   NED: 1310.
  Ess: Eilmer le Pessuner 1208 Cur 302. Sim. le Pessuner 1255 *Ass* 37. Rob. le Pessoner 1303 *2. GDR* 13. — *Sx:* Math. le Pessoner 1296 SR 17. Steph. Pessoner 1327 SR 206. Ad Pessoner 1332 SR 317. — *Ha:* Henr. le Pessoner 1280 *2. Ass* 87. Rog. le Pesshoner 1280 *3. Ass* 35. Will. Pessoner 1327 *SR* 17. *Wo:* J. le Pessoner 1286 Epi 280. — *La:* Rob. le Peysuner 1292 *3. Ass* 96 (le Pessouner ib. 113). — *Li:* Rob. de Hicham Pesshoner 1332 *Ass* 12. — *Nf:* Ran. le Pessouner 1275 RH 531.

  AF **pessoner, peiss-* = OF *poissonnier*. — *Fishmonger.*

Fishmongere. 1312.   NED: 1464.
  Lo: Master John le Fisshmongere 1320 CLB (E) 115. — *Nf:* Ralph le Fhismongere 1312 CDN 33.

OE *fisc* 'fish' + *mangere*. — *One who deals in fish.*

Heryngmongere. 1212. NED: 1614.
Sx: Is' Relicta Heryngmongere 1296 SR 123. — *Sr:* Joh. Herengmongar' 1332 SR 23. — *Berks:* Theodbaldus le Heringmongere 1212 Cur 390. — *Hu:* Agnes le Haringmongere 1294 CR Ramsey 222.

OE *hǣring* 'herring' + *mangere*. — *One who sells herrings.* — Cf the following surname: Rob. *Heryngkartere* 1332 SR 69 (Lo) 'one who carts herrings for sale'.

Lusmonger. 1293. NED: —
Y: Joh. le Lusmanger 1293 *Ass* 21 (Lusmonger ib. 69).

ME *lus* 'pike' (fr. OF *lus*) + ME *monger;* v. NED *luce* (1338). — *One who sells pike.* — Cf the following trade-name (same sense): Ric. Mounkton, *pykemonger* 1472 Free Y 193.

Laxman. 1281. NED: —
Sx: Rich. Laxman 1339 FF 93, 1342 ib. 105. — *Y:* Joh. Laxman 1301 SR 108. Rob. Laxman, piscarius 1318 Free Y 18. — *Li:* Rog. Laxman 1281 *1.Ass* 46. Will. laxman 1327 *4.SR* 3. Thom. laxman ib. Rog. Laxman 1332 *1. SR* 13.

OE *leax* 'salmon' + *mann*. — *Seller of salmon*; perhaps also *one who fishes salmon*. — *Laxman* was an ON byname (1442), v. Lind.

J. Brewer, Vintner, Taverner.

Brewere. 1263. NED: a1300.
Ess: Rob. le Brewere 1285 *Ass* 42. Joh. le *Briwere* 1311 CR 49. Galfr. le Brewer' 1319 *SR* 1. Ric. le Brewere 1327 *SR* 6. Rob. le Bruer 1332 *SR* 28. — *Sx:* Will. le Brouwere 1263 *Ass* 41. Thom. le Brewere 1288 *Ass* 38. Rob. le Brouwer' 1296 SR 67. Thom. le Brewer' 1315 *2. GDR* 12. Joh. le Bruar' 1327 SR 115. Hugo le Browar 1332 SR 225. — *Ha:* Thom. le Bruware 1327 *SR* 8. Nich. le Brewere ib. 7. Henr. le Brewere 1333 *SR* 8. Walt. le Bruer' 1340 *SR* 3. — *So:* Henry le Brewere 1278 Ass 162. Joh. Le Bruwer' 1305 *Ass* 12 (Le Brewer' 1307 *Ass* 9). Rich. le *Brywer* 1327 SR 103. Adam le Brewer' 1333 *SR* 11. Henr. le Brewere 1344 *Ass* 13. — *Wo:* Will. le Breware 1275 SR 76. Rob. Le Brewer' 1307 *Ass* 5. Gregorius le Brewere 1332 SR 26. — *Y:* Isabella Brewer 1319 Free Y 19. — *Li:* Walt. Le Brewer 1305 *Ass* 16. Walt. Brewer 1327 *2. SR* 14. Joh. Brewer 1332 *1. SR* 18. — *Nf:* Reg. Le Brewere 1286 *Ass* 111.

A der. of OE *brēowan* 'to brew'. The two instances of *Briwere* in *Ess* and *So* are early examples of the change from *eu* to *iu*. There is a still earlier instance under BREWSTERE (*Bryester' Wo*). Cf Luick § 407 and Jordan § 109. These forms speak in favour of Luick's opinion. NED has *brywer* 1393. — Signification: *One who brews.*

The occurrence of this surname should be compared with BREWSTERE, q. v. — *Brewere* very seldom occurs in compound surnames; I have only found one instance: Cristin le *Alebrewere* 1311 CLB (D) 249 (Lo).

Brewstere. 1284. NED: c1308.

Ess: Rob. Brouster 1332 *SR* 24. — *Ha:* Marg. la Bruwestre 1333 *SR* 4. — *Wo:* Agn. le *Bryester'* 1305 *Ass.* — *St:* Pet. le Brewestere 1305 7. Ass 130. John le Breuster 1306 ib. 174. Thom. le Breustere 1326 10. Ass 73. Adam le Breuster 1327 SR 242. Adam le Brouster' 1332 SR 115. — *La:* Will. le Breuster 1284 Ass 177. Galfr. le Brewstere 1292 *1. Ass* 21. — *Y:* Alice the Breustere 1316 4. Wake 138. Will. le Breuster 1332 *SR* 7. — *Li:* Rob. Breuster 1327 *1: SR* 2. Agnes la Breuster 1328 *Ass* 13. Galfr. Brewyster 1332 *1. SR* 5. Joh. Bruster 1332 *3. SR* 6. Adam Breuster 1340 *Ass* 7. — *Nf:* Joh. Breustere 1295 *GDR* 2 (le Broustere ib.). Bricius le Brewestere 1308 *GDR* 4. Mabil' le breuster' 1332 *SR* 26.

The fem. form of BREWERE. The form *Browster* is, according to NED, a northern form, but this does not agree with the above instances. — Signification: *Brewer.*

With the exception of three instances, this surname has only been found in the Anglian counties. The corresponding surname in the South is BREWERE, which occurs frequently there, but very seldom in other counties.

Brasur. 1202. NED :—

Ess: Thom. le Brachur 1255 *Ass* 23 (le Brasur ib. 32). Adam le **Brasur** 1285 *Ass* 33. — *Sx:* Joh. le Braseur 1272 FF 81. Fulco Le Bracur 1279 *Ass* 12. Rad. le Bracur 1296 SR 84. Will. Brassour 1332 SR 308. — *Ha:* Walt. le Brazur 1272 *Ass* 20. — *Wo:* Rob. le Bracur 1275 SR 3. Gilb. le Brasur ib. 90. Rob. le Braszour 1305 *Ass* 1. — *St:* Thom. le Bracur 1227 4. Ass 69. Hugo le Brasur 1327 SR 221. — *La:* Ad. le Bracur 1292 *1. Ass* 39. Bened. le Braceur 1292 *3. Ass* 107. — *Y:* Rob. le Bracur 1202 FF 58. Geoffrey le Brazur 1260 Ass 105. Hutredus le Brassour 1293 *Ass* 73. — *Li:* Ralph Le Brathur 1234 FF 255. Henr. le Brazour 1245 *Ass* 31. Thom. le Bracur 1281 *2. Ass* 5. Will. le Bracour 1305 *Ass* 16. Rad. le Braseur 1332 *2. SR* 7. — *Nf:* Ric. le Bracur 1250 *Ass* 23. Steph. le Bracour 1286 *Ass* 113. Rob. le Brascour ib. 117.

OF *braceor, brasseur* 'celui qui brasse la bière' (Godefroy). — *Brewer*. — The OF word also meant 'one who works with his arms, one who manufactures something', but this sense is not probable here.

Braceresse. 1255. NED: —
Ess: Ida la Braceresse 1255 *Ass* 6. Oliua la Braceresse ib. 18. Dionisia la Braceresse ib. 16. — *Wo:* Juliana la Braceresse 1297 Hal 362.

OF *braceresse*. — *Female brewer*.

Malter. 1319. NED: c1440.
Ess: Rog. le Malter' 1319 *SR* 4. Rad. le Malter' ib. 1. John le Malter 1336 CR 146.

A der. of *malt* 'to make malt', fr. *malt* sb (OE *mealt*) — *Maltster*. — Cf the following surnames in the other counties: Hugo le *Maltmakere* 1255 RH 31 (Bk). Margeria le *Maltmaker* 1292 RBL 221 (Le). Rog. *Maltmo(n)gere* 1199 RBL 17 (Le).

Maltestere. 1279. NED: c1370—80.
Y: Rob. le Maltester' 1279 *Ass* 75. Thom. le Maltster c1346 *SR* 3. — *Li:* Henr. Malster 1327 *1. SR* 1. — *Nf:* Ric. Maltestere 1332 *SR* 48.

The fem. form of MALTER. — *Maltster, maker of malt*.

Medemaker. 1332. NED: —
Nf: Joh. Medemaker' 1332 *SR* 27.

OE *meodu* 'mead' + a der. of *macian*. — *Maker of mead*. — Cf the MG surnames *medemechere, medebruer* 'Metbrauer' (Bücher).

Vineter. 1212. NED: 1297.
Ess: Rad. le Vineter 1255 *Ass* 12. Joh. Vyniter 1319 *SR* 8. Rog. Vynter 1327 *SR* 24. Matilda la Vinetere 1329 CR 91. Will. le Vynter 1332 *SR* 20. — *Sx:* Godefridus le Vineter 1249 *Ass* 39. Rob. le Vineter ib. Steph. le Veneter 1262 FF 46. — *Ha:* Joh. le Vineter 1280 *2. Ass* 64. Sim. le Vyneter 1289 *Ass* 13. — *So:* Adam le Vineter 1256 FF 161. Rob. Vyneter 1327 SR 250. Will. le Vyneter ib. — *Wo:* Will. Wineter 1212 Cur 396. Ph. Le Vyneter 1275 *2. Ass* 51. Pegun le Vineter' ib. — *St:* Eva la Vinitere 1286 6. Ass 161. Henry le Vineter 1306 7. Ass 154. — *Y:* Will. le Vineter 1251 Ass 82. Galfr. le Vineter 1268 *Ass* 30. — *Li:* Adam le Vineter 1248 FF 48. Math. le Vineter' 1281 *1.Ass* 10. Lambert' le Wyneter ib. 44. Joh. le Vineter 1281 *2.Ass* 22. Rog. le Vinter 1332 *2.SR* 16. — *Nf:* Steph. le Vineter 1286 *Ass* 118. Ric. le Vyneter ib. Henr. Vinter 1332 *SR* 57.

AF *viniter, vineter, vinter* = OF *vinet(t)ier*. — *Vintner, wine-merchant*.

Vyntener. 1327.   NED: c1430.
La: Ric. le Vyntener 1327 *SR* 14.

Alteration of Vineter (NED). — *One who deals in wine.*

Tauerner. 1175.   NED: 13..
Ess: Joh. le Tauerner 1282 *1.GDR* 10. Bened. le Tauerner 1285 *Ass* 39. Walt. Le Tauerner 1327 *SR* 4. — *Sx:* Will. Le Tauerner 1263 *Ass* 18. Gilb. le Tauerner 1296 SR 82. Joh. le Tauerner 1327 SR 109. — *Ha:* Hugo le Tauerner 1272 *Ass* 2. Adam Le Tauerner 1305 *Ass* 12. Joh. la Tauernere 1333 *SR* 4. — *So:* Rob. Le Tauerner 1307 *Ass* 1. Rob. le Taverner 1327 SR 104. — *Wo:* Will. le Taverner 1304 Reg 4. Rog. Taverner 1332 SR 12. — *St:* Will. le Taverner 1299 7.Ass 60. Joh. le Taverner 1332 SR 83. — *Y:* Walt. Tauerner 1175 P 174. Rob. le Taburner 1301 SR 67. Benedictus le taverner 1320 Free Y 19. — *Li:* Louekin' le Tauerner' 1281 *1.Ass* 6. Alicia Tauerner 1327 *2.SR* 7. Hugo le Tauerner 1332 *3.SR* 6. — *Nf:* Geoffrey le Taverner 1288 CDN 16. Will. Tauerner 1332 *SR* 18.

AF *taverner* = OF *tavernier.* — *Tavern-keeper, seller of ale and wine.* — *Tauerner* is a common surname during this period.

Tipelere. 1250.   NED: 1396.
Li: Ulphus le Tippeler 1256 FF 150. Will. le Typeler 1281 *1.Ass* 44. Ric. Typeler' 1327 *1.SR* 2. Joh. Tipeler 1332 *2.SR* 5. Lucas Typeler ib. 5. — *Nf:* Rob. le Tipelere 1250 *Ass* 14. Rog. Le tipeler' 1329 *SR* 57.

ME *tipeler;* v. NED *tipple* 'to sell ale'. — *A retailer of ale, a tapster.*

Gannoker. 1330.   NED: c1380.
Ess: Beatrix le Gannoker 1330 CR 97 (la Gannoker 1334 ib. 126).

Origin obscure. — *An alehouse-keeper* (NED).

CHAPTER III.

CLOTH WORKERS.

A. Manufacturers of Cloth.

1. Flax-Dresser, Comber, Carder.

Flaxbeter. 1246. NED: —
Wo: Thom. le Flaxbeter 1306 Hal 550. — *La:* Geoffrey le Flaxbeter 1246 Ass 89.

OE *fleax, flæx* 'flax' + *bēatere*. — *Flax-dresser.*

Flaxere. 1316. NED: —
Ess: Ric. Le Flexere 1316 *3.GDR* 36. Juliana le Flexere 1317 *2.GDR* 42. Rob. le Flexer' 1319 *SR* 18. Elias Le Flexere 1320 *3.GDR* 52. Walt. le Flexere 1326 *3.GDR* 9. Will. le Flexere 1327 *3.GDR* 5. — *Nf:* Rog. Flaxer 1329 *SR* 9.

A der. of OE *fleax, flæx, flex* 'flax'. — *One who dresses or sells flax.*

Flaxman. 1294. NED: 1509.
Ess: Walt. Flexman 1327 *SR* 10. — *Nf:* Thomas de Brandon le Flaxman 1294 CDN 53. Nich. Flaxman 1332 *SR* 40. — *Hu:* Will. Flexman 1279 RH 667.

OE *fleax, flæx, flex* 'flax' + *mann*. — Signification: = FLAXERE. — I have found one instance of the corresponding fem. surname, *Flaxwife:* Cristina Flexwyf 1378 CLB (H) 115 (Lo).

Lynman. 1296. NED: —
Sx: Joh. Lynman 1296 SR 29.

OE *līn* 'line, flax' + *mann*. — Signification: = FLAXMAN.

Lyneter. 1263. NED: —
Sx: Rob. le lynetier 1263 *Ass* 48. Al. Lyneter 1296 SR 77. Will. Lyneter ib. 83. John le Lynter 1325 FF 57. Gregor' Lynter 1327 SR 209. Will. le Lynetyr 1332 SR 259. Ric. Lyneter ib. 285. Rad. Lyneter' ib. 291. — *So:* Walt. le Lyneter 1327 SR 85. — *Wo:* Walt. le Lintere 1275 SR 10.

A der. of ME *lynet, lynt* 'flax-plant; flax prepared for spinning' (perh. fr. F *linette*); v. NED *lint* (1375). There may have been an OF *linetier. — Prob. *a flax-dresser*.

Hekelere. 1297.   NED: c1440.
Y: Will. le Hekelere 1297 1.Wake 292.

A der. of ME *hekel* 'to heckle' (fr. OE *hecel sb). — *Heckler, dresser of flax or hemp*.

Combere. 1202.   NED: 1646—82.
Ess: Ric. le Camber' 1319 *SR* 21. Joh. le Comber' 1327 *SR* 20. Will. Cambere 1341 *Ass* 12. Rog. le Comber 1341 CR 176. — *Sx:* Will. le Comber' 1263 *Ass* 41. Joh. Comber 1296 SR 51. Walt. Comber 1327 SR 181. — *Ha:* Walt. le Cambere 1280 2.*Ass* 96. Thom. le Combere 1327 *SR* 1. Ric. le Camber 1333 *SR* 7. — *So:* Rich. le Kamber 1243 Ass 238. Nich. le Kambere ib. — *Wo:* Patricius le Combar' 1275 SR 89. Adam le Kombar' 1292 Epi 414. Emma le Combar 1332 SR 21. — *St:* Thom. le Combere 1327 SR 246. — *Y:* Rich. the Camber 1246 FF 164. Thom. le Kamber' 1279 *Ass* 14. — *Li:* Rad. le Kamber' 1202 Ass 101. Sim. le Comber 1281 2.*Ass* 31. — *Nf:* Rad. le Combere 1286 *Ass* 110. Will. le Comere ib. 139. Barth. le Comber 1328 CDN 143. Galfr. komere 1329 *SR* 23.

The interpretation of this surname is not quite certain. NED has *comb* vb 1398 (in the sense 'to comb wool' not until 1577), which is formed fr. the sb *comb* (OE *comb, camb*). The early occurrence of the surname (first instance 1202) points to an OE *cambian, a side-form of *cemban;* this is also supported by the fem. form *Combestere*. The signification of the surname is therefore probably *one who combs wool or flax*. If, however, a verb did not exist at this early period, *Combere* must be a der. of OE *comb* sb and mean 'a maker of combs'. In the South of England the form spelt *Combere* may also be = *Cumber*, v. Toponymical surnames. — *Camber* occurs several times as a trade-name in Free Y, e. g. Adam de Popilton, camber 1312 p. 14.

Combestere. 1297.   NED:—
Ess: Helena la Cambstere 1310 CR 12. Nich. le Kambestere 1341 *Ass* 8 (le Cambestere ib. 12). — *Li:* Rog. Camester 1327 2.*SR* 13. — *Nf:* John le Combestere 1297 CDN 62 (le Combister 1315 ib. 63, le Comestere 1330 ib. 157). Thom. le Comestere 1334 ib. 183.

The fem. form of COMBERE. — Signification: = COMBERE.

Kembere. 1327. NED: 1511—2.
Sx: Rog. le Kembar' 1327 SR 116, 1332 SR 239. Joh. le Kembar' 1332 SR 240. — *Ha:* Pet. le Kembere 1333 *SR* 3. Adam le Kembere ib. 6. — *So:* Jurdanus le Kemere 1344 *Ass* 14. Lucia Kemere 1349 BBA 110.

A der. of OE *cemban* 'to comb'. — *Comber of wool or flax.*

Kembestere. 1275. NED: a1400.
Ess: Basilia le Kembestere 1287 *1. GDR* 4. — *Wo:* Dyicia la Kembestere 1275 SR 33. Joh. le Kembestere ib. 36. Ric. Le Kemester' 1307 *Ass* 3. Rob. le Kembestar' ib. — *La:* Beatrix la Kempster' 1300 *Ass* 7. — *Y:* Alic. Kembster c1346 *SR* 9.

The fem. form of Kembere. — Signification: = Kembere.

Tosere. 1249. NED: c1440.
Sx: Joh. Le Tosere 1249 *Ass* 25. — *So:* Will. le Thosere 1275 Ass 20. Will. le Tosere 1292 FF 285, 287.

A der. of OE **tāsian* 'to toze, tease'; this is a side-form of OE *tǣsan* (v. Tesere). — *A comber or carder of wool, etc.*

Tesere. 1275. NED: 1483.
So: Will. le Tesere 1275 Ass 4. — *Li:* Thom. le Tessere 1281 *2.Ass* 54.

A der. of OE *tǣsan* 'to tease'. — Signification: = Tosere.

Peyneresse. 1250. NED: —
Wo: Juliana le Pineresse 1281 3.Hal 81 (J. Bele le Peyneresse ib. 84). — *Nf:* Agatha la Peyneresse 1250 *Ass* 14.

OF *peigneresse, pein-* 'celle qui peigne la laine, le chanvre, le lin' (Godefroy). — *A woman who combs wool, hemp, or flax.*

Carder. 1332. NED: c1450.
Y: Joh. le carder 1332 Free Y 27.

A der. of ME *card* vb (fr. OF *carder* 'to card'). Cf OF *cardeur* 'one who cards', which, however, does not correspond to the English form. — *One who cards wool, etc.*

Cardestere. 1337. NED: —
Ess: Elena Cardester 1337 CR 152 (Cardestere 1340 ib. 167). Elicia la Cardestere 1341 ib. 185 (le Cardestere ib. 186).

The fem. form of Carder. — Signification: = Carder.

2. Spinner, Roper.

a. Spinner, Winder and Packer of Wool.

Spinnere. 1270.   NED: 1393.

Ess: Maur. le Spinnere 1332 *SR* 22. — *Sx:* Ph. le Spynnere 1327 SR 205. — *So:* Mich. le Spinner 1327 SR 177. — *Wo:* Joh. le Spinner 1270 Hal 23. Will. Spyner 1327 SR 17. — *St:* Will. le spynnere 1327 SR 234. — *La:* John le Spynner 1323 CR 126.

A der. of OE *spinnan* 'to spin'. — *One who spins wool, yarn, etc.* — This surname is very rare, the above instances being all that I have found. The spinner's occupation was probably performed by the weavers, who were very numerous.

Filour. 1275.   NED: —

So: Will: Filour 1327 SR 178. — *Wo:* Joh. le Filur 1275 SR 37. Rob. le Felur ib. 1. Rog. le Felour 1286 Inq 26. — *Li:* Joh. le Felur 1281 *2.Ass* 58.

OF *fileur* 'celui qui file' (Godefroy). The form *Felur*, which probably belongs here, is not evidenced in Godefroy. — *Spinner*.

Windere. 1275.   NED: 1552.

Li: Ric. le Windere 1275 RH 306. — *Nf:* Joh. Le Winder 1332 *SR* 48.

A der. of OE *windan* 'to wind'. — *One who winds wool, etc.* — Cf Thom. Panett, *wolwynder* 1409 Free Y 113. — This surname may also mean the same as FLEKEWYNDER, q. v.

Throwere. 1292.   NED: c1450.

Ess: Rob. le Thrawer' 1319 *SR* 12. Rob. le Twrawer' ib. 18. Will. Le Trowere 1327 *SR* 9 (le Throwere dupl. 9). Joh. Thrower 1341 *Ass* 16. — *St:* ..... oma le Throwere 1327 SR 198. — *La:* Will. le Threwere 1292 *1.Ass* 25 (Le Threwere 1292 *2.Ass* 14). — *Y:* Will. le Trower 1332 *SR* 11. — *Nf:* Thom. le Throwere 1316 *GDR* 35.

A der. of OE *prāwan* 'to throw'. — Prob. *one who converts raw silk into silk thread*. The signification, however, is not easy to fix at this early period. It may also have been 'turner' and 'potter'; this does not seem probable, since these trades are represented by many other very common surnames. — NED has *throwster* 1455 'one who twists silk fibres into raw silk or raw silk into thread'.

Sorter. 1275.   NED: 1554.

Wo: Joh. Sorter 1275 SR 38. — *Nf:* Walt. le Sorter 1300 CDN 76.

A der. of ME *sorte* 'to arrange, classify' (fr. L *sortiri* or OF *sortir*). — *One who sorts, arranges; esp. a wool-sorter* (NED).

Packere. 1275. NED: 1353.
Sx: Joh. le Packere 1296 SR 35. Joh. Packer' 1327 SR 190 (Packer 1332 SR 301). — *So:* Edmund. Le Pakere 1305 *Ass* 11. Galfr. le Packere 1307 *Ass* 8. — *Wo:* Juliana la Packare 1275 SR 70. Henr. le Packare ib. 79. Joh. le Pakkare ib. 91. Thom. le Pakkere ib. — *Y:* Pet. Packer 1297 SR 119. — *Li:* Walt. Russel Packer 1327 *3.SR* 2. — *Nf:* Walt. le Paker' 1301 *GDR* 21.

A der. of ME *packe* 'to pack' (fr. ME *packe* sb, v. NED *pack*). — *One who packs wool, etc.* — *Packer* and *wollepacker* are both frequent as trade-names in Free Y: Rob. de Lyndesay, pakker 1314 p. 16. Henr. de Misen, wollepacker 1351 p. 46. — In *Lo:* John Parker, »wolpakker» 1393 CLB (H) 396.

b. Maker of Ropes, Strings, Nets.

Ropere. 1249. NED: 1226.
Ess: Rog. le Ropere 1255 *Ass* 26. Will. le Ropere 1324 *3.GDR* 20. Joh. le Ropere 1332 *SR* 25. — *Sx:* Will. le Ropere 1249 *Ass* 34. Joh. Le Ropere 1288 *Ass* 9. Walt. le Ropere 1296 SR 81. Rob. le Ropere 1327 SR 152. — *Ha:* Joh. le Ropere 1272 *Ass* 20. Rog. le Ropere 1327 *SR* 13. Rob. le Ropere 1333 *SR* 6. Thom. le Ropere 1340 *SR* 7. — *So:* Rob. Le Ropere 1307 *Ass* 9. Will. Roper 1327 SR 257. Joh. le Ropere 1333 *SR* 17. — *Wo:* Will. le Ropere 1275 SR 61. — *St:* Rich. le Roper 1272 4.*Ass* 211. Will. le Ropere 1327 SR 225. Adam le Roper ib. 235. Elyas le Roper 1332 SR 99. — *La:* Jord. le Ropere 1292 *1.Ass* 21. Ran. le Rapere ib. 17. Al. le Ropere 1292 *2.Ass* 26. Will. le Roper 1332 *Ass* 2. — *Y:* Thom. le Raper 1268 *Ass* 30. Adam le Ropere 1293 *Ass* 31. Rob. Raper 1297 SR 138. Gilb. Raper 1301 SR 42. Joh. Rapar 1332 *SR* 12. Will. le Roper c1346 *SR* 3. — *Li:* Ric. Raper 1327 *2.SR* 14. Alan. Raper ib. 18. Hugo le Raper 1328 *Ass* 14. Adam le Roper 1328 *Ass* 47. Joh. Raper 1328 *Ass* 60 (le Roper ib. 45). Thom. le Roper 1332 *2.SR* 3. Steph. Raper 1332 *3.SR* 18. — *Nf:* Sim. le Roper 1275 RH 486. Ric. Le Ropere 1286 *Ass* 139. Lucia la Ropere 1313 *GDR* 18.

A der. of OE *rāp* 'rope'. As is to be expected, the form *Raper* occurs in the North: *Li:* 10 inst. (9 Roper). *Y:* 9 inst. (7 Roper). *La:* 2 inst. (6 Roper). — *Rope-maker*.

Ropestere. 1280. NED: —
Ha: Alic. la Ropestre 1280 *2.Ass* 62, 1280 *3.Ass* 10.

The fem. form of ROPERE. — Signification: = ROPERE.

Corder. 1231. NED: (c1430).

Sx: Joh. Corder 1296 SR 103. — *Wo:* Joh. le Cordur 1275 SR 13. Pet. Corder ib. 58. — *St:* Adam le Cordur 1280 6.Ass 104. — *Y:* Rob. le Corder 1231 FF 158. — *Nf:* Rog. le Cordur 1250 *Ass* 14. Joh. le Corder 1329 *SR* 19.

OF *cordier* 'celui qui fabrique et vend des cordes' (Godefroy); the form *Cordur* prob. belongs here; cf, however, OF *cordeur* 'arpenteur' (Godefroy, 1 inst.). — *Rope-maker.* — I have found one early instance of another synonymous surname: Augustinus *Cordemaker* 1199 Cur 74 (Sf).

Lacebreyder. 1329. NED: —

Nf: Will. le Lacebreyder' 1329 *SR* 10.

ME *lace* 'cord' (fr. OF *laz, las*) + a der. of ME *breyde* 'to braid, plait' (fr. OE *bregdan*). — *Maker of cords, strings.*

Lacer. 1298. NED: —

Ess: Rich. le Lacer 1333 CR 109. — *Y:* Will. le Lacer 1298 2.Wake 31. Nich. le lacer 1303 Free Y 10. Henr. le lacer 1311 ib. 14. Joh. le lacer 1325 ib. 23. Hugo Lasser c1346 *SR* 5. — *Li:* Joh. Lasur 1327 *1.SR* 5.

OF *laceor, lasseur* 'faiseur de lacets' (Godefroy); the forms in *-er* perhaps come fr. an OF **lacier*, otherwise fr. ME *lace* 'cord' (OF *laz, las*). — Signification: = LACEBREYDER.

Brayder. 1286. NED: (1866).

La: John le Brayder 1324 CR 80. — *Nf:* Rob. Le Bredere 1286 *Ass* 34.

A der. of OE *bregdan* 'to braid, plait'. Signification: = LACEBREYDER; it may also be 'net-maker', cf Prompt. P.: Nette breydare: reciarius. — Another interpretation of the form *Bredere* is illustrated by the following surname: Sim. *Haryngbredere* 1275 RH 423 (Lo) 'one who roasts herrings' (OE *hǣring* + a der. of *brǣdan* 'to roast').

Trender, Trinder. 1275. NED: 1828.

So: John le Trendare 1278 Ass 139. — *Nf:* Hugo le Trinder 1275 RH 532.

A der. of OE *trendan* 'to turn round, roll'. For the change of $e > i$ (no such form in NED), v. Jordan § 34. — Prob. = BRAYDER, LACEBREYDER.

Strenger. 1293. NED: 1420.

So: Godwyna Strenger 1327 SR 100. Rob. le Strengare 1344 *Ass* 13, 14. — *St:* Will. le Strenger 1334 14.Ass 39, 1335 ib. 45, 1348 12.Ass 90. — *Y:* Rog. le Strenger 1293 *Ass* 84.

A der. of OE *streng* 'string, cord'. — *Stringer, maker of strings for bows* (NED). — Cf Joh. de Huntyngton, *stringer* 1364 Free Y 60. — The following surname is synonymous: Gilb. le *Strengmakere* 1338 PMR 188 (Lo).

Haltrere. 1296. NED: c1425.
Ess: Walt. le Haltrere 1303 *2.GDR* 13. — *Lo:* Rob. le Haltrere 1296 CLB (B) 61.

A der. of OE *hælftre* 'halter'. — *Halter-maker*.

Netmaker. 1288. NED: 1380.
Ess: John le Netmaker 1336 CR 143 (bis). — *Sx:* Godefridus Le Netmakyer' 1288 *Ass* 12.

OE *net(t)* 'a net' + a der. of *macian*. — *Maker of nets*.

Nettere. 1298. NED: 1481—90.
Lo: John le Nettere, paternostrer 1298 CLB (B) 69. — *Sx:* Osbertus le Nettar' 1332 SR 232.

A der. of OE *net(t)* 'a net'. — *Netmaker*.

3. Weaver or Seller of Cloth.

a. Weaver, Webster.

Webbe. 1243. NED: c1100.
Ess: Adam le Webbe 1274 RH 145. Margar. la Webbe 1300 *2.GDR* 10. Hugo le Webbe 1327 *SR* 5. Mich. le Webbe 1341 *Ass* 24. — *Sx:* Ric. le Webbe 1263 *Ass* 39. Joh. le Webbe 1279 *Ass* 34. Rob. le Webbe 1296 SR 7. Reg. le Webbe 1327 SR 113. — *Ha:* Agnes la Webbe 1272 *Ass* 1. Nich. le Webbe 1327 *SR* 9. Agnes la Webbe 1333 *SR* 2. — *So:* Will. le Webb 1243 Ass 281. Nich. le Webbe 1301 FF 317. Rob. Le Webbe 1305 *Ass* 10. Nich. le Webbe 1333 *SR* 9. — *Wo:* Thom. Webbe 1266 Inq 9. Will. Le Webbe 1275 *1.Ass* 5. Alicia la Webbe 1294 Hal 272. Rad. Le Webbe 1327 SR 17. — *St:* Thom. le Webbe 1327 SR 231. Thom' le Webbe 1332 SR 110. Will. le Webbe 1341 11.Ass 115. — *Nf:* Will. le Webbe 1286 *Ass* 115. Joh. Webbe 1332 *SR* 51.

OE *webba* masc. or *webbe* fem. — *Weaver* (male or female). NED has only the signification 'male weaver' during this period ('female weaver' 1377), but I have several instances applied to women, the first one being from 1272 (Wo). In the same way NED has only the signification 'female weaver' for *webster* ('male weaver' 1362). But to judge from my material, the distribution of these two words is quite another: it is geographical. *Webbester* is an *Anglian* surname (I have only found a single instance in the Saxon counties). *Webbe,* however, is a *Saxon* surname, which is very common in these counties; in the other counties I have only found five instances (2 in *St* and 3 in *Nf*).

Webbester. 1275. NED: c1100.

So: Galfr. Webster' 1333 *SR* 6. — *La:* Will. le Webbster 1284 Ass 183. Rob. le Webbestere 1292 *3.Ass* 46. Rog. le Webbester' 1303 *Ass* 8. John le Webster 1324 CR 69. Henr. le Webester 1332 SR 44. Adam le Webbester 1332 FF 83. — *Y:* Thom. the Webester 1277 1.Wake 177. Hugo le Webester' 1305 *Ass* 1. Agnes the Webester 1316 4.Wake 100. Thom. le Webester 1332 *SR* 6. Hugo Webster c1346 *SR* 8. — *Li:* Will. le Webester 1305 *Ass* 1. Walt. Webester 1327 *2.SR* 1. Will. Le Webster ib. 8. Rog. Webester 1332 *3.SR* 8. — *Nf:* Joh. le Webestere 1275 RH 444. Thom. le Webestere 1286 *Ass* 122. Alan. Le Webbester' 1301 *GDR* 22. Alic. Webester' 1332 *SR* 70. Henr. Le Webester' ib. 75. Sim. le Webestere 1338 CDN 215.

OE *webbestre* 'female weaver'. The corresponding masc. form would be *webbere (not *webba,* as NED says, the fem. of which is *webbe*), but this has not been found in OE. v. Webbere. — *Weaver.* — Cf Webbe.

Webbere. 1340. NED: c1440.

Lo: Cristina Webbere 1378 CLB (H) 114. — *So:* Henry le Webbere 1340 SR for Bath (VH So vol. II p. 407).

This may be a der. of OE *webbian* (in OE only in a figurative sense: 'to weave, contrive'), but it seems more prob. that this word disappeared, and that a new verb was formed fr. the subst. *web* (OE *web*). The verb *to web* is not evidenced in NED until c1440. The surname *Webbere* must be very rare during this early period, as the above instances, which are both very late, are the only ones that I have found. — Signification: *Weaver.*

Weuere. 1296. NED: 1362.

Sx: Will. Weuere 1296 SR 13. Joh. le Weuere ib. Nic. le Weuere ib. 18. Rosa Weuere 1327 SR 199. Sym. Weuere 1332 SR 310. — *Wo:* Rich. le Wevur 1303 Reg 32.

A der. of OE *wefan* 'to weave'. — *Weaver.*

Tyssur. 1327. NED: —

Li: Joh. Tyssur' 1327 *1.SR* 9. Rob. Tyssour 1328 *Ass* 26.

OF *tisseur* 'ouvrier qui tisse' (Godefroy). — *Weaver.*

Tystour. 1295. NED: —
Wo: Walt. le Tystour 1304 Reg 204. Will. le Tystour ib. — *Nf:* Joh. le Tistur 1295 *GDR* 10.

A der. of AF *tister* 'to weave' (Lib. Alb. 273) = OF *tistre*; the subst. *tisteor is not evidenced in Godefroy. — *Weaver.* — Cf Joh. de Pontefract, junr., *tistour* 1333 Free Y 28.

Tisterer. 1255. NED: —
Ess: Henr. le Tisterer 1255 *Ass* 10.

A der. of OF *tistrer* 'to weave'; it corresponds to an OF *tistrier. — *Weaver.*

b. **Maker or Seller of Woollen Cloth.**

Draper. 1148. NED: 1362.
Ess: Nich. le Draper 1255 *Ass* 1. Matth. le Draper 1285 *Ass* 1. Fina le Draper 1332 *SR* 24. — *Sx:* Ph. le Draper 1249 *Ass* 38. Joh. le Draper 1263 *Ass* 39. Adam le Draper 1279 *Ass* 12. Alex' Draper 1296 SR 31. — *Ha:* Walt' draper 1148 LWint 560. Edredus le drapier 1200 P 204. Sim. le Draper 1280 *2.Ass* 3. Alic. la Draper 1333 *SR* 5. — *So:* Alex. le Draper 1263 FF 196. Rob. Le Draper 1320 *Ass* 8. Rob. le Drapere 1327 SR 147. Joh. le Drapere 1333 *SR* 34. — *Wo:* Joh. le Draper 1275 SR 65. Will. le Draper 1303 Reg 40. — *St:* Ric. le Drapur 1327 SR 203 (le Draper 1332 SR 100). Will. le Draper 1327 SR 245. — *La:* Egideus le Draper 1292 *3.Ass* 57. Henr. le Draper 1332 SR 51. — *Y:* Parus le Drapere 1268 *Ass* 37. Rob. le Drapur 1297 1.Wake 279. John the Drapour 1314 3.Wake 66. — *Li:* Rob. le Drapier 1181 P 63. Joh. Drapur' 1327 *1.SR* 2. Henr. le Drapour 1328 *Ass* 50. Rob. le Drapur 1332 *2.SR* 3. — *Nf:* Marth. le Draper 1286 *Ass* 125. Hubert le Draper 1303 CDN 94.

AF *draper* = OF *drapier*; the form *Drapur* certainly belongs here (the same person is called both *Drapur* and *Draper*, v. *St*); cf Godefroy *drapeur* 'railleur' (1 inst.). — *One who makes or sells woollen cloth.*

Clothere. 1286. NED: 1362.
So: Joh. le Clothere 1344 *Ass* 17. — *Nf:* Rob. le Clother 1286 *Ass* 114.

A der. of OE *clāp* 'cloth'. — *Clothier, maker or seller of woollen cloth.* — Cf the following synonymous surname: Thom. *Clothman* 1416 CLB (I) 150 (Lo).

Clothmangere. 1327. NED: —
Ha: Joh. le Clothmangere 1327 *SR* 15. 1333 *SR* 1.

OE *clāp* 'cloth' + *mangere*. — *One who sells cloth*. — Cf Hugh le *Clothseller* 1357 FF 154 (La). It is noteworthy that this surname is the only compound in *-seller* that I have found. Compounds in *-mongere*, however, are very numerous; v. List of compound surnames.

Wollere. 1319.   NED: —

Ess: Will. le Woller' 1319 *SR* 20. — *Ha:* Rob. Wolere 1333 *SR* 5. — *So:* M-na le Wollares 1333 *SR* 6.

A der. of OE *wull* 'wool'. — *One who dresses, weaves, or sells wool.*

Wollestere. 1297.   NED: —

Y: Thom. le Wollestere 1297 1.Wake 291.

The fem. form of WOLLERE. — Signification: = WOLLERE.

Wolmongere. 1250.   NED: 1297.

Ess: Mich. le Wulmangere 1255 *Ass* 33. Will. le Wlmoggere 1319 *SR* 15. Joh. le Wolmongere 1324 *2.GDR* 29. Ric. le Wolmonger' 1332 *SR* 23. Sim. le Wollemongere 1334 CR 119. Rog. le Wollemonger 1340 CR 171. — *Ha:* Nich. le Wolmongere 1280 *3.Ass* 22. Ric. le Wolmangere 1333 *SR* 1. Joh. Wolmongere ib. Juliana la Wolmongere ib. — *Nf:* Joh. le Wolmonger 1250 *Ass* 28. Rog. de Hoocton le wollemonegere 1296 CDN 60.

OE *wull* 'wool' + *mangere*. — *One who sells wool.*

Laner. 1279.   NED: —

Ess: Thom. Layner 1285 *Ass* 17. — *Sx:* Joh. le Laner' 1309 *1.GDR* 4. Henr. le Lanere 1310 *2.GDR* 4. Johanna lanere ib. John Lanour 1327 SR 122. — *So:* Rich. Lanour 1327 SR 131. Joh. Lanour ib. — *Y:* Hugo le Layner 1279 *Ass* 71. — *Li:* Ric. Lanour 1305 *Ass* 12.

OF *lanier, lainier* and *laneor* 'apprêteur et marchand de laine' (Godefroy). — Signification: = WOLLERE. — Cf LANER p. 199.

c. **Maker or Seller of Linen or Hempen Cloth**.

Teler. 1193.   NED: c1400.

Ess: Will. le Teler 1255 *Ass* 5. Rich. le Teler 1311 CR 32. — *Sx:* Reg. le Teler 1229 FF 63. Jord. Le Teler 1288 *Ass* 8. — *Ha:* Rob. le Teler 1280 *2.Ass* 91. Will. le Tellare 1327 *SR* 1. — *So:* Reg. le telier 1243 *Ass* 191. Rich. le Teler ib. 229. Thom. le Teller ib. 241. Adam le Teler 1306 FF 341. Joh. Teler 1327 SR 272. — *Wo:* Warinus le Teler 1212 Cur 396. Ric. le Teler 1275 SR 6. — *St:* Rob. le Teler 1227 4.Ass 54. — *Y:* Joh. le Teler 1268 *Ass* 29. Ric. le Teler 1279 *Ass* 67. Nich. le Teler 1301 SR 108. — *Li:* Rog. le teler 1193 P 47. Walt. Le Teler 1226 FF 190. Ric. le Teler 1245 *Ass* 24. — *Nf:* Thurstanus le Telier 1250 *Ass* 23. Will. Le Teler 1286 *Ass* 91. Alic. Teler 1332 *SR* 73. Reg. Teler ib.

OF *telier, teillier* 'fabricant de toiles, commerçant en toiles' (Godefroy). — *Maker or seller of (linen) cloth.*

Lyndraper. 1183.   NED: 1436.
Ess: Galfr. le Lyndraper 1318 *3.GDR* 45. Will. Lyndraper 1330 CR 98. Nich. Lyndraper 1333 ib. 107. John le Lyndraper 1341 ib. 181. — *Ha:* Nich. Le Lyngedraper 1305 *Ass* 17 (Le Lynnedraper ib., Le Lyngedrapere ib. 13). Joh. Lyndraper 1333 *SR* 8 (le Lyndraper 1340 *SR* 6). — *Oxf:* Walt. le Lingedrapier 1183 P 103. — *Wo:* Joh. le Lyndrapere 1305 *Ass* 1. — *Y:* Will. le lynge daper (sic) 1313 Free Y 15. — *Li:* Lucia Linedraper 1332 *1.SR* 19. — *Nf:* Joh. Le Lyndraper 1286 *Ass* 91. Rog. le Lindraper 1294 CDN 54. Will. le Lyndraper 1305 ib. 108. Walt. le Lyndraper 1317 ib. 80. Margaret le Lyndraper 1322 ib. 115.

OE *līn* 'line, flax' + *draper* (v. DRAPER). The form *Lynge*draper is apparently influenced by F *linge* 'linen cloth'; cf LYNER, LYNGER. — *Maker or seller of linen cloth.*

Lyner, Lynger. 1279.   NED: —
Sx: Ad. Le Lyngere 1288 *Ass* 37. Joh. Lynar 1327 SR 114 (le Lynar' 1332 SR 238). — *Y:* Will. Lynger 1301 SR 84. Rog. Lynger c1346 *SR* 5. — *Li:* Margar. Lynger 1332 *3.SR* 9. — *Hu:* Gilb. le Lyner 1279 RH 621.

OF *linier, lingier* 'marchand de lin, fabricant de toile de lin' (Godefroy). Cf LYNDRAPER (Lyngedraper). — *Maker or seller of linen cloth.* — Free Y has *lyner* as a trade-name, e. g. Ric. de Wymondham, lyner 1334 p. 29.

Lakensnither. 1350.   NED: —
Y: Arnaldus de Lakensnither 1350 Free Y 44. Henr., fil. Arnaldi Lakensnyder 1380 ib. 79. Henr. Lakensnyder 1392 1.YMB 173.

MDu *lakensnider(e)* 'lakenkooper, linnenkoopman' (Verwijs). The *de* preceding this surname may be the MDu article. — *One who sells cloths and sheets.* — Cf the MG surname (Lübeck): gozwinus *lakensnidere,* hermannus *lakensnidere* (Reimpell p. 88).

This surname does not seem to be of native origin, though both elements might be OE. For the first element v. Anglia 42 (p. 357 ff), where O. B. Schlutter points out that there existed an OE *lacen* 'sheet'. Cf Holthausen OE *lacen* 'Mantel', C. Hall *lacen?* 'a cloak', and NED *lake* c1386 'fine linen'. The second element corresponds to a der. of OE *snīðan* 'to cut, kill, mow'.

Flaxmongere. 1305. NED: —
Wo: Adam Le Flexmangre 1307 *Ass* 4 (Le Flexmongere ib. 6). — *Li:* Thom. le Flaxmonger 1305 *Ass* 22.

OE *fleax, flœx, flex* 'flax' + *mangere*. — *One who sells flax.*

Caneuacer. 1274. NED: —
Ha: Joh. le Caneuacere 1274 RH 222. Henr. le Canauacer 1325 *Ass* 1 (le Caneuacir 1327 *SR* 17, le Caneuaser 1333 *SR* 9, le Caneuacer 1340 *SR* 6). Ric. le Caneuacer 1333 *SR* 8.

AF **canevacer*, OF *chanevacier* 'marchand ou fabricant de canevas' (Godefroy). — *Maker or seller of canvas or hempen cloth.*

Pavilloner. 1322. NED: c1600.
Y: Joh. le pavilloner 1322 Free Y 21.

A der. of ME *pauillon* (fr. OF *paveillun* 'tent'), or there may have been an OF **paveillunier*. — *Maker or seller of pavilions or tents.* — Cf Thom. de Thornton, »*pavilloner*» 1364 PMR 271, 272 (Lo).

d. **Maker or Seller of Silk, Pall, Curtains.**

Mercer. 1168. NED: [c1123].
Ess: Anketillus le Mercer 1274 RH 157. John le Mercer 1310 CR 9. — *Sx:* Will. le Mercer 1241 FF 101. Gwydo le Merser 1263 *Ass* 44. Thom. le Mercer 1296 SR 85. Lambert le Mercer 1313 FF 16. — *Ha:* Joh. le Mercer 1280 *2.Ass* 4. Will. le Mercir 1327 *SR* 3. Emeric. le Mercer 1340 *SR* 4. — *So:* Thom. le Mercer 1243 Ass 208. Henr. le Merzour 1327 SR 183. Will. le Mercer 1333 *SR* 24. — *Wo:* Adam le Mercer 1255 *Ass* 16. Agnes la Mercere 1275 SR 4. Galfr. Le Mercer 1327 SR 35. — *St:* Will. le Mercer 1227 4.Ass 41. Walt. le Merser 1327 SR 245. Nich. le Mercer 1332 SR 119. — *La:* Walt. le Mercer 1246 Ass 63. Hugo le Mercer 1292 *1.Ass* 1. Will. le Mercer 1332 SR 34. — *Y:* Adam le mercerer 1176 P 120. Iuo le Mercer 1268 *Ass* 6. Rob. Merchier 1301 SR 103. Nich. Mercer 1332 SR 11. — *Li:* Gamel mercer 1168 P 70. Will. le Mercer 1245 *Ass* 47. Wydo Le Mercer 1332 *1.SR* 19. — *Nf:* Hildebrand' le Mercer 1275 RH 530. Geoffrey le Mercer 1309 CDN 12. Margareta Mercer 1329 *SR* 23.

OF *mercier, -sier, -chier* 'marchand en général' (Godefroy). — *One who deals in textile fabrics, esp. a dealer in silks, velvets, and other costly materials; a small-ware dealer* (NED). — Mercer is a common surname in all counties.

Setere. 1262. NED: —
Ha: Steph. le Setere 1262 Gross: Gild M. II 4. Symon le Setere ib. Phil. le Setere ib. Henr. le Setere 1280 *1.Ass* 33. Hugo le Setare 1327 *SR* 5.

Prob. fr. OF *saietier* 'ouvrier employé à tisser la saie' (Godefroy). — *Silk weaver.* — Cf CLB (E) p. 50: a silk-embroidered cope was valued by John Heyroun, »settere», and Will. le *Settere* at 18 marks (cf Weekley: Surnames p. 113). This seems to point to the above interpretation. — *Setter* sometimes occurs as a trade-name in Free Y, e. g. Joh. de Belegame, setter 1343 p. 37.

Silkwoman. 1334. NED: c1440.
Ess: Alice la Selkwimman 1334 CR 123.

OE *seoloc, seolc* 'silk' + *wīfman* 'woman'. — *A woman who makes or sells silk.* — As a trade-name: Elena Arnald, *silkwoman* 1435 Free Y 150. — The following surname, *Silkwife*, is synonymous: Margareta Selkewif 1332 SR 92 (Lo). Cf also Johanna Tayllour, »*selkwyf*» 1348 CLB (F) 187 (Lo).

Pallere, Pellere. 1263. NED: —
Sx: Will. le Peller' 1263 *Ass* 48, 28. Ric. Le Pellere 1279 *Ass* 1. — *St:* Joh. le Pallere 1327 SR 238 (le Paller' 1332 SR 118).

A der. of OE *pæll, pell* 'costly cloak, purple cloth'. In NED *pall* is spelt *pall* and *pell* at this time. — *Maker or seller of pall, a fine and rich cloth, or a robe of this.* — In the following instance *peller* occurs as a trade-name: Rog. Dun, peller 1332 SR 87 (Lo).

Courtener. 1333. NED: —
Ha: Joh. le Courtenyr 1333 *SR* 2. — *Le:* Adam Courtanier 1345 RBL 64.

A der. of ME *courtyn, -ayn* (fr. OF *co(u)rtine*) 'curtain'. — *Maker of curtains.*

Tapicer. 1275. NED: c1386.
Lo: Ralph le Tapicer 1282 CLB (A) 59. — *Wo:* Adam Tapicer 1275 SR 112. Adam the Tapyser (undated) OCW 92.

AF *tapicer* = OF *tapicier*. — *A maker or weaver of figured cloth or tapestry* (NED).

e. **Maker of Sacks, Bags, Pouches.**

Sacker. 1225.   NED: —

So: Hugh le Saker 1225 Ass 103. — *Y:* Rog. Saker 1230 P 278. Eva la Seckere 1277 1.Wake 179. Joh. le Sekere 1293 *Ass* 57 (le Seckere ib.). Henr. le Sekere ib. 33 (le Seckere ib.). Joh. le sekker 1334 Free Y 29. — *Li:* Thom. le Sakker 1327 *2.SR* 15. Reg. le Saker ib. (Sekker 1332 *3.SR* 18). — *Nf:* Will. le Sekere 1286 *Ass* 141. Ric. Le Sekker 1332 *SR* 84.

A der. of OE *sacc* or ON *sekkr* 'sack'. — *Maker of sacks.*

Sakwebbe. 1279.   NED: —

So: Henry le Sacwebbe 1279 Ass 194. Jurdanus Sakwebbe 1327 SR 276.

OE *sacc* 'sack' + *webba* 'weaver'. — *One who weaves sacks.*

Sakman. 1333.   NED: —

So: Joh. Sakman 1333 *SR* 30.

OE *sacc* 'sack' + *mann*. — Prob. = Sacker.

Sachere. 1280.   NED: —

Ha: Henr. le Sachiere 1280 *3.Ass* 27. — *La:* Rob. le Sascher 1338 *Ass* 2. — *Hu:* Joh. le Sachere 1294 CR Ramsey 219, 220.

OF *sachier* 'fabricant de sacs' (Godefroy). — Signification: = Sacker.

Bagger, Badger. 1246.   NED: a1500.

Wo: Matilda la Baggar' 1275 SR 52. Henr. Le Bagger 1327 SR 7. Joh. Bagger ib. 26. Will. Le Bagger ib. 63 (Baggare 1332 SR 10). Joh. Badgare 1332 SR 24. — *St:* Emma le Baggere 1307 7.Ass 180. — *La:* Ivo le Bagger 1246 Ass 115. Pet. le Bagger 1324 CR 5. — *Y:* Hugo le Bager 1293 *Ass* 33. Rich. le Bagger 1297 1.Wake 280. Emma le Baggere ib. 287 (la Baggere 1306 2.Wake 55). Nich. le Baggere 1306 2.Wake 55. Henry le Bagger 1307 ib. 102. John le Bagger 1308 ib. 186. Alice la Bagere ib. Amabilla the Baggere 1316 3.Wake 106. Joh. le Badger c1346 *SR* 12. — *Li:* Ric. Bagare 1332 *3.SR* 25. — *Nf:* Joh. Baghar' 1329 *SR* 10.

The interpretation of this surname is uncertain. The general spelling is *Bagger(e)*, but a few instances spelt *Badger, Badgare* occur in *Y* and *Wo*. These three forms seem to belong together and may be the same as *badger* NED a1500 'one who buys corn and other commodities and carries them elsewhere to sell; a hawker, huckster'. The origin of this word is unknown, and this is also the case with the related verb *to badge*, which has not been found before 1552.

The most common form of the surname, *Bagger,* however, points to a der. of ME *bagge* 'a bag, small sack'. This is supported by a street-name in York: »[John de] *Bagergate* 1243 Yorksh. Inq.; *Baggergate* 1303 charter, 1489 Brown, Yo. Deeds II, p. 216; *Beggergate* 16th cent. Chantry Survey» (Lindkvist, Anglia 50, p. 363). The first element can hardly have been pronounced like *badger.* The normal signification of the surname *Baggere* during the period before 1350 will therefore be *a maker of bags* (not 'one who encloses in bags, a miser', as Lindkvist suggests; this is quite improbable); cf SACKER, PURSER, POUCHER. — There may have developed another sense, which is also probable, especially at a later time, viz. 'one who carries goods in a bag, a hawker, *badger*'. If this is right, the change in pronunciation from *bagger* to *badger* (which, for some reason or other, does not seem to have taken place in the street-name) is difficult to account for. The connection with *bag*, however, may have been forgotten, which would facilitate the change. Another thing that points to a change of pronunciation is that in modern times there is a surname spelt *Badger*, but no *Bagger* exists.

Another street-name which contains the same element is *Baggerawe* 1332 SR 50 (Cu).

The surname *Baggere,* which is most common in Yorkshire, has not been found in southern counties (*Ess, Sx, Ha, So*).

Poghwebbe. 1306. NED: —
St: John le Poghwebbesone [1] 1306 7.Ass 157.

OE *pohha* (v. NED *pough*) + *webba* 'weaver'. — *One who weaves bags.* — The instance given above properly means 'the son of a person called Poghwebbe'.

Pouchemaker. 1349. NED: 1362.
Y: Rich. Pouchemaker 1349 Free Y 43. Peterkyn Pouchemaker 1350 ib. 45.

ME *pouche* (fr. ONF *pouche*) + ME *maker*. — *Maker of pouches or bags.*

Poucher. 1317. NED: 1401.
So: Rad. Pucher 1333 *SR* 7 (bis). — *Li:* Joh. Poucher 1340 *Ass* 13. — *Le:* Rob. Poucher 1317 RBL 317.

A der. of ME *pouche* (fr. ONF *pouche*). — *Pouch-maker.*

---
[1] Printed *Poghwelbesone.*

Pocheler. 1327. NED: —

Sx: Walt. Pochelyr 1327 SR 127. Will. le Pocheler ib. 132. — *Li:* Will. Pocheler 1332 *3.SR* 13.

Prob. fr. an OF *pochelier, formed fr. *pochele, diminutive of *poche*. — *Maker of pouches.*

Poker. 1314. NED: —

St: Ithel Poker 1314 10.Ass 15 (le Poker 1323 9.Ass 100). Joh. le Poker' 1332 SR 114.

A der. of ME *poke* 'bag' (v. NED *poke*). — Prob. *a maker of pokes* (bags, small sacks).

f. Maker of Quilts, Blankets, Mats.

Quilter. 1255. NED: 1563.

Ess: Ric. le Culleter 1255 *Ass* 33. Will. le Quilter 1316 *2.GDR* 45. Henr. le Quylter 1319 *SR* 14. Walt. le Quylter 1323 *3.GDR* 21. Eadmund' Le Quylter 1328 ib. 42. — *St:* Rich. le Quylter 1300 7.Ass 69 (le Coylter 1306 ib. 173, le Qwilter 1325 9.Ass 111). — *Li:* Henr. le Qwylter 1281 *1.Ass* 48. Rob. le Quilter 1321 *Ass* 40. — *Nf:* Rob. Le Qylter 1286 *Ass* 111. Will. de Suthkarleton le Qwelter 1294 CDN 52. Ralph le Quilter 1315 ib. 58. Rob. Quilleter 1332 *SR* 34. Henr. Le Quilter' ib.

A der. of ME *quilte, cowlte, coylte* 'a quilt' (fr. OF *cuilte, coilte*). — *Maker of quilts, mattresses.* — Cf the following synonymous surname: Edm. *Quyltmaker*, de Fossegate 1379 Free Y 77.

Custere. 1254. NED: —

St: Sibilla la Custere 1254 4.Ass 129.

OF *coustier* masc., *coustiere* fem. 'faiseur de *coutes* ou lits de plumes, de coussins' (Godefroy). — *Maker of feather-beds and cushions.*

Chaloner. 1255. NED: 1372.

Ess: Galfr. le Chaloner 1274 RH 142. Walt. le Chaloner 1300 *2.GDR* 10. Johanna la Chalonere 1319 *3.GDR* 47. Pet. le Chaloner 1319 *SR* 12. Edm. le Chalouner 1327 *SR* 4. Rob. le Chaloner 1332 *SR* 24. — *Sx:* Will. Chaloner 1296 SR 67. Will. le Chalener ib. 68. Walt le Chaloner 1327 SR 154. Ric. le Chaloner ib. — *Ha:* Will. le Chaloner 1333 *SR* 3. — *So:* Walt. le Chal'uner 1278 Ass 174. Rog. Le Chaloner 1305 *Ass* 3. Joh. le Chaloner 1327 SR 194. Walt. le Chalner 1333 *SR* 9. Thom. le Chaloner 1344 *Ass* 15. — *Wo:* Will. le Chaloner 1255 *Ass* 32. Rad. le Chaluner 1275 *1.Ass* 13. Joh. le Chaloner 1275 SR 42. Thom. le Chalener 1280 Hal 159. — *St:* Henry le Chaloner 1294

6.Ass 299. Rich. le Chaloner 1306 7.Ass 168. Sym. le Chaloner 1327 SR 216 (le Chalner 1332 SR 117). Ric. le Chalner 1332 SR 121. — *La:* Joh. le Chaluner 1292 *1.Ass* 4. — *Y:* Will. the Chalunner 1272 FF 184. Rog. le Chaloner 1301 SR 118. Will. le chaloner 1323 Free Y 21. Rob. Chaloner 1343 FF 170. — *Li:* Will. Chaloner 1327 *3.SR* 3. Ric. Chaloner 1328 *Ass* 4. Rad. Chaloner 1332 *1.SR* 13. — *Nf:* Will. le Chaluner 1286 CDN 4. Rob. le Chaloner 1329 SR 31. Edmundus Chaluner 1332 *SR* 20. Thom. Le Schaluner ib. 34. Joh. le Chalouner ib. 67.

A der. of ME *chaloun, -one, -un* 'blanket' (fr. its place of manufacture, Châlons-sur-Marne). — *Maker of blankets or coverlets.* — *Chaloner* occurs frequently in *Ess, So,* and *Y.* — Cf Ric. le *Chalunmaker* 1359 FF 72 (Y).

Tapener. 1272.   NED: a1400.
Sx: Ric. le Taponer 1288 *Ass* 24. Rad. le Tauponer 1309 *1.GDR* 5. Margareta le Taupenire 1327 SR 126. Henr' le Tapenyr ib. 130 (le Taupenyr 1332 SR 252). Joh. Taupener 1332 SR 277. — *Ha:* Gregor' le Tapiner 1272 *Ass* 24. Humfr. le Tapyner 1280 *2.Ass* 32. Ric. le Tappenyr 1280 *3.Ass* 43. Steph. Le Tapiner 1305 *Ass* 17. Will. le Tapenir 1327 *SR* 17. Thom. Tapener 1333 *SR* 7.

Derivation obscure (NED). Cf OF *taponner* 'tapisser'. — *Maker of chalons and burel.* — This name is common in *Ha* and *Sx,* but no instance has been found in any other county.

Couchur. 1295.   NED: c1400.
Ess: Amicia Cochour 1316 *2.GDR* 49. — *Sx:* Sim. le Cochur 1327 SR 156 (Cochur 1332 SR 271). — *Ha:* Joh. le Cochor 1333 *SR* 2. — *So:* Walt. Cochour 1344 *Ass* 7, 8. — *Wo:* Nich. le Couchur 1295 *Ass* 8.

AF **coucheour*; cf F *coucheur* 'a coucher' (NED). — *?A couchmaker, an upholsterer* (NED). — *Couchur* is common as a tradename in Free Y, e. g. Joh. del Wodde, coucheour 1368 p. 66.

Mattere. 1263.   NED: 14..
Ess: Joh. le Mattere 1341 *Ass* 12, 8. — *Sx:* Muriell' la Mattere 1263 *Ass* 45. Joh. Le Mattere 1288 *Ass* 21. — *Wo:* Ric. Le Matter 1327 SR 46.

A der. of OE *matt, meatt* 'a mat'. — *Mat-maker.* Mats were made of rushes, sedge, straw, bast, etc.

Seggemaker. 1306.   NED: —
St: Rich. le Seggemaker 1306 7.Ass 155.

OE *secg* 'sedge' + a der. of *macian.* — *One who makes mats etc. of sedge.*

Segger. 1292. NED: —
La: Ric. le Segger' 1292 *1.Ass* 8 (le Seggere ib. 39, le Segger' 1292 *2.Ass* 8). — *Y:* Milisanta le Segger' 1293 *Ass* 10.

A der. of OE *secg* 'sedge'. — Prob. = SEGGEMAKER. This surname might also be derived from OE *secgan* 'to say', and the signification would be 'one who tells stories' or something similar, but this does not seem very probable.

Rischere. 1255. NED: (1630).
Ess: Ric. le Risser 1255 *Ass* 13. — *Sx:* Geruas' le Rischere 1296 SR 35. Joh. le Russere ib. 73.

A der. of OE *risc* 'rush'. — Prob. *one who cuts and sells rushes*, or *one who makes mats of rushes*. — In London (early 14th century) there was a special place, Oystergate, which appears to have been a place of great resort for the sellers of rushes, in these times much in use for strewing on the floors of houses (Lib. Cust. Intr. p. 110). Cf *huxsteres cirporum* 'sellers of rushes' London 1365 (2.PMR p. 36).

g. Felt-Maker, Worker in Horsehair.

Feltere. 1275. NED: 1605.
Sx: Rad. le Veltere 1279 *Ass* 27 (Le Feltere 1288 *Ass* 28, le Feltere ib. 25). — *Ha:* Rob. le Feltere 1287 *Ass* 6 (le Faltere ib.). Rad. le Feltere ib. — *So:* Rog. le Velter 1327 SR 260. — *Li:* Rob. le Felter 1275 RH 338, 375. — *Nf:* Isabella Felter 1332 *SR* 71.

A der. of OE *felt* 'felt'. — *One who makes or works with felt* (NED).

Feutrer. 1198. NED: 14..
Sx: Thom. le Feutrier 1198 P 227. — *Ha:* Walt. le Feuterer 1274 RH 220. Walt. le Feutrer 1280 *2.Ass* 70. Galfr. le Feutrer ib. 87. Gilb. le Feuterer 1280 *3.Ass* 35. — *Wo:* Ric. le feutrer 1221 Ass 604. Reg. le Feutrer 1275 SR 91. — *Nf:* Budric le Feutreer 1297 CDN 62.

OF *feutrier* 'ouvrier en feutre' (Godefroy). — *Felt-maker, worker in felt.*

Hayremaker. 1328. NED: —
Ess: John le Hayremaker 1337 CR 150 (le Heyremaker ib. 152, 154). — *Li:* Alex. Hayremakere 1328 *Ass* 2.

ME *haire* 'cloth made of hair' (a mixture of OE *hǣre, hēre* and OF *haire* 'hair-shirt') + ME *makere*; v. NED *haire*. — *Maker of haircloth, hair-shirts.* — Cf the following synonymous trade-name: Ric. Nicholson, *hayrwever* & porter 1501 Free Y 226. Cf also the MG surname *harmakere* (Reimpell p. 88).

Hayrwright. 1279. NED: —
Le: Rich. le Hayrewritte ?1283—4 RBL 388. — *Y:* Ric. le Hayrwrithe 1279 *Ass* 64.

There has prob. been an OE *hǣrewyrhta*, and the spelling has later been influenced by OF *haire*. — Signification: = HAYREMAKER.

Hayrere. 1252. NED: —
Ess: Ric. le Hayrere 1317 *3.GDR* 39, 1317 *2.GDR* 43. — *Le:* Rich. le Heyrere c1292 RBL 392 (le *Hayrewritte* ?1283—4 ib. 388). — *Y:* John the Hayrer 1252 FF 78.

A der. of ME *haire* (v. HAYREMAKER), or perhaps fr. an OF *hairier*. — Signification: = HAYREMAKER. Note that the same person is called both *Heyrere* and *Hayrewritte* in *Le*.

The corresponding fem. form, *hairester*, often occurs as a trade-name in Free Y, e. g. Rog. de Beverlay, hairster 1299 p. 8. Ran. de Mellmerby, hairester 1349 p. 43. This word is also recorded in NED (1415) and translated by 'a worker in horsehair' (derived fr. *hair* sb). This explanation does not seem quite satisfactory; the spelling of the much earlier *Hayrere* (above) and *hairester* (in Free Y) prove this; *hair* got its modern spelling (with *ai*) in the 15th century.

Taylmongere. 1329. NED: —
Nf: Thom. Talmonghere 1329 *SR* 27. Pet. Taylmonger 1332 *SR* 27.

OE *tæg(e)l* 'tail' + *mangere;* cf ON *tagl* 'a horse's tail'. — *One who sells tails, prob. horses' tails, horsehair.* — Cf the following surname, which apparently means 'one who sells hair': Hugo le *Hermonger* 1279 RH 628 (Hu).

Tailman. 1319. NED: —
Ess: Jacob' Taleman 1319 *SR* 9. — *So:* Walt. Talman 1327 SR 186 (Tailman 1333 *SR* 13).

OE *tæg(e)l* + *mann*. — Signification: = TAYLMONGERE.

4. Fuller, Teaseler, Shearman.

Fullere, Fulur. 1221. NED: c1000.

Ess: Henr. le Folur 1255 *Ass* 4. Ad. Le Fuller' 1316 *2.GDR* 50. Galfr. le Fuller' 1319 *SR* 2. Joh. Le Fullere 1327 *SR* 6. Alan le Fullere 1341 *Ass* 22. — *Sx:* Joh. le Fuller' 1249 *Ass* 37. Ric. Le Folur 1279 *Ass* 4. Henr' le Fullere 1296 SR 26. Ph. le Fuller ib. 57. Walt. le Fuller 1327 SR 138. — *Ha:* Walt. le Fulur 1272 *Ass* 16. Henr. le Fullere 1280 *3.Ass* 6. Sim. le Fullere 1340 *SR* 6. — *So:* Will. le Fulur 1243 Ass 303. Pet. le Fulur 1256 FF 168. — *Wo:* Theobaldus le Fulur 1221 Ass 591. Joh. le Fulur 1255 *Ass* 23. Will. Le Folour 1307 *Ass* 4. — *St:* Will. le Fullere 1307 7.Ass 183. — *La:* Walt. le Folur 1292 *1.Ass* 1. Henr. le Fulere ib. 22. Ric. le Foulour 1333 *Ass* 15. — *Y:* Alan. le Folur 1268 *Ass* 27. Ric. le Fullur 1293 *Ass* 83. Will. Fullour 1332 *SR* 6. — *Li:* Gilb. le Fulur 1245 *Ass* 24. Henr. le Fulur 1281 *1.Ass* 13. Joh. le Foler ib. 37. — *Nf:* Barth. le Fuller' 1286 *Ass* 58. Thom. le Fullere 1300 *GDR* 21. Elueredus le Fulere 1307 ib. 1. Sim. Le fuller' 1329 *SR* 33. Ric. Fuller' 1332 *SR* 9. Rog. le Fullere ib. 25. Agnes Fulere ib. 47.

It has been considered suitable to put these two surnames together; their significations are identical, but their origin is different: one comes fr. OE, the other fr. OF. But as the forms are much alike some confusion in spelling has sometimes arisen; moreover, the same person is not seldom called by both names. — There are two other such pairs of surnames, *Tannere, Tanur* and *Tyghelere, Tiulur*, which I have treated in the same way.

1. OE *fullere*. 2. OF *fouleor, foleur* 'celui qui foule le raisin'; cf the corresponding adj. *fouleor, follour* 'qui sert à fouler les draps' (Godefroy). NED has only the native form. — *One who fulls cloth, a walker*.

Fullere is a southern and eastern surname; most instances have been found in *Nf* and *Ess*. The French form, however, occurs in the whole of England; v. WALKERE.

Fullester. 1327. NED: —

Sx: Emma Fullestr' 1327 SR 203. — *Li:* Galfr. Fulster 1327 *4.SR* 2.

The fem. form of OE *fullere*. — Signification: = FULLERE.

Fulun. 1219. NED: —

La: Mich. le Fulun 1246 Ass 11. Hugh le Fulun ib. 73. — *Li:* Rad. le fullun 1219 Ass 346.

OF *foulon, fulun, foullon* 'fuller' (Godefroy). — *Fuller, walker*.

Walkere. 1260. NED: c1050.

So: Joh. Batte de Were Walkere 1344 *Ass* 13. — *Wo:* Henr. le Walker' 1275 SR 57. Ric. le Walkere 1277 Hal 78. Will. Le Walker 1307 *Ass* 3. Ric. Le Walkere 1327 SR 1. Joh. le Walkar 1332 SR 7. — *St:* Rob. Walkere 1266 4.Ass 160. Ric. Le Walkere 1309 *GDR* 3. Rog. le Walkere 1327 SR 225. Thom' le Walker 1332 SR 129. — *La:* Joh. le Walker 1292 *1.Ass* 39. Will. le Walkere 1300 *Ass* 7. Mich. le Walker 1324 CR 4. Pet. le Walker 1327 *SR* 15. Adam le Walker 1332 SR 3. — *Y:* Hubert le Walker 1260 Ass 117. Elena Walker 1297 SR 139. Rog. le Walker 1301 SR 52. Rob. the Walkere 1316 3.Wake 102. Thom. le Walker 1332 *SR* 3. — *Li:* Sim. le Walker 1281 *1.Ass* 41. Hugo Walker 1327 *2.SR* 1. Ric. le Walker 1332 *3.SR* 12. Steph. le Walker ib.

OE *wealcere*. — *One who fulls cloth, a fuller*.

The occurrence of *Walkere* should be compared with the other common synonyms, *Fullere* and *Toukere*; they belong to different parts of England. With the exception of one instance in *So*, *Walkere* only occurs in *Wo, St, La, Y*, and *Li*, i. e. in the West and North of England. *Fullere*, on the other hand, is common in *Nf, Ess, Sx*, and *Ha*, i. e. in the East and South-East (the French instances, *Fulur, Folour*, in the other counties should not be taken into consideration, as they are probably translations of *Walkere* or *Toukere*). The third name, *Toukere*, seems to belong to the South-West, for it occurs very frequently in *So*, and only a few instances have been found in the other counties; v. below.

Toukere. 1243. NED: [1273].

Sx: Thom. le Toker 1326 *Ass* 8. — *Ha:* Walt. le Touker' 1280 *2.Ass* 88. Nich. le Toukare 1327 *SR* 1. Walt. le Toukere 1333 *SR* 2. — *So:* Wolward le Tukare 1243 Ass 262. Joh. le Tokere 1305 *Ass* 2. Walt. Le Touker' 1307 *Ass* 6. Rob. dictus le Toukere 1310 BBA 46. Ric. le Touker 1327 SR 127. Sim. le Touker ib. 177. Laur. Toukere 1333 *SR* 1. Joh. le Toukere ib. 2. Will. Touker' ib. 13. Edith la Toukere 1347 FF 6. — *Wo:* Thom. le Tukkere 1255 *Ass* 25. Adam Le Tukere 1275 *2.Ass* 49. — *Y:* Henr. Tuker 1279 *Ass* 55.

A der. of OE *tūcian* 'to torment', later 'to tuck, full'. — *Tucker, fuller*. — As is seen above, *Toukere* belongs chiefly to *So;* v. WALKERE.

Wolbetere. 1271. NED: —

So: Rich. le Wolbetere 1271 Ass 163. — *Wo:* Alan. Le Wlbetere 1275 *1.Ass* 5. Ernald of (sic) Wlbetere (undated) OCW 119. — *Nf:* Joh. le Wllebetere 1332 *SR* 57.

OE *wull* 'wool' + *bēatere*. — *One who fulls woollen cloth*.

Betere. 1200.   NED: 1483.
Ha: Walt. Betare 1327 *SR* 14. Ric. le Betare ib. Hugo le Betare ib. Will. le Betere 1333 *SR* 8. Alic. la Betere ib. (la Bettere 1340 *SR* 6). — *Li:* Jord. le Bettere 1200 Cur 317.

OE *bēatere.* — Signification: = Batour. Cf. Wolbetere, Flaxbeter; v. also Betere p. 134.

Batour. 1199.   NED: —
Ess: Joh. le Batur 1255 *Ass* 8. Mich. le Batour 1285 *Ass* 18. Sym. le Batur ib. 34. Joh. Batour 1341 *Ass* 5. — *Sx:* Ric. le Batur 1249 *Ass* 20. Osbertus le Batur ib. 36. Rog. le Batur 1296 SR 45. — *Ha:* Rog. le batur 1230 P 192. Ric. le Batur 1272 *Ass* 4. Walt. le Batour 1280 *3.Ass* 31. Derbes Le Batour 1305 *Ass* 8. — *So:* Rob. le Batur' 1225 Ass 98. Joh. le Batour 1327 SR 112. — *Gl:* Edmundus le batur 1199 P 30. — *Y:* Adam le Batur 1268 *Ass* 38. Nich. le Batur 1279 *Ass* 9. Walt. le Batour 1301 SR 118. Pet. le batour, zonarius 1314 Free Y 15. — *Li:* Rog. Batour 1275 RH 374. Hugo le Batur 1281 *1.Ass* 44. Thom. le Batur 1281 *2.Ass* 40. Christiana Batour' 1327 *2.SR* 21. — *Nf:* Pet. le Batur 1275 RH 520. Thom. le Batur 1286 *Ass* 80. Eda Batour 1316 *GDR* 32.

OF *bateor* 'ouvrier qui bat certaines matières' (Godefroy). — Signification: 1. *Beater of cloth, wool, flax, etc.; fuller.* 2. Short for Orbatour, q. v., or *one who beats other metals;* v. Batour p. 134.

Dreyster. 1292.   NED: 14..
La: Alic. le Dreyster' 1292 *1.Ass* 17, 1292 *2.Ass* 31. Alice le Dristar 1324 CR 68, 69. — *Y:* Adam Dreyster 1301 SR 103. Agnes le dreystr' ib. 10. — *Li:* Hawysia Dryestere 1328 *Ass* 3.

A fem. der. of OE *drȳgean, drīgean* 'to dry'. — *One who dries something;* prob. *a drier of cloth* (as a process in bleaching or fulling). »The cloth, having been fulled, had to be stretched on tenters to dry» (Salzman: Med. Ind. p. 224).

Teseler, Taseler. 1230.   NED: 14..
Ess: Galfr. Taseler 1230 P 152 (Taslere ib.). Rog. le Taselere 1324 *2.GDR* 29. — *Sr:* Ric. le Tesler'(?) 1332 SR 14.

A der. of OE *tǣsel, tǣsl* 'teasel'; AF *teizeler.* — *Teaseler, one who teasels cloth.* The business of the teaseler was to draw up from the body of the cloth all the loose fibres with teasels, the dried heads of the 'fuller's thistle' (Salzman: Med. Ind. 225).

Cf NED tasseller 'one who makes tassels'; there are only two instances consisting of surnames (Matilda la Taselere, Gilbert le

Taselere), and the spelling of these (the -a- is of course regular in *Lo* and *Ess)*, I think, indicates that the signification is *teaseler*.

Cf the river-name *Salary Brook Ess, Taseleresbrok* 1333, which contains the present surname (v. Pl. Soc. Ess p. 11).

Sherman. 1275. NED: c1275.

Ess: Joh. Scharman 1312 *4.GDR* 2. Rob. Sherman 1319 *SR* 15. Phil. Sharman 1327 *SR* 1. John Shereman 1337 CR 154. — *Wo:* Thom. Scheremon 1275 SR 79. Joh. Scherman 1306 *Ass* 3. Will. Le Sheremon 1327 SR 35. Thom. le Sheremon 1343 OCW 52. — *St:* Henry le Schermon 1306 7.Ass 164. — *La:* Henr. le Shermon 1332 SR 54. Will. le Shermon 1338 *Ass* 1. — *Y:* Sim. le Sherman 1295 Free Y 6. Joh. Le Schereman 1305 *Ass* 21. — *Li:* Will. le Scherman 1317 *Ass* 11. Rad. Scherman 1327 *2.SR* 12. Thom. Sherman 1327 *3.SR* 1. Hugo Cherman 1328 *Ass* 51. Andr. Scherman 1332 *1.SR* 15. Laur. Sherman 1332 *3.SR* 2. Rob. le Scherman ib. 4. — *Nf:* Will. Scherman 1299 GDR 18. Galfr. Scherman 1329 *SR* 32. Reg. Shereman 1332 *SR* 47.

According to NED, *shearman* is a compound of OE *sceran* and *mann*. But it is far more probable that the first element is OE *scēar* 'scissors'. The form *Sharman* (Ess), in which the *a* corresponds to an OE *ǣ*, points in this direction. Moreover, a compound of *a verb + man* seems to be very rare; I have no instance among my compounds in *-man*. — One who shears woollen cloth (NED). The shearman used a pair of large shears to cut off the loose portions of the cloth raised by the teaseler.

Sherere. 1275. NED: 1318—9.

Sx: Will. le Scherar 1284 FF 130. Galfr. Le Sherere 1288 *Ass* 35. Will. Sherar 1332 SR 246. — *Ha:* Will. Le Scherer' 1305 *Ass* 6 (Le Schirere ib. 15). Rad. Le Shyrere ib. Steph. le Sherare 1327 *SR* 17. Rob. le Sherere 1333 *SR* 1. — *So:* Rob. le Sherere 1336 FF 183. Joh. Scherere 1344 *Ass* 7. — *Li:* Matild' le Scherher 1275 RH 312. — *Nf:* Nich. le Sherere 1318 CDN 85. Pet. le Sherere ib.

A der. of OE *sceran* 'to shear, cut'. — Signification: = SHERMAN. It may also mean 'reaper' and 'one who removes the fleece from an animal'. — I have found one instance of the corresponding fem. form: Juliana la »*Scherestere*» 1282 CLB (A) 58 (Lo).

Poller. 1288. NED: 1578.

Sx: Ric. Le Pollere 1288 *Ass* 30. — *Ha:* Barth. le Pollare 1327 *SR* 10. — *Li:* Gilb. le Poller 1327 *4.SR* 8. Hugo Poller 1328 *Ass* 50.

A der. of ME *pollen* 'to poll, clip, shear'; v. NED *poll*. — Signification: = SHERERE. It may also be synonymous with FELPOLLARE, q. v.

Tundur. 1275. NED: —

Sx: Walt. Le Tundur 1288 *Ass* 28. Henr. Le Tundur ib. Will. le Tundur 1296 SR 82. — *Nf:* Hugo le Tundur 1275 RH 468 (*Tonsor* ib). Ric. Le Tundur 1286 *Ass* 91. Pet. le Tundur 1286 CDN 5. Nich. le Tundur 1298 ib. 64. Edmund le Toundur 1319 ib. 89. John le Tundour 1321 ib. 105.

AF *toundour* (Lib. Alb. 724) = OF *tondeur*. — Signification: = SHERMAN. — *Toundour* is common as a trade-name in Free Y, e. g. Joh. de Tikhill, toundour 1320 p. 19. — The following surname has a prefix, otherwise it is identical with *Tundur:* Will. le »*retundur*» 1276 CLB (A) 8 (Lo).

Tonsur. 1252. NED: 1656.
Y: Thom. the Tonsur 1252 FF 67.

OF *tonsour* 'rogneur' (Godefroy). — Prob. = SHERMAN. The same person is called both *Tonsor* and *Tundur* in Nf, v. TUNDUR. Cf NED *tonsor* 1656 'a barber'.

5. Dyer and Bleacher of Cloth.

a. Dyer, Litster.

Deyer, Dyer. 1260. NED: 1369.

Ess: Rich. le Deyer 1310 CR 11. Adam le Dyer' 1319 *SR* 15. Gilb. le Degher' ib. 16. Cristiana le Deyer' 1327 *SR* 3. Nich. le Deyer' 1332 *SR* 7. Joh. le Dyere 1341 *Ass* 7. — *Sx:* Rad. Le Deyere 1288 *Ass* 40. Alex' Dyghere 1296 SR 93. Will. Le Degher' 1310 2.*GDR* 5. Rog. le Degher' 1325 *Ass* 14. Joh. le Digher 1327 SR 134. Ric. Digher 1332 SR 225. — *Ha:* Walt. le Deghere 1280 2.*Ass* 80. Alan. le Dyghere 1325 *Ass* 2. Joh. le Dyare 1327 *SR* 17. Galfr. le Dyghere 1333 *SR* 7. Ad. le Deyer 1340 *SR* 7. — *So:* Henr. le Deghar 1260 BBA 7. Elias Le Deygher' 1307 *Ass* 1. Thom. Le Deyere 1320 *Ass* 9. Alex. le Degher 1327 SR 271. Alicia Deghere ib. 281. Alan. le Digher ib. 135. Rich. le Dyare ib. 279. Joh. le Degher' 1333 *SR* 20. — *Wo:* Rob. le Deyare 1275 SR 65. Will. Le Dayer 1304 Reg 8. Rog. Le Dyer 1327 SR 16. Joh. Le Dyere ib. 17. Ric. Le Dir ib. 72. Nich. le Diyare 1350 OCW 53. — *St:* Ralph le Deyer 1321 10.Ass 40. — *Nf:* Joh. Le Dyere 1286 *Ass* 77.

OE **dēagere* fr. *dēagian* 'to dye'. The two forms *Deyer* and *Dyer* occur side by side, but not in the same proportion in all counties. I here give a survey of all the instances I have found:

Ess: Deyer 19 inst., Dyer 9. *Sx:* Deyer 5, Dier 7. *Ha:* Deghere 6, Dighere 9. *So:* Deyer 31, Dier 13. *Wo:* Deyer 5, Dyer 7. *St:* Deyer 1. *Nf:* Dyere 1.

Signification: *One who dyes cloth*. — As is seen above, this surname is restricted to the Saxon counties; the corresponding Anglian surname is LITESTER, q. v.

Deyster. 1280. NED: a1350.
Sx: Eua Dygestre 1296 SR 93. — *Wo:* Henr. le Deystere 1280 Hal 141. Ric. le Deyster 1304 ib. 475. Thom. le Deystore ib. 478. Godith la Deyster ib. 479. — *St:* Ralph le Deystere 1298 7.Ass 49. Will. le Deyghester 1326 9.Ass 114.

The fem. form of OE *dēagere. — *Dyester, dyer*.

Litester. 1279. NED: c1374.
Ess: Nich. le Littestere 1327 2.GDR 18. — *St:* Ralph le Listere 1338 FF 144. — *La:* Will. le Lister 1292 *1.Ass* 16. Henry le Lister 1323 CR 7. Alice le Lister 1325 ib. 143. Ric. le Lister 1332 SR 2. Joh. Litester 1338 *Ass* 2. Hugo le Lytster 1341 *SR* 4. — *Y:* Thom. le litestere 1279 *Ass* 78. Ric. le Listere 1293 *Ass* 78. Jord. the Littester 1316 3.Wake 126. Rad. le Letestere 1332 *SR* 7. Rad. Lister ib. 15. Patricius le litester 1344 Free Y 38. Ph. le litster c1346 *SR* 10. — *Li:* Thom. le Littester 1281 *1.Ass* 13. Joh. Lytster 1327 *2.SR* 5. Custancia Litster ib. 12. Rob. litester' 1327 *4.SR* 7. Henr. le Litester 1328 *Ass* 58. Reg. le Lister 1332 *2.SR* 1. Ric. Litester 1332 *3.SR* 14. — *Nf:* Joh. le litestere 1316 *GDR* 36. Thom. Lytestere 1329 *SR* 27. Matild. Le litester' 1332 *SR* 19. Galfr. le Litester' ib. 26. Ric. le litester' ib. Will. Le Litester' ib. 65.

A fem. der. of ME *lite, litte* 'to colour, dye' (fr. ON *lita* 'to dye'). — *Dyer*. — *Litester* is an Anglian surname; it occurs frequently in *La, Y, Li* and *Nf*, but not at all in the West Saxon counties. Cf DEYER.

Teynturer. 1196. NED: —
Ess: Galfr. le Teynturer 1255 *Ass* 9. Adam le Teynturer 1282 *2.GDR* 1. Henr. le Thenturer 1285 *Ass* 45. Ric. le Teynturer 1312 *4.GDR* 1. — *Sx:* Rob. le Teynturer 1263 *Ass* 49. Will. Le Teynturer 1279 *Ass* 1. Henr' le Tenterer 1296 SR 12. Will. le Teynturer 1316 FF 27. — *Ha:* Will. le Tenterur 1272 *Ass* 20. Galfr. le Teynturer 1280 *2.Ass* 75. Adam le Tenturer ib. 87. — *So:* Rich. le Teyntrer 1243 Ass 188. Steph. le Teinturer 1254 Ass 438. Henry le Teynturer 1263 FF 201. Adam le Teinturer 1301 FF 317. Will. Le Teingturer 1305 *Ass* 2 (Le Teynturer ib. 7). — *Wo:* Will. le Teinturer 1275 SR 2. Rad. le Teynturer 1275 *1.Ass* 18. Henr. le Teyturer 1294 Hal 283 (le Teynterel ib. 287). Magister Ric. dictus Teyntrier 1295 ib. 328. Walt. le Teynturer 1305 Reg 112. — *St:* Magister Henry le Teynturer 1272 4.Ass 188. John le Teynturer 1304 7.Ass 118. Ralph le Tenturer 1306 ib. 131. Adam le Teynturer 1307 ib. 176. — *La:* Hugh le Teynturer 1285 Ass 215. Ric. le Teynturer 1292 *3.Ass* 54. Joh. le Taynturer ib. 94. — *Y:* Hugh le teinturer 1226 FF 93. Angnes la taynturer 1279 *Ass* 49. Alan. le Teynturer

ib. 54. Will. le Taynturer 1305 *Ass* 14. — *Nt:* Thom. le teinturer 1196 P 269.
— *Li:* Warnerus le tunterer 1202 Ass 167. Gilb. le Taynturer 1245 *Ass* 46.
Alan. le Teynturer 1281 *2.Ass* 33. — *Nf:* Joh. le Teinturier 1250 *Ass* 28.
Barth. le Teynterer 1295 *GDR* 14. Geruas. le Teynturer 1329 *SR* 32.

OF *teinturier, tainterier.* — Dyer.

Teyntur. 1268. NED: —
Ha: Will. le Teyntur 1280 *3.Ass* 40. — *So:* Pet. le Teyntur 1268 Ass 20.
Will. le Teintur 1278 Ass 135. — *Wo:* Rob. Le Teyntour 1313 OCW 96. — *St:*
Mich. le Teinter 1255 FF 246. — *Nf:* Maur. le Teyntour 1332 *SR* 40.

AF *teyntour* (Lib. Alb. 723) = OF *teindeor, teintur* 'teinturier'.
— Dyer.

Heustere. 1288. NED: 1600.
Sx: Rob. le Huster' 1296 SR 29. — *St:* Rog. le Heuster 1306 7.Ass 159.
Ric. le Heustere 1327 SR 205. Joh. le Heustere ib. 224. Rog. le Heustere ib.
236. Nich. le Heustere ib. 237. Ric. le Heustere ib. 244. Will. le Heuster'
1332 SR 82. Will. le Hewestere 1346 12.Ass 51. — *Ch:* Rich. le Heuster 1288
Court 104.

A fem. der. of *hew, hu* 'hue, colour' (OE *hīew, hīw*). — *Colourer,
dyer* (NED). — This is the only surname meaning 'dyer' that is
common in *St.* — *Heustere* may perhaps also mean 'one who hews
or hacks'.

b. **Dyer with Woad, Cork, Madder.**

Wayder. 1185. NED:—
Ha: Barth. Le Weyder 1305 *Ass* 17. — *So:* Phil. le Wayder 1243 Ass
293. Galfr. le Weyder 1276 RH 134. — *Wo:* Joh. Le Wayder 1327 SR 35.
— *Y:* Will. le Waisdier 1185 P 69. Erkenbaldus Wesdier 1191 P 70 (le Wais-
der 1195 P 84, le Weisdier 1196 P 167). Joh. le waider, junior 1293 Free
Y 5. Elias Wayder 1297 SR 151. — *Li:* Reinerius le Waider 1202 Ass 162.
Rog. Wayder 1230 P 301. Will. le Wayder 1281 *1.Ass* 37. — *Nf:* Ric. Le
Weyder 1286 *Ass* 138. Pet. Pyremund le Weyder 1287 CDN 14. Adenet le
Wayder 1293 Free L 1. Thorald le Weyder 1296 CDN 59. John Chirsesy le
Weyder 1299 ib. 72.

OF *wesdier, guesdier, waisdier* 'marchand de guède' (Godefroy). The disappearance of -*s*- is quite regular; note that -*s*- occurs in the earliest instances. — Signification: = Wadere.

Wadere, Wodere. 1275. NED: 1415.
a. W a d e r e:
Sx: Rob. le Wadere 1296 SR 43. Walt. le Wadere ib. 83. — *La:* Joh. le
Wadder 1332 SR 71. Rad. Wadder 1338 *Ass* 3. Joh. Wadder ib. 5 (le Wadder

ib). Rad. le Wadd'r 1341 *SR* 8. — *Cu:* Nich. le Wadder 1332 SR 65. Joh. le Wadder ib. — *Nf:* Thorald de Cawston le *Wader* 1290 CDN 30 (T. de Causton le *Weyder* 1293 ib. 47). Geradm' Le Wader 1329 *SR* 61.

b. W o d e r e:

Sx: Andr' le Wodere 1275 RH 210 (Le Wodere 1288 *Ass* 17). — *Ha:* Barth. le Wodere 1327 *SR* 17, 1333 *SR* 9. — *So:* Rich. le Wodere 1293 FF 288, 1296 ib. 297. Thom. le Wodere 1327 SR 263, 1333 *SR* 2.

A der. of OE *wād* 'woad'. One would not expect the form *Wader(e)* in *Sx* and *Nf*, but this must be an early shortened form ($\bar{a} > \breve{a}$); note that the same person is called both *Weyder* and *Wader* (v. *Nf*). This is also borne out by the Lancashire spelling, *Wadder*.

Signification: a. *One who dyes with woad*. b. *One who sells woad*. c. Less prob. *one who cultivates woad*. — Woad is a blue dye-stuff obtained from the plant of the same name.

The form *Wodere* might also come from OE *wudere* 'woodman, wood-carrier'. Cf, however, the following instance, in which the sense 'woader' is obvious: Rob. le »*Woder*» de Merthone, Rob. de Merthone, »*wayder*» 1276 CLB (B) 257 (Lo).

I have found another surname which might be mentioned here: Thom. le *Wodebetere* 1275 RH 167, 168 (Sf); the signification is apparently 'one who beats or dresses woad'. Cf FLAXBETER and WOLBETERE.

Wadester, Wodester. 1256. NED: —

Nb: Will. Wodester' 1256 Ass 118. *Li:* Rob. le Waddester 1305 *Ass* 16 (Le Waddester ib. 10). Henr. le Wadester 1318 *Ass* 20, 1327 *3.SR* 1. Ric. Wadester 1327 *3.SR* 3 (le Wadester 1332 *3.SR* 25).

The fem. form of WADERE, WODERE. — Signification: = WADERE.

Wademan, Wodeman. 1296. NED: 14..

a. W a d e m a n:

Nf: Symon le Wademan 1296 *GDR* 1. — *Y:* Will. Wadman 1417 2.YMB 82.

b. W o d e m a n:

Sx: Joh. Wodeman 1296 SR 69. — *So:* Rich. Wodeman 1327 SR 139. — *St:* Reg. Wodemon 1332 SR 83.

OE *wād* 'woad' + *mann*. — Signification: = WADERE.

Of the form *Wodeman* I have only included a few of the instances found, because there is another more probable interpretation: in most cases it certainly means 'woodman'.

Cf Ric. de Norham, *waddeman* 1375 Free Y 74.

Corklittster. 1279. NED: —

Y: Will. le Corklittster 1279 *Ass* 37.

ME *cork* (fr. Gaelic and Irish *corcur*) 'a purple or red dye-stuff obtained from certain lichens growing on rocks in Scotland and the north of England' (NED) + ME *litester* 'dyer'. NED has *cork* 1483, q. v. — *One who dyes cloth with 'cork'.*

Cf Joh. Bekwith, *blaklitster* 1506 Free Y 231.

Corker. 1297. NED: —

La: Galfr. le Corker 1338 *Ass* 1 (G. Corker ib. 3). Thom. le Corker ib. 7. — Y: Adam le Corker 1297 2.Wake 11.

A der. of ME *cork* 'a purple or red dye-stuff'. Signification: = CORKLITTSTER; perhaps also *one who sells purple dye.*

Madrer. 1333. NED: —

La: Ric. le Madrer 1333 *Ass* 14.

A der. of OE *mædere* 'madder'. — *One who dyes with madder* or *one who sells madder.* Madder is a plant from which a red dye-stuff is obtained. — Cf the following surname, which means 'one who sells madder': Rob. *madermanger* 1230 P 323 (Np).

Madster. 1332. NED: —

La: Rob. le Madster 1332 *Ass* 13, 1333 *Ass* 16.

Prob. the fem. form of MADRER. The form evidenced in the surname is abridged; it ought to have been **Maderster.* — Signification: = MADRER.

c. **Blacker, Bleacher, Washer.**

Blacker. 1246. NED: 1632.

Ess: Rad. le blaker' 1291 2.*GDR* 4. Joh. Blaker' 1319 *SR* 5. Joh. le Blakiere 1332 *SR* 23. — Sx: Will. Blaker 1327 SR 177. — So: Walt. le Blacker 1327 SR 225. Steph. le Blakar ib. 263. Ric. le Blacker' 1333 *SR* 31. — La: Rog. Blacker 1246 Ass 75.

A der. of ME *bla(c)ken* 'to make black' (fr. OE *blæc* 'black'). — *One who blacks.*

Blakestere. 1199.   NED: —
Wo: Ric. le Blakestare 1275 SR 15. Joh. Blakestre ib. 87. — *St:* Will. de Blakestere 1199 3.Ass 40.

The fem. form of BLACKER. — Signification: = BLACKER.

Blacchere. 1305.   NED: —
So: Rob. Le Blacchere 1305 *Ass* 9 (Le Blaccher' ib. 2).

A der. of *blatch* 'to black' (fr. OE **blæcce* 'blacking'). — *One who blacks.*

Blacchester. 1305.   NED: —
Ess: John le Blachester 1334 CR 121 (J. Blachester 1346 ib. 212). — *Wo:* Felic' la Blacchester' 1305 *Ass* 1. Thom. le Blacchester' ib.

The fem. form of BLACCHERE. — Signification: = BLACCHERE.

Blextere. 1275.   NED: c1440.
Nf: Joh. le Bleckestere 1275 RH 531. Alex. Le Blexstere 1286 *Ass* 43. Will. le Blexstere 1306 CDN 110. Thom. le Blexstere 1309 ib. 14. Rob. le Blextere 1329 ib. 146. Mich. le Blexter ib. 147.

A fem. der. of ME *bleck* 'to make black' (fr. ME *bleck* sb, prob. fr. ON *blek* 'ink'). — *One who blackens.* — Cf BLEYKESTERE, which is much alike in form; both these words, however, are well evidenced in Prompt. P. (which prob. also is fr. *Nf*). v. NED.

Bleykestere. 1286.   NED: c1440.
Li: Hugo le Bleykster' 1286 *Ass* 1. Ric. Blaykster 1327 *2.SR* 14. Will. Blaikester 1332 *3. SR* 23. — *Nf:* Will. Bleykestere 1329 SR 8. Joh. Bleykestere ib. 9. Rob. Le Blikester 1332 *SR* 65.

A fem. der. of ON *bleikja* 'to whiten, bleach'. — *Bleacher.*

Blechere. 1327.   NED: 1550.
Ha: Rob. le Blechere 1327 *SR* 18 (le Blechare 1333 *SR* 9).

A der. of OE *blǣcan* 'to bleach'. — *Bleacher, one who bleaches.*

Boukere. 1229.   NED: —
Sx: Rob. le Bukere 1229 FF 65. Walt. Bukere 1262 FF 43. Rob. le Bukere 1279 *Ass* 27. Ric. le Bukere 1288 *Ass* 24. Elias le Boukere 1296 SR 60. Ad' le Bokere ib. 89. Thom' le Boucar' ib. 98. Will. le Bouker 1327 SR 123. Elena le Bouker ib. 178. Relicta le Buker 1332 SR 242. John Bouker 1341 FF 102. — *St:* Rog. le Boukere 1327 SR 207. Ric. le Boukere ib. 225. — *La:* Will. le Buker 1246 Ass 7. Thom. le Buker 1277 Ass 141. Rob. le Bouker 1325 CR 106. Thom. le Bouker 1332 SR 37. Alan. le Bouker 1338 *Ass* 7. Henr. le Bouker ib.

A der. of ME *bouken* (OE *būcian) 'to steep in lye, to bleach'. The first instance of the verb *buck* in NED is fr. 1377, but it has apparently been in common use much earlier, especially in *Sx*, where I have found many instances of the surname.

Signification: *Buck-washer, bleacher.*

Stepere. 1327.   NED: 1611.

Sx: Alic' Relicta le Stepere 1327 SR 114. Rob. le Stupere ib. 153. Joh. le Stupar' 1332 SR 238.

A der. of ME *stepe, stipe,* *stupe 'to steep' (OE **stīepan,* *stēpan). — *One who steeps flax, cloth, etc., in order to wash or bleach it, a bleacher*; prob. synonymous with BOUKERE.

Lavender, Launder. 1268.   NED: [a1300].

Ess: Amicia la Lavendere 1311 CR 48. Sarra le Lauender' 1317 *2.GDR* 39. Rob. le Lauender' 1332 *SR* 6. — *So:* Ralf la Lavendere 1268 Ass 21. Steph. le Lauender 1344 *Ass* 7. — *St:* Sim. de Lavender 1332 SR 106. — *La:* Adam Lauender 1325 CR 82. Matilda le Launder 1326 CR 75. — *Y:* Eva la Lavender 1285 1.Wake 195. Thom. Launder, mariner 1330 Free Y 26. — *Li:* Beatrix le Lauender 1281 *1.Ass* 24. Isabella Lauender 1327 *2.SR* 25. Henr. Lauender 1332 *3.SR* 25. — *Nf:* Walt. Lauender 1329 *SR* 22.

OF *lavandier* masc., *lavandiere* fem.; the form *Launder* is a contraction of these. — *One who washes.* This surname is prob. connected with the wool industry, and refers to the washing and bleaching of flax, wool, cloth, etc. As is seen above, the lavender was often a man. Cf SKYNWASHERE.

Waschere. 1293.   NED: c1440.

Y: Henr. le Wassere 1293 *Ass* 85. Will. le Wassar 1297 SR 85. Steph. Wascher, mercer 1350 Free Y 44. — *Nf:* Alan. le Wascere 1295 *GDR* 8. Beatr. le Waschere 1310 ib. 11.

A der. of OE *wæscan* 'to wash'. OE had the fem. form *wæscestre.* — Signification: = LAVENDER.

B. Manufacturers of Clothes.

1. Tailor, Renovator of Old Clothes.

Taillour. 1182.   NED: [1296].

Ess: Rob. le taylur 1255 *Ass* 4. Clemens Le taylur 1316 *2.GDR* 50. Will. le Taillour 1332 *SR* 6. — *Sx:* Thom. le Taillur 1249 *Ass* 6. Rad. Taliur 1296 SR 36. Walt. le Taylour 1327 SR 115. — *Ha:* Nich. le Taylur 1272

Ass 4. Thom. le Tayllur 1305 *Ass* 7. Alic. la Tayllour 1333 *SR* 7. — *So:* Will. Le Taillur 1182 P 113. Rich. le Tailur 1243 Ass 278. Ric. le Taillour 1333 *SR* 2. — *Wo:* Nich. le taillur 1221 Ass 447. Ric. le Tayllur 1255 *Ass* 24. Matilda Le Taillour 1327 SR 7. — *St:* Thom. le Taillur 1200 3.Ass 69. Thom. le Taylour 1332 SR 92 (Cissor 1327 SR 197). Will. le Taylour 1332 SR 96. — *La:* Rob. le Tayllur 1246 Ass 53. Joh. le Talyur 1292 *1.Ass* 2. Rob. le Taillour 1332 SR 32. — *Y:* Adam le Taylur 1260 Ass 121. Rob. le Taylur 1268 *Ass* 19. Hugo le Taillur c1346 *SR* 3. — *Li:* Rob. le taillur 1197 P 105. Rob. le Tayllur 1245 *Ass* 3. Andreas Tayliour' 1327 *1.SR* 1. — *Nf:* Rog. le taillur 1199 P 287. Galfr. le Taliur 1296 *GDR* 1. Matild. Taliour 1329 *SR* 9. Rad. Talliour 1332 *SR* 14.

AF *taillour* = OF *tailleor, -eur*. — *Tailor*. — This surname is one of the most common during this period.

Parmenter. 1176.   NED: [1301].
Ess: Ric. le Parmenter 1255 *Ass* 12. Thom. le Parmunter 1299 *2.GDR* 8. Will. le Parmentier 1332 *SR* 26. — *Sx:* Mancerus le Parmenter 1296 SR 92. Joh. le Parmenter 1332 SR 261. — *Ha:* Ric. parmenter 1176 P 196. Maynet. le Parmenter 1272 *Ass* 24. Will. le Parmentier 1327 *SR* 1. — *So:* Hamo le parmenter 1243 Ass 143. Joh. le Permonter 1327 SR 220. Henr. Parmunter 1333 *SR* 21. — *Wo:* Henr. le parmentier 1199 P 82. Rob. le parminter 1221 Ass 520. Ric. Le Parmonter 1327 SR 55. — *St:* Osbert le Parmentur 1227 4.Ass 53. Adam le Parmenter 1327 SR 236. Will. Parmonter 1332 SR 120. — *La:* Adam le Parmenter 1292 *3.Ass* 21. Rob. le Parmenter ib. 107. — *Y:* Will. le Parmenter 1297 1.Wake 286. John le Permenter 1297 2.Wake 14. Rob. le Parmenter c1346 *SR* 7. — *Li:* Gerardus Parmenter 1186 P 80. Rob. le Parmenter 1245 *Ass* 46. Rad. Parmounter 1327 *2.SR* 7. — *Nf:* Hamo le parmenter 1250 *Ass* 10. Joh. Parmonter 1329 *SR* 32.

OF *parmentier, parmetier* 'tailleur' (Godefroy). — *Tailor*. — This surname is common, especially in *Ess, Ha,* and *So*.

Sartour. 1333.   NED: 1656.
So: Ric. le Sartour 1333 *SR* 27.

OF *sartor* 'couturier' (Godefroy). — *Tailor*.

Coussur. 1286.   NED: —
Wo: Will. le Coussur 1286 Epi 289.

OF *couseor, couss-* 'couturier, tailleur' (Godefroy). — *Tailor*. — As a trade-name: Walt. de Harwedon, *Coseour* 1332 SR 75 (Lo).

Sewstere. 1292.   NED: 1391.
La: Agnes le Seuster' 1292 *1.Ass* 12 (le Sewestere ib. 29, 4). — *Y:* Alicia Sewstere 1301 SR 5. Pet. le Seuster 1305 *Ass* 22.

A fem. der. of OE *seowian* 'to sew'. — *Sempstress, tailor*.

Sewere. 1279.   NED: 1399.
Ha: Will. le Seware 1322 *Ass* 1. Walt. le Seuare 1327 *SR* 8. Steph. le Seuare ib. — *So:* Rob. Seuere 1307 FF 354, 357. — *Y:* Ric. le Sewer 1279 *Ass* 47.

A der. of OE *seowian* 'to sew'. — *One who sews, a tailor*. The signification of this name may also be 'sewer, attendant'.

Semester. 1275.   NED: c995.
Y: Alicia Semester 1376 1.YMB 10. — *Li:* Will. le Semestre 1275 RH 327. Pet. le Semester ib. 318 (P. dictus Semester ib. 310).

OE *sēamestre* 'one who sews', the fem. form of *sēamere*. — *Tailor, seamstress*.

Semere. 1327.   NED: —
Ha: Joh. le Semere 1340 *SR* 7. — *So:* Joh. Semere 1327 SR 198. Thom. Semere 1333 *SR* 34.

OE *sēamere* (only found in OE). — *Tailor*.

Sheppestere. 1296.   NED: 1377.
Ess: Alicia le Schepstere 1317 *2.GDR* 39. Sibil la Sheppester 1334 CR 137 (la Sheppestere ib. 138). — *Sx:* Alic' La Seppestre 1296 SR 81. — *So:* Johanna La Scheppester' 1307 *Ass* 9. Alicia La Scheppester' ib. — *Wo:* Sarra Le Shapester 1327 SR 25. — *Nf:* Claricia la Sheppestr' 1300 *GDR* 21.

A fem. der. of OE *scieppan* 'to create, form'. — *Shepster, dressmaker*.

Shepper. 1327.   NED: (a1175).
Sx: Rob. le Shuppar' 1327 SR 125. Will. Shupper 1332 SR 275. — *So:* Walt. le Schepper 1333 *SR* 9. — *Li:* Rob. Shepere 1327 *2.SR* 8. Will. Schepper 1332 *3.SR* 8.

A der. of OE *scieppan* 'to create, form'. This seems to be the masc. correspondence to SHEPPESTERE, and the signification is prob. the same. NED has *shepper*, but only in the sense of 'the Creator'.

Trymmere. 1327.   NED: 1555.
Ha: Will. le Trymmare 1327 *SR* 8. Henr. le Trymmere ib. 6, 1333 *SR* 7.

A der. of *trim* vb; v. NED. — *One who trims*, prob. *a kind of tailor;* but the signification is difficult to establish, as the corresponding verb has not been found in ME.

Dubbere. 1249.   NED: 1225—6.
Ess: John Dubber 1340 CR 173. — *Sx:* Pet. le Dubber 1249 *Ass* 20. Will. Dubbere 1296 SR 81. Thom. le Dubbar 1332 SR 226. — *Ha:* Joh. Le Dubbere 1305 *Ass* 7 (le dobber ib. 12). Henr. le Dubbere 1327 *SR* 7. Galfr. le Dubbere 1340 *SR* 6. — *So:* Adam le Dubbere 1333 *SR* 5. — *La:* Walt. le Dubbere 1292 *1.Ass* 37, 3. — *Y:* Joh. le Dobber 1293 *Ass* 86. — *Li:* Joh. Dubber 1327 *3.SR* 3. — *Nf:* Pet. le Dubbere 1286 *Ass* 125. Symon le dubber' 1332 *SR* 43.

A der. of late OE *dubban* 'to dub'; ME *dubbe* also had the sense 'to renovate old clothes'. Cf NED *dubber* (fr. OF *doubeur*). — *A renovator of old clothes.*

Pacher. 1241.   NED: 1528.
Ess: Reg. le Pacher 1285 *Ass* 51. Joh. le Paccher' 1319 *SR* 19. — *Sx:* Rad. le Pacher 1241 FF 100.

A der. of ME *pac(c)he* 'a patch', or rather fr. a ME vb **pac(c)hen* (NED *patch* vb c1500). — *One who patches or mends something.*

Feliper. 1277.   NED: —
Lo: Aunger the Pheliper 1277 CLB (A) 16. — *Nf:* Sim. le Feliper 1295 CDN 56.

AF *pheliper* (Lib. Alb. p. 279, 718). Not in Godefroy. It corresponds to L *pheliparius* (= fripperer). — *Fripperer, dealer in second-hand clothes.* — Cf Rog. le Lung, »*feliper*« 1278 CLB (A) 19 (Lo).

Upholdere. 1280.   NED: 1333.
Ess: Bertolomeus le Ophelder' 1317 *2.GDR* 42. — *Ha:* Laur. le Vpholdere 1280 *2.Ass* 87 (le Vpheldere 1280 *3.Ass* 35). — *Nf:* Will. Le Vpheldere 1286 *Ass* 90. Petronilla le Hupholdere 1295 *GDR* 17. Rob. Baroun le Hupholder 1329 CDN 147 (le Opholder 1333 ib. 178).

A der. of ME *upholden* 'to support, keep in repair' (OE *up-* + *healdan*). — *One who makes, repairs, or sells small wares or second-hand articles of clothing, furniture, etc.* (NED).

Upholdestere. 1316.   NED: 1411.
Ess: Isabella La Hopheldestere 1316 *3.GDR* 36 (la Opheldestere 1317 *2.GDR* 41). — *Lo:* Joan Upholdestere 1366 PMR 57.

The fem. form of Upholdere. — Signification: = Upholdere.

2. Maker of Cowls, Jackets, Pantaloons.

Culewright. 1292. NED: —
Ess: Thom. Kulewricth' 1299 *2.GDR* 9. — *La:* Joh. le Collowrighte 1292 *1.Ass* 19.

The first element of this surname presents some difficulties; there is a word *cowl* (ME *cuvel, couel, colle,* etc.) 'a tub or similar large vessel for water' (NED c1250), the sense of which would suit excellently with the second element, OE *wyrhta*. *Cowl* is of French origin, however, and compounds in *-wright* seem to be formed only from OE words. It is even possible that all such compounds date from the OE period, and that there were no new formations in ME. Cf List of compound surnames. The spelling, moreover, of the early forms of *cowl* does not correspond very well to the forms of the surname.

It is more probable, therefore, that the first element is OE *cug(e)le, cūle* (Me *cule, couel, cole,* etc.) 'a garment for monks, a cowl, cloak'. It is true that the first element of the compounds in *-wright* generally is some wooden article, but not in all cases; this may, in fact, be of any material. I have among my surnames one in *-wright* that corresponds fairly well to the present one, i. e. HAYRWRIGHT 'maker of haircloth, hair-shirts'. The signification of *Culewright* will thus be *one who makes cowls or cloaks*.

Aketonmaker. 1328. NED: —
Li: Ric. le Aketonmaker 1328 *Ass* 12.

ME *aketon* (fr. OF *auqueton*) + ME *maker*. — *Maker of actons* (stuffed jackets or jerkins).

Slopere. 1279. NED: 1854.
Hu: Agatha la Slopere 1279 RH 638. — *Nf:* Galfr. Le Slopere 1286 *Ass* 58. Adam le Slopere 1291 CDN 40. Ric. Sloper' 1332 *SR* 15.

Prob. a der. of ME *slop(e)* 'slop, outer garment, loose jacket, tunic, etc.' (cf MDu *slop,* ON *sloppr*). — *Maker or seller of slops.*

Smokere. 1279. NED: —
So: Thom. le Smokere 1279 3.Ass 191. Rob. le Smoker 1327 SR 136. Will. Smoker ib. 159. Joh. smokare 1333 *SR* 6. Joh. le Smokere ib. 25. — *Li:* Joh. Smoker' 1327 *1.SR* 10, 1332 *2.SR* 13.

Prob. a der. of OE *smoc* 'smock, a woman's undergarment'.
— *One who makes or sells smocks.*

Chaucer. 1256. NED:—
Ess: Gerardus le Chaucer 1311 CR 18. Bartholomeus le Chaucer ib. 31. Rich. le Chaucer 1312 CR 64. — *Lo:* Steph. le Chaucer 1281 CLB (B) 5. — *Nb:* Rob. le Chauser 1256 Ass 11. — *Nf:* Pet. le Chaucer 1286 CDN 5. Henry le Chaucer ib. 6. Walt. Le Chauser 1286 *Ass* 94. Ran. le Chaucer 1289 CDN 29. Nich. le Chaucer 1321 ib. 105.

OF *chaucier* 'chaussetier, fabricant de chausses'. — *Maker or seller of pantaloons or tight coverings for the legs and feet.* Cf NED *chausses* (1484).

Hosiere. 1197. NED: [1403].
Ess: Gerard le Hosiere 1311 CR 48. Margr. Hosyer' 1319 *SR* 16. Steph. le Hosyer' ib. 17. Walt. le Hosyer' ib. 23. Bartholomew le Hosyer 1329 CR 95 (le Osyere ib. 93). — *Sx:* Alex. le Hoser 1204 Cur 195. Rob. le Hoser 1249 *Ass* 34 (le Huser ib. 35, Le Husiere 1279 *Ass* 1). Will. Le Hosier' 1288 *Ass* 30. Rob. le Hosiere 1325 *Ass* 10. Joh. le Hosiar 1332 SR 229. — *So:* Sim. Le Hosier 1305 *Ass* 2. — *Y:* Yuo le hosier 1197 P 44. Nich. the Huser 1268 FF 146. Sim. le Hoser 1279 *Ass* 77. Alan. le Hosier 1341 Free Y 35. — *Li:* Rob. le Hoser 1281 *1.Ass* 37. Isabella Hoyser 1332 *3.SR* 9. — *Nf:* Nich. Le Hosyere 1286 *Ass* 71. Pct. le Hosiere 1301 *GDR* 20. Joh. Le Hosyere 1332 *SR* 64.

A der. of OE *hosa* 'hose' (NED). — *One who makes or deals in hose* (stockings and socks) (NED). — The early forms, especially the spelling *Husier,* point to an OF **hosier*; cf OF *heuse* (*huese, house, hose*) 'botte' (Godefroy). In this case the signification would prob. be 'shoemaker'.

3. **Maker or Seller of Hats, Caps, Hoods, Plumes.**

Hattere. 1268. NED: 1389.
Ess: Emma le Hattere 1316 *2.GDR* 49. — *Sx:* Thom. Le Hattere 1288 *Ass* 40. Joh. le Hattere ib. 30. Nicol le Hettere 1296 SR 49. Will. le Hattere ib. 100. — *Ha:* Alex. le Hattere 1280 *2.Ass* 69. Joh. le Hettere 1280 *1.Ass* 69. Ph. le Hattere 1333 *SR* 8. Joh. le Hatter 1340 *SR* 7. — *So:* Walt. Le Hattere 1307 *Ass* 9. Ric. le Hattere 1320 *Ass* 11. Edw. le Hattere 1327 SR 276. — *Wo:* Reg. le Hattere 1275 SR 4. Will. le Hatter 1285 Epi 264. — *Y:* Rog. le Hattere 1268 *Ass* 24. Nich. le hatter 1305 Free Y 10. Galfr. le hatter 1321 ib. 20. — *Li:* Sim. le Hatter 1281 *1.Ass* 16. Margareta le Hatter 1332 2. SR 1. Cecilia Hattere 1332 *3.SR* 25. — *Nf:* Joh. le Hattere 1299 *GDR* 19. Rog. le Hattere 1311 CDN 31. Walt. le Hattere 1315 ib. 56.

A der. of OE *hæt* 'hat'. — *Maker or seller of hats*. — Cf the ON synonymous surname *Hattari*, 1398 (Lind).

Chapeler. 1249.   NED: 1601.
Ess: Hugo le Chapeler 1285 *Ass* 20. — *Sx:* Ham' le Chapeler 1249 *Ass* 34. Walt. le Chapeler 1255 FF 16. Rog. le Chapeler 1279 *Ass* 27. Ric. le Chapeler 1309 *1.GDR* 7. — *Ha:* Joh. le Chapeler 1280 *2.Ass* 32. Rad. le Chapeler ib. 87. — *Y:* Pet. le Capeler 1279 *Ass* 49. — *Li:* Sim. le Chapeler 1281 *2.Ass* 54. — *Nf:* Thom. le chapeller 1250 *Ass* 21. Wydo le Chapeller 1286 CDN 7. Adam le Chapeler 1288 ib. 22. Rog. the Chapeller 1290 ib. 37. Nich. le Chapeler 1303 ib. 96.

OF *chapelier, cap-* 'celui qui fabrique ou vend des chapeaux' (Godefroy). — *Maker or seller of hats*.

Capiere. 1275.   NED: 1389.
Ess: Ric. le Capier 1285 *Ass* 36. — *Ha:* Joh. Le Capiere 1305 *Ass* 9. Will. le Capiere 1333 *SR* 5. — *Wo:* Nich. le Capyare 1275 SR 7. Ric. le Kapiare ib. 24. Rob. le Kapiare ib. — *Y:* Adam Capper 1314 *3.Wake* 53.

A der. of OE *cæppe* 'cap'. — *One who makes or sells caps*.

Capiestere. 1280.   NED: —
Ha: Agnes la Capiastre 1280 *3.Ass* 4.

The fem. form of CAPIERE. — Signification: = CAPIERE.

Capman. 1285.   NED: 1647.
Ess: Ric. le Capman 1285 *Ass* 36. — *Y:* Joh. Capman c1346 *SR* 9. — *Nf:* Letic' Capman 1332 *SR* 28.

OE *cæppe* 'cap' + *mann*. — Signification: = CAPIERE.

Hurrer. 1281.   NED: 1403.
Lo: Geoffrey le Hurer 1288 CLB (A) 110. Will. le Hurrer 1289 ib. 111. Henr. le Herrere 1332 SR 62. — *Li:* Sewallus le Hurrer 1281 *2.Ass* 46.

A der. of ME *hure* 'cap' (fr. OF *hure* 'hair of the head'). — *Maker or seller of hats and caps* (NED).

Caperoner. 1327.   NED: —
So: Will. Caperoner 1327 SR 88.

AF *caperonner = OF *chaperonnier*. — *Maker of chaperons*.

Coyfer. 1281.   NED: —
Sx: Ric. le Coyfer 1296 SR 30. — *Li:* Marger' la Coyfere 1281 *1.Ass* 41.

OF *coifier* 'faiseur ou marchand de coiffes' (Godefroy). — *Maker of coifs* (a kind of close-fitting cap for both sexes).

Hodere. 1275. NED: —

Lo: Pet. le Hoder 1275 RH 424. Elias le Hodere 1283 CLB (A) 59. — *Sr:* Will. le hoder' 1332 SR 91. — *Sx:* Joh. Le Hodere 1288 *Ass* 2. Pet. le Houdere 1324 *Ass* 19 (le Hoder 1325 ib. 14).

A der. of OE *hōd* 'hood'. — *Maker of hoods.* — The following surname is synonymous: Will. *Hodemaker* 1393 CLB (H) 403 (Lo). — I have also found another similar compound: Rad. *Hudsmyth* 1582 RG Prest. 45 (La), the signification of which apparently is 'a smith who makes hoods or helmets'.

Callemaker. 1336. NED: —

Ess: Alice Callemaker 1336 CR 142 (la Callemaker ib. 146).

ME *calle* 'caul' (F *cale* 'a kind of cap') + ME *maker.* NED has caul (*calle*) a1327. — *Maker of cauls* (a kind of cap or hair-net for women).

Kallemakestere. 1311. NED: —

Ess: Stacy la Kallemakestere 1311 CR 42.

The fem. form of CALLEMAKER. — Signification: = CALLEMAKER.

Caller, Keller. 1281. NED: —

a. Caller:

Lo: Henry le Callere 1281 CLB (B) 3. Rob. le Callere 1332 SR 70. — *Sr:* Thom. Caller' 1332 SR 36. — *Sx:* Will. Callere 1327 SR 167. Walt. le Caller 1332 SR 281.

b. Keller:

La: Ric. le Keller 1332 *Ass* 7 (R. Keller 1338 *Ass* 1). — *Y:* Nich. Keller 1317 Free Y 17. Symon le keller 1322 ib. 20. — *Li:* Will. Keller 1327 *2.SR* 21, 1332 *3.SR* 2. — *Nf:* Will. le Kellerer 1285 CDN 3.

A der. of ME *calle* and *kelle* (fr. F *cale* 'a kind of cap'); *kelle* is a northern form; v. NED caul and kell. — *Maker of cauls or kells* (a cap or hair-net for women). — As is seen above, *Caller* has only been found in the South of England, and *Keller* only in Anglian counties.

Wympler. 1183. NED: 1260.

Sx: Rob. Le Wympler 1279 *Ass* 13, 1. — *Ha:* Hamo le Wymplere 1280 *2.Ass* 47 (le Wympler 1280 *1.Ass* 62). — *So:* Will. le Whimpler 1333 *SR* 35. — *Y:* Eda the Wimpler 1225 FF 61. — *Li:* Will. le Wimpler 1202 Ass 161 (Winplarius ib. 187). Albrid' le Wimpler 1219 Ass 169. — *Np:* Sim. le Wimpler 1183 P 123.

AF *wimpler or a der. of OE wimpel 'veil'. Godefroy has the fem. form guimpliere 'femme qui fait des guimples'. — Maker of wimples, veils.

Courcheuer. 1328. NED: —
Li: Agnes le Courcheuer 1328 *Ass* 6.

A der. of ME *courchef* 'kerchief' (fr. OF *couvrechief*). — Maker of kerchiefs.

Cokeler. 1281. NED: —
Li: Will. le Cokeler 1281 *1.Ass* 44 (le coclere ib.). Will. Cokeler 1332 *1.SR* 6.

OF *coquillier* 'fabricant de coquilles' (Godefroy). — Maker of a kind of head-covering for women.

Plumer. NED: 1282.
The spelling of this surname coincides with some of the forms of PLUMER 'plumber', viz. those spelt *Plumer, Plomer*. I have included all instances under that name, q. v. Most of them prob. mean 'plumber', but some certainly belong here.

AF or OF *plumier (L *plumarius*). — A dealer in plumes or feathers (NED). — Cf the names of the following person: John de Cestrehunte, »*plumer*» 1282 CLB (A) 46 (Lo); John de »Chesthunte», called »*Fethermongere*» ib.

Fetherman. 1275. NED: 1621.
Nf: Will. le fetherman 1275 Nf Arch I 350. Margareta le Fetherman 1305 CDN 105.

OE *feðer* + *mann*. — One who deals in feathers or plumes (NED).

Fetherbycger. 1304. NED: —
Ess: Rob. Le Feþerbycger 1304 *2.GDR* 14.

OE *feðer* + a der. of OE *bycgan* 'to buy'. — One who buys feathers and sells them at a higher price, a dealer in feathers.

In this surname — and in SHOUBIGGERE, q. v. — the last element apparently means 'one who sells'. This sense is not recorded in NED, but it is not unparalleled; cf NED *cop* vb 1430 'to buy', 1570 'to barter'; *coper* 1609 'dealer'; *chap* vb 'to buy', 'to buy and sell', 'to barter'. Cf CHAPPERE. Cf also MG compounds in *-koufer* meaning 'Verkäufer', e. g. *sleierkoufer, messerkoufer* (Bücher p. 12); *Holtcopere* 'Holzhändler', *Yserencopere* 'Eisenhändler' (Mahnken p. 52).

CHAPTER IV.

LEATHER WORKERS.

A. Tanner, Skinner, Currier.

Tannere, Tanur. 1166.   NED: a975.
Ess: Joh. le Tanur 1205 Cur 324. Ric. le Tanur 1255 *Ass* 30. Andr. le Tannur 1285 *Ass* 21. Adam Tannere 1327 *SR* 7. Sim. le Tannere 1332 *SR* 22. — *Sx:* Rob. le tanur 1192 P 204. Will. le Tanur 1263 *Ass* 49. Ric. le Tanner' 1296 SR 72. Rob. le Tannere 1327 SR 192. — *Ha:* Nich. le Tannur 1272 *Ass* 4. Joh. Le Tannere 1305 *Ass* 6. Adam le Tannere 1327 *SR* 8. Pet. le Tannere 1333 *SR* 1. — *So:* Henry le Tanur 1243 Ass 195. Gocelin le Tannur 1268 FF 219. Alic. la Tannere 1305 *Ass* 1. Martinus le Tanner' 1333 *SR* 9. — *Wo:* Osbertus le tanur 1197 P 190. Ran. le Tanner 1304 Hal 477. Joh. Le Tanner 1327 SR 65. — *St:* Rob. le Tanur 1227 4.Ass 48. Rad. Le Tannor 1327 SR 209. — *La:* John le Tanur 1246 Ass 101. Adam le Tanour 1327 *SR* 8. — *Y:* Gerardus le Tanur 1178 P 77. Pet. le Tanur 1279 *Ass* 24. Adam le Tanour 1301 SR 30. — *Li:* Stanhardus Tanur 1180 P 59. Haket le Tanur 1245 *Ass* 24. Joh. le Tannour 1320 *Ass* 36. Gilb. le Tannour 1332 *3.SR* 5. — *Nf:* Henr. Taneur 1166 P 23. Sim. le Tanur 1250 *Ass* 16. Constantine le tanner 1288 CDN 22. Alan. Tannur Junior 1332 *SR* 7.

OE *tannere* or OF *taneor, tanour.* Cf Fullere, Fulur. — *Tanner.* — This surname is very common, especially in the South of England.

Tannestere. 1339.   NED: —
Sx: Maud le Tannestre 1339 FF 94.
The fem. form of OE *tannere.* — *Tanner.*

Taneresse. 1290.   NED: —
Nf: Margaret la taneresse 1290 CDN 32 (le *Tannere* 1291 ib. 41).
OF *taneresse* 'femme du tanneur' (Godefroy). — *Female tanner.* — Note that the same person is also called 'Tannere'.

Skynnere. 1263.   NED: 1398.
Ess: Will. le Skinnere 1281 *1.GDR* 12. Auicia le Skinere 1285 *Ass* 14. Rog. le Schynnere 1317 *2.GDR* 39. Joh. Skynner' 1319 *SR* 12. Steph. le

Skynner' 1327 *SR* 9. Alic. la Skynnere 1332 *SR* 20. — *Sx:* Rob. le Skynnere 1263 *Ass* 42. Galfr. le Schinnere 1296 SR 98. Will. le Skinnere 1296 SR 68. Joh. le Skynner 1327 SR 147. Agath' le Skynnar 1332 SR 233. Juliana Skynnar ib. 244. Rob. le Skynnere 1343 FF 106. — *Ha:* Henr. le Scinnere 1272 *Ass* 21. Gilb. le Skiniere 1280 *2.Ass* 51. Galfr. le Skynnere 1287 *Ass* 2. Joh. Schynnere 1305 *Ass* 9. Adam Le Skynner' 1306 *Ass* 3. Nich. le Skynnare 1327 *SR* 8. Bernardus le Skynnere ib. 15. Henr. le Skynnere 1333 *SR* 8. Semannus le Skynner 1340 *SR* 6. — *So:* Rich. le Skynnere 1276 Ass 70. Rog. le Scynnere 1299 BBA 35. Ad. Le Schinner 1305 *Ass* 1 (Le Skynnere ib. 9). Will. le Skynnere 1320 *Ass* 20. Rob. le Skynnar 1327 SR 105. Joh. le Skynnere 1333 *SR* 8. — *Wo:* Ric. Le Skynnere 1305 *Ass* 6. Nich. Le Skynner' 1307 *Ass* 4. Alan. Le Skynnere 1327 SR 40. Bernard the Scynnere 1345 OCW 144. — *St:* Rob. le Skinner 1279 6.Ass 101. Adam le Skynner 1306 7.Ass 159. Thom. le Skynnere 1327 SR 201. — *La:* Alan. le Skinner' 1292 *1.Ass* 20. Adam le Skinner 1324 CR 25. Thom. le Skynner 1341 *SR* 4. — *Y:* Steph. le Skinnere 1279 *Ass* 49. Ric. le Skynnere 1293 *Ass* 6. Rob. Skynner 1332 *SR* 9. — *Li:* Will. le Skynnere 1281 *1.Ass* 12. Thom. le Skynner 1305 *Ass* 19. Bernardus Skynner 1327 *2.SR* 4. Hamo le Skynner 1327 *3.SR* 1. Will. Skynere 1332 *1.SR* 18. Ric. le Skynner 1332 *3.SR* 26. — *Nf:* Henr. le skynnere 1286 *Ass* 118. Beatrix la Skinyere 1295 *GDR* 11. Galfr. le Skynnere 1312 ib. 13. Gilb. le Skynnere 1329 *SR* 38. Thom. Skynner' 1332 *SR* 15. Ric. Skinnere ib. 20.

The origin and history of this surname is not quite clear. There seem to have existed two different words in OE: *scynn* 'skin, fur' of Scandinavian origin (ON *skinn*) and *scinn* 'skin', a native word. Neither of these, however, is evidenced in NED or BT, but the Scandinavian word is given by Holthausen and Björkman (Scand. Loan-Words), and both are recorded by C. Hall. The native word is also supposed by Schlutter to have existed in OE; he thinks that this word, OE *scinn*, corresponds to a ME and NE *shin;* v. Anglia 40 p. 260 ff. NED has the forms *schin, scin* under *skin* sb in the 14th century. — The present surname is generally spelt *Skynnere*, but there also occur some instances in the South of England spelt *Schinnere, Scinnere*. These latter forms may be derived fr. the native word, OE *scinn;* the other form is either a der. of OE *scynn* (of ON origin) or comes directly fr. ON *skinnari* 'skinner'.

The occurrence of *Skynnere* is surprising; one would expect to find it only in those counties that show Scandinavian influence. The case is, however, that it occurs in all the counties dealt with and most frequently in the South and East. The earliest instance (fr. 1263) has been found in Sussex. The ON word must have been borrowed early and spread rapidly over the whole of England.

Signification: *Skinner, one who prepares skins.* — *Skinnari* was a surname in ON (v. Lind).

Skinner is the first element of *Skinningrove* Y (*Scineregrive* c1175), which means »the skinner's pit» (v. Ekwall: Trades in Eng. Pl. N. p. 86). — Cf *Shearston* (Pl. Soc. De p. 316), *Shynnerston* 1330, the first element of which is alleged to be a surname derived fr. OE *scinnere* 'magician'.

Barkere. 1255. NED: 1402.

Ess: Jord. le Barkere 1255 *Ass* 26. Petronilla la Barkere 1311 CR 47. Ric. le Barkere 1317 *3.GDR* 28. Joh. le Barkere 1327 *SR* 14. Adam Barkere 1341 *Ass* 17. — *Sx:* Rad. le Barkere 1263 *Ass* 48. — *Wo:* Alicia la Barcar' 1275 SR 89. Nich. Le Barkere 1305 *Ass* 5. Thom. Le Barker 1327 SR 37. Nich. le Barkar 1332 SR 20. — *St:* Rich. le Barker 1306 7.Ass 173. Nic. le Barker 1316 9.Ass 62. Joh. le Barkere 1327 SR 209. Marg' le Barkere ib. 242. Will. le Barker' 1332 SR 119. — *La:* Rog. le Barkere 1292 *1.Ass* 6. Rich. le Barker 1324 CR 61. Rob. le Barker 1327 *SR* 13. Elias le Barker 1332 SR 7. — *Y:* Will. le Barker 1279 *Ass* 56. Rad. le Barker 1301 SR 102. John the Barkere 1306 2.Wake 57. Rob. le Barker 1332 *SR* 1. — *Li:* Joh. le Barker 1281 *2.Ass* 46. Hugo le Barker 1327 *2.SR* 4. Alan. Barker 1327 *1.SR* 1. Adam le Barker 1332 *2.SR* 5. Thom. le Barker ib. 11. — *Nf:* Walt. le Barkere 1275 RH 456. Emma la Barkere 1286 *Ass* 2. Rog. le Barkere 1299 *GDR* 18. Alan. Barkare 1332 *SR* 19. Cater' Barker' 1337 *SR* 5.

A der. of ME *bark* 'to tan', fr. *bark* sb (fr. ON *bǫrkr* 'bark'). — *Tanner* (NED). — Some instances of this surname may come fr. OF *berkier, barcher* 'shepherd'; in the form *Berker* this surname is common in early rolls.

Barkere is very common in the Anglian counties, particularly in *Li* and *Nf*, but only one instance has been found in the WS counties.

Tawyere. 1280. NED: [1311].

Ess: Will. le Tawyer' 1327 SR 21 (le Tawiere 1332 *SR* 20). — *Ha:* Will. le Tawyare 1280 *2.Ass* 67. Nich. le Tawyare 1327 *SR* 9. Joh. le Tawere ib. 18. Henr. le Tawyere 1333 *SR* 3. Ric. le Tawyere ib. — *So:* Math. le Tawyare 1344 *Ass* 15. — *Le:* Ric. le Tawere 1286 RBL 210.

A der. of OE *tawian* 'to taw' (NED). — *One who taws; one who prepares white leather* (NED). — This surname (just as Towere) is common only in *Ha*.

Tewere. 1275. NED: c1440.

Wo: Nich. le Teware 1275 SR 1. — *Li:* Will. Tewer 1327 *3.SR* 1. Joh. le Tewer ib. Will. Le Teuwer 1328 *Ass* 24. — *Nf:* Mich. le Tewere 1295 *GDR* 11.

A der. of ME *tewe* 'to taw': »a later collateral, derivative, or altered form of *taw* vb; the form-history is obscure» (NED). An explanation of the origin is given under Towere, q. v. — Signification: = Tawyere. — *Tewer* is common as a trade-name in Free Y, e. g. Will. de Alverton, tewer 1299 p. 7.

Towere. 1255. NED: —

Ha: Thom. le Touere 1274 RH 221. Will. Le *Towyere* 1280 *3.Ass* 50 (Le *Tawyere* ib.). Adam le Toware 1306 *Ass* 1. Will. le Towere 1327 *SR* 11. Ad. le Towere ib. Walt. le Towere ib. Iuo le Towere ib. 6. Ric. le Towyere 1333 *SR* 3. — *Wi:* Gilb. le Tower 1255 RH 241. — *Nf:* Nich. le Towere 1310 *GDR* 10.

West Germanic *$t\bar{a}w\bar{o}jan$ becomes WS $t\bar{a}wian$, Anglian *$t\bar{e}wian$; West Germanic $\bar{a}$ remains before $w + a$ *velar vowel* in WS (Bülbring § 129), but becomes $\bar{e}$ in Anglian. The latter form, *$t\bar{e}wian$, is the basis of Tewere, q. v., and *Towere* is a der. of $t\bar{a}wian$. This form, which is not recorded in NED (nor are *tow* vb and *tower*) is given by Bülbring (§ 129); cf Gothic *gatewjan* 'anordnen'.

Signification: = Tawyere. — That the explanation given here for *Towere* is right, is proved by the fact that the same person is called both *Tawyere* and *Towyere* (v. *Ha* above), and also by the three compound forms Whittawyere, Whittewere, Whittowere, v. below.

I have found one instance of the corresponding fem. surname: Juliana la *Touestre* 1279 RH 787 (Oxf).

Whittawyere, Whittewere, Whittowere. 1279. NED: 1284.

Lo: Humphrey le »Wyttowier» 1281 CLB (A) 38. Walt. le Whitawyer 1311 CLB (D) 258. — *Sx:* Will. Le Wytawere 1288 *Ass* 29 (Le Whittawiere ib. 16). Joh. le Wytthauwere 1296 SR 46. Rob. le Wytheuere ib. 105. — *Ha:* Ric. le Witthawyere 1280 *2.Ass* 87 (le Whytauwyere 1280 *3.Ass* 35). — *So:* John le Whyttewere 1313 FF 38. — *Nf:* John Payn le Whyttowere 1298 CDN 70. Laurence Qwytteuwer 1315 ib. 62 (le Quyttower 1316 ib. 69). — *Ca:* Thom. le Wytewere 1279 RH 580. — *Hu:* Eustach. le Wittowere 1279 RH 665. — *Le:* Augustinus le Whyttawere 1300 RBL 229.

The first element is OE $hw\bar{\imath}t$ 'white'; the second el. is equivalent to the three preceding surnames: Tawyere, Tewere, Towere. NED has only the first of these forms, *Whittawer*. — *One who taws skins into whitleather* (NED). — Cf Joh. Prychet, *whit-lether-tewer* 1384 Free Y 82.

Beauderer. 1276. NED: —
Y: Rog. Beuderer 1276 RH 115. Joh. Beauderer 1297 SR 151.

OF *baudroier* 'apprêteur de cuir épais, corroyeur' (Godefroy); cf *bauderier*, the adj. belonging to this noun. — *Tanner*.

Couraour, Cunreyour. 1286. NED: c1380.
So: Joh. le Cunreyour 1344 *Ass* 12. — Y: Mauricius le couraour 1293 Free Y 5. Joh. le couraur 1327 ib. 24. Will. le couraour 1332 ib. 27. — Li: Joh. Currayour 1340 *Ass* 7. — Nf: Rog. de Bradefeud le Conreur 1286 CDN 6. Henry Kyng le Cunreur 1298 ib. 64.

F *couraieur* (16th cent.), OF *conreeur* 'currier' (NED). — *Currier, one who dresses and colours leather after it is tanned* (NED).

Felpollare. 1302. NED: —
So: Walt. le Velpollare 1302 BBA 39.

OE *fel(l)* 'skin or hide' + *poller* (v. POLLER). — *One who removes the hair from skins before they are tanned*.

Skynwashere. 1281. NED: —
Li: Joh. Le Skynwassere 1281 *1.Ass* 37 (le skynwassere 1281 *2.Ass* 33).

ME *skin* 'skin, hide' (ON *skinn*) + ME *wassher* (fr. OE *wæscan* 'to wash'). — *One who washes skins* (as a process in tanning). — Cf Salzman (Med. Ind. p. 247): »The raw hides had first to be soaked, then treated with lime to remove the hair, and then washed again before being placed in the tan vat».

B. Saddler, Girdler.

Sadelere. 1288. NED: 1389.
Ess: Joh. Sadeler' 1327 *SR* 23. Walt. le Sadelere 1329 CR 91. James Sadeler 1345 CR 199. — *Sx:* Sim. le Sadelere 1288 *Ass* 36. Adam le Sadeler 1325 *Ass* 14. Henr' le Sadelar 1332 SR 257. — *Ha:* Humfr. le Sadeler' 1323 *Ass* 8. — *So:* Rob. le Sadelere 1320 *Ass* 11. Joh. le Sadeler 1327 SR 104. Ric. le Sadeler' 1333 *SR* 20. Will. le Sadeler' ib. 33. — *Wo:* Thom. le Sadeler' 1305 *Ass* 1. — *St:* Rad. le Sadelere 1327 SR 235. — *La:* Emma le Sadelere 1292 *1.Ass* 29. Will. le Sadelere 1338 *Ass* 1. — *Y:* Pet. le

Sadelare 1296 1.Wake 256. Rob. Sadelere 1332 *SR* 13. Ric. le sadeler 1335 Free Y 31. — *Li:* Nich. Sadeler 1327 *2.SR* 15. Joh. le Sadeler 1327 *3.SR* 1. Galfr. Sadelere 1328 *Ass* 28. Rob. le Sadeler 1332 *3.SR* 25. Joh. Sadiller 1332 *Ass* 8. — *Nf:* Ric. le sadelere 1308 *GDR* 4. Charles Sadlere 1332 CDN 167.

A der. of OE *sadol* 'saddle'. — *One who makes or deals in saddles.*

Seler, Seller. 1227.   NED: 1311.
Ess: Edm. le Seler 1255 *Ass* 25. Thom. Le Seller 1304 *2.GDR* 14. Walt. Seler 1310 CR 3. Will. le Seler 1332 *SR* 25. — *Sx:* Moys' le Seler 1263 *Ass* 41. Will. le Selyr 1296 SR 98. Joh. Sellere 1327 SR 187. Henr. Seller 1332 SR 300. — *Ha:* Rob. le Seler 1280 *3.Ass* 36. Humfr. le Seler 1323 *Ass* 7. — *So:* John le Seler 1277 *3.Ass* 85. Henr. Le Seler 1305 *Ass* 4. — *Wo:* Rob. le Seler 1275 SR 9. Payn Le Celer 1305 *Ass* 3. — *St:* Ric. Le Seler 1309 *GDR* 3. — *La:* Benedictus le Seler 1292 *3.Ass* 97. — *Y:* Thom. Le Celer 1227 FF 100 (Le Seler 1240 ib. 60). Rob. le Seler 1293 *Ass* 39. Ric. le Seler 1301 SR 108. Phil. le seler 1327 Free Y 24. — *Li:* Will. le Seler 1281 *1.Ass* 11. Joh. le Seller 1305 *Ass* 22. Galfr. le Seler 1328 *Ass* 50. — *Nf:* Ric. le Seler 1286 *Ass* 111. Rog. le Seler 1313 *GDR* 18. Henr. Le Celer 1332 *SR* 65.

OF *selier, seller* 'fabricant de selles' (Godefroy). — *Saddler.* — The form *Seler* may also mean 'a maker of seals', v. SEELER; and the signification of *Seller* might also be 'one who sells', but this is not probable; cf CLOTHSELLER.

Bastere. 1230.   NED: —
De: Baldwynus le bastere 1230 P 18. — *St:* Pet. le Bastere 1327 SR 203. Adam le Bastere ib. (le Baster 1332 SR 99). — *Nf:* Rob. Baster 1332 *SR* 77.

OF *bastier* 'bâtier' (Godefroy). — *Saddler.* — Another possibility would be to derive this name fr. OE *bæst* 'bast', and the signification would be 'one who makes ropes or mats of bast'.

Fuster. 1280.   NED: [1309].
Ha: Joh. Fuster 1280 *2.Ass* 87 (le Fuster 1280 *3.Ass* 35). — *Wo:* Gilb. Le Furstare 1305 *Ass* 6 (le Fuster ib. 1). — *Y:* Galfr. le fufster 1283 Free Y 4 (le Fuster 1293 *Ass* 91). Thom. le fufster 1345 Free Y 38.

AF *fuster, fuyster;* OF *fustier, fuyster, fustrier* 'charpentier' (Godefroy). The form *Fufster* is difficult to explain; it occurs frequently in Free Y, especially as a trade-name, and can therefore hardly be a misreading. — *Saddle-tree-maker* (NED).

Girdeler. 1295. NED: c1400.

Ess: Ellen Gerdlere 1310 CR 1. Will. le Gerdler 1311 ib. 24. Phil. le Gerdler ib. 51. Sim. le Gerdler 1315 *3.GDR* 31. Beatrix la Gerdler 1333 CR 108. — *Sx:* Reg. le Gerdlere 1296 SR 50. Joh. le Gerdler 1327 SR 121. Will. Gurdlar 1332 SR 244. — *Ha:* Rob. Le Gurdelere 1306 *Ass* 2. — *So:* Gilb. Gurdlere 1327 SR 273. — *Wo:* Henr. Le Gurdler 1327 SR 35. — *Li:* Nich. le Girdeler 1327 *3.SR* 3. Rob. Girdeler 1329 *GDR* 2. — *Nf:* Henr. le Girdlere 1295 *GDR* 15. Will. le Girdelere 1315 CDN 59.

A der. of OE *gyrdel* 'girdle'. — *Maker of girdles* (NED). A girdler also made small articles in metal work (York Pl. Intr. 40, 76).

Girdelester. 1321. NED: —

Sx: Cristina le Gurdelestr' 1321 *2.GDR* 27.

The fem. form of GIRDELER. — Signification: = GIRDELER. — As a trade-name: Matilda Bakere, *gurdlestere* 1377 PMR 244 (Lo).

Ceynturer. 1275. NED: —

Wo: Joh. le Ceinturer 1275 *1.Ass* 1, 33. Sim. le Seynterer (undated) OCW 120. — *Li:* Will. le Ceynturer 1305 *Ass* 16. — *Nf:* John le Ceynturer 1285 CDN 4. Rog. le Ceynturer 1290 ib. 33. Cristiania le Ceynturere 1293 ib. 50. Rob. le Ceynturer 1305 ib. 106. Will. le Ceynturer 1306 ib. 109.

OF *ceinturier, saint-* 'fabricant, marchand de ceinturons, de baudriers' (Godefroy). — *Maker of 'seyntures'* (waist-belts).

Beltere. c1260. NED: —

Y: Benedictus le belter 1295 Free Y 6. — *Le:* Will. le beltere c1260 RBL 118.

A der. of OE *belt*. — *Maker of belts*. — Cf the ON surname *Beltari* (1414) 'belt-maker' (Lind).

C. Furrier, Glover, Purse-Maker.

Peleter. 1248. NED: 1389.

Ess: Ad. le Peleter 1255 *Ass* 36. Edm. le peleter 1285 *Ass* 48. Ric. le Pelleter 1302 *2.GDR* 12. Joh. Le peleter 1319 ib. 34. — *Sx:* Rob. le Peleter 1263 *Ass* 49. Henr. le Peleter 1279 *Ass* 29. Joh. le Peleter 1288 FF 149. Ad' le Peletur 1296 SR 56. Thom. le Peleter 1317 FF 30. — *Ha:* Alan. le Peleter 1272 *Ass* 20. Will. le Peleter 1288 *Ass* 4. Semannus le Peleter 1333 SR 8. — *So:* Rog. le Peleter 1276 Ass 64. John le Peleter 1278 Ass 130. — *Wo:* Joh. le Peleter 1275 SR 48. Will. le Pelter 1281 3.Hal 109. — *St:* Will. le Peleter 1266 4.Ass 160. Henry le Peleter 1323 10.Ass

52. — *La:* Alan. le Peleter 1277 Ass 141. — *Y:* Walt. le Peleter 1268 FF 132. Rob. le Pelter 1293 *Ass* 104. Henr. le Pelter 1301 SR 108. — *Li:* Adam le Peleter 1248 FF 48. Warinus Pelter 1327 *2.SR* 1. Lucas le Pelter 1328 *Ass* 3. — *Nf:* Sim. le peletter 1250 *Ass* 28. Edm. le Pelter 1332 *SR* 66. Joh. le Pelter ib.

OF *peletier* 'celui qui prépare, qui vend des fourrures' (Godefroy). — *Fellmonger, furrier* (NED); also *one who dresses fells.*

Pilchere. 1214. NED: —

Sx: Mabilia Pullchare 1214 FF 35. Rad. Le Pilcher' 1288 *Ass* 40. Ric. le Pylechere 1296 SR 29. Hamo le Pilchere 1310 *2.GDR* 1 (le Pulchere ib.). Godefr. le Pilcher 1321 *Ass* 33. Adam le Pilicher 1327 SR 174. Cristina Pulcher 1332 SR 309. — *Wo:* Henr. le Pilchere 1275 SR 2. — *St:* Petronilla la Pilcher 1303 *GDR* 1. Henry le Pylchere 1306 7.Ass 170. — *Nf:* Pet. Le Pilcher' 1332 *SR* 76.

A der. of OE *pylece* 'a pilch'. — *Maker or seller of pilches* (an outer garment made of skin dressed with hair). — This name is very common in *Sx*, but not in any other county.

Glouere. 1250. NED: c1400.

Ess: Joh. le Glouer 1302 *2.GDR* 12. Galfr. le Glouere 1327 *SR* 21. Reg. le Glouer' ib. Vincent' le Glouer' 1332 *SR* 6. — *Sx:* Sim. Glouere 1296 SR 36. Andr. le Glouere 1325 *Ass* 14. Rob. le Glouare 1327 SR 152. Joh. Glower 1332 SR 282. — *Ha:* Nich. le Glouere 1272 *Ass* 2. Thom. le Glouere 1327 *SR* 14. Joh. le Glouare 1333 *SR* 7. Steph. le Glouer 1340 *SR* 6. — *So:* Joh. le Glouere 1320 *Ass* 23. Nich. Glover 1327 SR 198. Walt. le Glouere 1333 *SR* 11. — *Wo:* Will. le Glovere 1294 Inq 49. Rog. Le Glouer' 1306 *Ass* 1. Pet. Le Glover 1327 SR 72. — *St:* Ric. le Glover 1327 SR 206. Joh. le Glovere ib. 235. Rob. le Glover 1350 14.Ass 74. — *La:* Ric. le Glouere 1292 *1.Ass* 29. Rob. le Glouer 1338 *Ass* 2. — *Y:* Patricius le Glover 1301 SR 27. Rad. le Glover ib. 27. Adam the Glover 1308 2.Wake 177. — *Li:* Will. Glouer 1327 *2.SR* 15. Sim. le Glouere 1328 *Ass* 18. Joh. Glouer 1332 *2.SR* 9. — *Nf:* Gilb. le Glouere 1250 *Ass* 19. Thom. le Glouere 1286 *Ass* 111. Reg. Glouer' 1332 *SR* 30.

A der. of OE *glōf* 'glove'. — *One who makes or sells gloves.*

Gaunter, Wanter. 1191. NED: 1415.

a. G a u n t e r:

Ess: Gilb. le Gaunter 1311 CR 34. — *Sx:* Barth. Le Gaunter 1288 *Ass* 12. Joh. Gantyr 1332 SR 277. — *Ha:* Dauid le Gaunter 1280 *3.Ass* 35. Rog. le Gaunter ib. 4. Walt. le Ganter 1333 *SR* 5. — *Wo:* Will. le Gaunter 1275 SR 9. Symon le Gaunter ib. 51. — *St:* John le Gaunter 1295 7.Ass 30. Alan le Gaunter 1306 ib. 156. — *Y:* Gervasius le Gaunter 1301 SR 119. (R)ich. le gaunter 1317 Free Y 17. — *Li:* Rob. le Gaunter 1275 RH 272.

Rog. le Gaunter 1281 2.*Ass* 49. Iuo le Ganter ib. 58. — *Nf:* Hermannus Le Gaunter 1286 *Ass* 91. Elueredus Le Gaunter ib. Rad. Le Gaunter ib. 105.

b. W a n t e r:
Ess: Galfr. le Waunter 1255 *Ass* 8. Joh. le Waunter ib. 9. — *Wo:* Walt. le wanter 1221 Ass 647. — *Y:* [Rad.] Palmer le wantier 1191 P 69 (R. le Palmer le Wantier 1194 ib. 152). — *Nf:* Will. Wanter' 1332 *SR* 75.

OF *gantier, wantier* 'fabricant, marchand de gants' (Godefroy). — *Glove maker or seller.* — NED has only *gaunter* (1 inst.). — The form *Gaunter* is most common, but *Wanter* occurs earlier.

Purser. 1305.   NED: c1440.
Ess: Will. le Pursere 1341 *Ass* 12. — *So:* Thom. Le Pursere 1305 *Ass* 3. — *La:* Adam le Purser 1327 *SR* 8, 1332 SR 88. — *Y:* Joh. le Purser c1346 *SR* 5. — *Li:* Sim. le Purser 1328 *Ass* 13. — *Nf:* Rob. purser' 1329 *SR* 45.

A der. of OE *purs* 'a purse'. — *Maker of purses;* perhaps also *a purse-bearer, treasurer*.

Burser. 1208.   NED: 1587.
Ess: Joh. le Boursser 1341 *Ass* 3. — *Ha:* Galfr. le Burser 1287 *Ass* 11. — *So:* Joh. Bursar' 1333 *SR* 6. — *Y:* Rob. le Burser 1208 Cur 263. — *Li:* Rob. le Bourser 1332 2.*SR* 1. — *Nf:* Walt. Plukkerose of London le Bursere 1301 CDN 83.

OF *borsier, boursier* 'fabricant de bourses' (Godefroy). — *Maker of purses;* perhaps sometimes *a treasurer*. NED has only the latter sense (1587); but the former is more prob. at this time. Cf Rob. Neel, *burser* 1344 PMR 159 (Lo), Rob. Neel, *pouchmaker* ib. 211 (same person).

Bulgere. 1300.   NED:—
Wo: John Bulgere 1300 Epi 533.

OF **boulgier* or a der. of ME *bulge* (OF *boulge* 'leathern bag'). — *Maker of leather wallets or bags.* — Cf Joh. Milne, *boulgemaker* 1465 Free Y 185.

D. Maker of Bellows or Bottles.

Belgmakere. 1289.   NED: 1715.
Nf: Hugo de Denton le Bellghe makere 1289 CDN 25. Geoffrey le Belgmakere 1294 ib. 54.

ON *belgr* 'skin-bag, bellows' + a der. of OE *macian*. — *Maker of bellows or, less prob., skin-bags.*

Belger. 1275. NED: —
  Li: Hugo Belger 1275 RH 314. Rog. Belger 1327 *3.SR* 3. Joh. Belger ib. 1. Nich. Belger ib. Joh. Belger 1340 *Ass* 11.

A der. of ON *belgr* 'skin-bag, bellows'. — Prob. = BELGMAKERE. — Cf MG *blasbelger* (1346) 'Blasbalgmacher' (Bücher).

Botelmaker. 1346. NED: 1483.
  Ess: Steph. Botelmaker 1346 CR 215.

ME *botel* (fr. OF *bouteille*) + ME *maker*. — *Maker of leather bottles.* — Cf Joh. de Shirwode, *botelmaker* 1383 Free Y 81. This trade-name is common in York in the 15th century.

NED has one instance of *bottler* (1415) 'bottle-maker'. It is not improbable that this word occurred as a surname during this period; but unfortunately the spelling coincides with another very common surname, *Butler* (spelt *Buteler, Boteler,* etc.).

Gourdmaker. 1336. NED: —
  Y: Martin le gourdmaker 1336 Free Y 32.

ME *gourde* 'a kind of cucumber', later 'bottle or cup' (OF *gourde*) + ME *maker*. — *Bottle or cup maker.* — In Free Y there is a synonymous trade-name: Phil. de Turnay, *gourder* 1328 p. 25.

E. **Parchmenter, Bookbinder, Copyist**.

Parcheminer. 1275. NED: 1415.
  Ha: Rog. le Parcheminer 1280 *3.Ass* 42. Rob. le Parchemener 1333 *SR* 8. Juliana le Parchemyner 1340 *SR* 7. — *So:* Andreas le Parchemener 1319 BBA 68. — *Wo:* Rog. le Parcheminer 1275 SR 1. Rich. le Parchemener 1338 OCW 26. — *St:* Elyas le parcheminer 1327 SR 214. — *Y:* Rob. le parchemyner, pistor 1296 Free Y 6. Thom. le Parcheminer 1301 SR 119. Ric. le parchminer 1327 Free Y 24. Nich. Parchemynere 1332 *SR* 7. — *Li:* Henr. le parcheminer 1281 *2.Ass* 53. Idonea la Parchemynere 1328 *Ass* 58. Galfr. le Parcheminer 1332 *2.SR* 1. Rad. Parcheminer 1332 *3.SR* 25. — *Nf:* Will. Le parcheminer 1286 *Ass* 91. Rob. le Parcheminer, butcher 1295 CDN 57. Sim. le Parcheminer 1324 ib. 128.

OF *parcheminier* 'celui qui prépare et vend le parchemin' (Godefroy). — *Maker or seller of parchment*.

Rollere. 1274.   NED: (1591).
So: Phil. le Rouller 1337 FF 192. — *Y:* Joh. le Rollere 1274 1.Wake 11. Rob. le Roller 1297 ib. 280. Rob. le Roller 1297 SR 115. Thom. le Rollere 1309 2.Wake 217. — *Nf:* Will. Roller 1337 CDN 207.

A der. of ME *rolle* 'a roll, piece of parchment' (fr. OF *ro(o)lle, roulle*). — Prob. *a maker or seller of parchment rolls for manuscripts*.

Bokbynder. 1286.   NED: 1389.
Ha: Thom. le Bokbynder' 1323 *Ass* 7. — *Nb:* Will. Buckbindere 1292—4 Newc. Deeds 142 (Bockbinder 1296—7 ib. 144). — *Li:* Ric. Lumpnur Bokbynder 1340 *Ass* 7. — *Nf:* Will. le *Bokbondere* 1286 *Ass* 139. Margareta le Bokbynder 1332 *SR* 57.

OE *bōc* 'book' + *bindere*. The form Bokbondere *Nf* perhaps owes its *o* (= *u*) to the influence of the preceding *b*; the form *buschop* (bishop) is particularly common in *Nf* and *Sf*. — Signification: *One who binds books*.

Bokmakere. 1293.   NED: 1515.
Y: Will. le Bokmakere 1293 *Ass* 24.

OE *bōc* 'book' + a der. of *macian*. — *One who copies books; bookbinder*. — Cf the ON surname *Bóksmiðr* (1327) 'maker of books' (Lind).

Scriueyn, Escriueyn. 1246.   NED: a1300.
Ess: Rich. le Skryveyn 1334 CR 137. — *Ha:* Joh. Scryueyn 1280 *3.Ass* 26. Rog. Scryuayn 1333 *SR* 1. — *So:* Gervase le Escriuein 1278 Ass 177. — *St:* Thom. le Scryveyn 1304 7.Ass 134 (le Screvayn 1306 ib. 154). John le Escreveyn 1306 ib. 168. Rich. le Scriveyn of Stone, Chaplain 1323 10.Ass 52. — *La:* Will. le Escruaynt 1246 Ass 100. Rob. Skryuin 1332 SR 63. Rob. Le Scryveyn 1334 FF 94. — *Y:* Alex. le Scryueyn 1293 *Ass* 23. Will. le Skriveyn 1301 SR 119. Joh. le Skreueyn 1332 *SR* 13. — *Li:* Geoffrey Le Escryuein 1260 FF 181. Rob. le Scryuayn 1305 *Ass* 21. Thom. Skryuayn 1327 *3.SR* 3. Margeria le Scriueyne 1328 *Ass* 60. — *Nf:* Joh. le Escryueyn 1286 *Ass* 118. Cristiana le screueyn 1312 *GDR* 15. Alic. Scryuein 1329 *SR* 32. Edm. Skryueyn 1332 *SR* 17.

OF *escrivain, -ein*. — *Writer, one who writes and copies books, manuscripts, etc.; also a clerk*. The 'scriueyn' belonged to artisans, and corresponded to our modern printer. — The writers of London formed two separate crafts in 1422: the writers of the ordinary bookhand (»textscriveyns») and the writers of the court-hands (PMR p. 199). Cf John Ruddok, *textscriveyn* 1393 PMR 199 (Lo).

Scriuener. 1311. NED: c1375.
Ess: Kemma Scriuener 1311 CR 49. — *Y:* Jurdanus le scrivayner 1317 Free Y 17. Rich. le Scryvayner 1345 FF 183.

Scriueyn (q. v.) + er. — Signification: = SCRIUEYN.

Wrytere. 1275. NED: c888.
Wo: Will. le Wrytere 1275 SR 99. Adam le Wrytar ib. Will. Le Wrytar' 1327 SR 46.

OE *writere.* — Signification: = SCRIUEYN.

Luminur. 1275. NED: 1330—1.
Wo: Joh. le Leominur 1275 SR 30. Ric. Lemner ib. 90. — *St:* Edm. le lumner 1327 SR 236. — *Y:* Will. le Lumenur 1293 *Ass* 103. Rog. le Lomenur ib. 61. — *Li:* Will. Lumnour' 1327 *1.SR* 1. Rob. Lumnour 1328 *Ass* 54 (le Lompnour ib. 58, le Lumenour ib.). Ric. Lumpnur 1340 *Ass* 7. — *Nf:* John le Luminur 1287 CDN 12. Rog. le Lumynour 1317 CDN 73 (le Lomynour 1324 ib. 127). Will. le Leminer' 1332 *SR* 27.

OF *enlumineor* 'celui qui éclaire'; *luminier* 'clerc chargé d'éclairer l'église' (Godefroy). In SR 1292 for Paris Géraud has found 13 instances of *enluminéeurs*, which he translates by 'enlumineurs pour les manuscrits et les images'. In ME the prefix was dropped; cf GYNOUR, ENGYNOUR. — *Illuminator of manuscripts* (NED). According to Riley (Lib. Alb. Glossary) the business of the limner also consisted in transcribing books.

A rest of the French prefix is seen in the following example: Joh. le *Aluminour* 1318 RBL 311 (Le). Cf AMELOUR.

F. Shoemaker, Cobbler.

Cordewaner. 1175. NED: a1100.
Ess: Rad. le Cordewaner 1255 *Ass* 27. Ric. Cordewaner 1327 *SR* 3. — *Sx:* Reg. le cordewanier 1200 P 247. Godefr. le Cordewaner 1279 *Ass* 27. Pet. le Cordewaner 1332 SR 225. — *Ha:* Godefr. le Corduwaner 1280 *1.Ass* 68. Thom. le Cordewaner 1287 *Ass* 5. Nich. Le Cordewaner 1305 *Ass* 7. Andr. le Cordewaner 1333 *SR* 8. — *Wo:* Mauricius le corduaner 1221 Ass 604. Rad. le Cordwaner 1275 SR 5. — *Y:* Marsilius le Cordewaner 1175 P 180. Durandus cordewanar' 1193 P 72. Nich. Cordewaner 1301

SR 72. — *Li:* Martin' le Cordewaner 1281 *1.Ass* 37. Barth. le Cordenewaner 1281 *2.Ass* 36 (le Cordewaner 1287 *Ass* 41). Gilb. Le Cordewanier 1305 *Ass* 5. — *Nf:* Will. le cordewanier 1250 *Ass* 10. Edmund le Cordewaner 1286 CDN 7. Ric. Corwaner 1332 *SR* 43.

AF *cordewaner* = OF *cordoanier*. — *Cordwainer, shoemaker.*

Corueyser. 1202.   NED: 1401.

Sx: Alex. le Corueisier 1202 FF 17. Will. Le Corueyser 1288 *Ass* 2. Thom. le Coruiser 1321 *Ass* 35. Rob. Coruayser 1327 FF 65. — *Ha:* Barth. le Corueser 1280 *2.Ass* 91. Alicia Corueser 1327 *SR* 18. Henr. Coruesyr 1333 *SR* 9. — *So:* Walt. Coruyser 1327 *SR* 25. Cristina Corueiser 1333 *SR* 7. Ric. le Coruiser ib. 31. — *Wo:* Galfr. le Corviser 1332 SR 26. Will. the Corviser 1335 OCW 132. Martin le Corviser 1347 ib. 126. — *St:* Adam le Coruiser 1327 SR 207 (le *Souter'* 1332 SR 101). Geoffrey le Corviser 1342 FF 151. — *La:* Joh. le Corueyser' 1341 *SR* 1. — *Li:* Thom. Coruayser 1327 *1.SR* 3. Joh. Coruayser ib. Rob. Corueyser 1332 *2.SR* 3. — *Nf:* Steph. le coruiser 1286 *Ass* 80.

AF *corviser, corveser* = OF *corveisier* 'cordonnier'. — *Shoemaker.*

Suour. 1255.   NED: —

Ess: Joh. le Suur 1255 *Ass* 33. Adam le Suour 1312 *4.GDR* 2. — *Sx:* Geruas' le Sour 1263 *Ass* 36. Rob. le Suur 1279 *Ass* 35. John le Suour 1333 FF 83. — *Ha:* Barth. le Suur 1272 *Ass* 20. Karelus le Suur 1280 *3.Ass* 35. Will. Le Suwor 1305 *Ass* 13. — *So:* Steph. Le Suor 1305 *Ass* 2. Thom. le Suour 1333 *SR* 29. — *Wo:* Rob. le Suur 1275 *1.Ass* 20. Adam le Suur ib. 15. — *St:* Rob. Suour 1334 11.Ass 50. — *La:* Henry le Suur 1277 Ass 141. Joh. le Suur 1292 *1.Ass* 25. Will. le Suour 1338 *Ass* 8. — *Y:* Alan. le Suur 1268 *Ass* 22. Rob. le Sour 1279 *Ass* 27. Ric. le Suour 1293 *Ass* 35. — *Li:* Henry Le Suur 1256 FF 136. Bened. le suur 1320 *Ass* 36. Eudo le Suour' 1328 *Ass* 48. — *Nf:* Galfr. Le Suur 1286 *Ass* 91. Joh. le Suer ib. 106. Ric. le Sour 1309 *GDR* 8.

OF *suor, suour, suur, seur* 'cordonnier' (Godefroy). — *Shoemaker.*

Soutere. 1263.   NED: c1000.

Ess: Joh. le Sutur 1285 *Ass* 33. Alic. la Souter' 1319 *SR* 3. Andr. Le Souter' 1327 *SR* 1. — *Sx:* Nich. le Soutere 1263 *Ass* 39. Joh. le Sutere 1296 SR 64. Will. le Soutare 1327 SR 151. — *Ha:* Joh. le Soutere 1327 *SR* 6. Elias le Sutere 1333 *SR* 4. Henr. le Sutere ib. 5. — *So:* Rob. Le Souter 1305 *Ass* 1. Walt. le Soutere 1320 *Ass* 13. Joh. le Soutere 1333 *SR* 8. — *Wo:* Ric. Le Soutere 1307 *Ass* 6. Margareta Le Souter' 1327 SR 8. Galfr. Le Souter ib. 66. — *St:* Joh. le Soutere 1327 SR 207. Adam le Souter' 1332 SR 101. — *La:* Rog. le Sutere 1292 *1.Ass* 24. Rich. le Souter 1324 CR 9. Ad. le Souter 1338 *Ass* 7. — *Y:* Will. le Souter 1301

SR 20. Rob. Souter 1344 FF 172. — *Li:* Adam Le Souter 1327 2.*SR* 5. Will. Le Souter 1328 *Ass* 47. — *Nf:* Joh. le sutere 1286 *Ass* 133. Cristiana le Sutere 1310 *GDR* 11. Andreas Le Souter' 1332 *SR* 63.

OE *sūtere*. — *Shoemaker, cobbler*. — This surname is common, especially in *Ha* and *Nf*. — *Sútari* was a surname in ON (Lind).

Cobelere. 1295.   NED: 1362.
Ess: Adam Cobbelre 1300 2.*GDR* 10. Will. le Cobelere 1332 *SR* 27. — *Y:* Joh. le Cobelur 1301 SR 51. Mariota Cobelur ib. — *Nf:* Hugo le Cobeler 1295 *GDR* 6. Walt. le Cobbelere 1300 ib. 21. Rog. le Cobelere 1315 ib. 31. Sim. Cobblere 1329 *SR* 15. Thom. le Cobeler' 1332 *SR* 71.

Of uncertain derivation. — *Cobbler, one who mends shoes*. — In London (early 14th cent.) it was strictly regulated »not only that shoemakers (= cordewaners) should use new leather in making shoes, but that *cobblers* should be restricted wholly to the use of old leather in mending them» (Lib. Cust. Intr. p. 70).

Specker. 1324.   NED: —
La: Cecily le Specker 1324 CR 59.

A der. of ME *spekke* (of obscure origin) 'a patch of leather'. NED has *speck* vb 1681 'to patch or mend (shoes) with specks'; this would suit better, and perhaps it existed already in ME. — *One who mends shoes, a cobbler*. — I have found one instance of a surname which seems to be the fem. form of the above name: Laurencius *Spexter* 1301 SR 71 (Y).

Cloutere. 1286.   NED: c1440.
Y: Adam Clouter 1307 2.Wake 77 (the Clouter 1309 ib. 193). — *Li:* Will. le Clouter 1328 *Ass* 36. — *Nf:* Ad. Le Clutere 1286 *Ass* 78. Sarra la Cluter' 1301 *GDR* 20. Galfr. Clouter' 1332 *SR* 52.

A der. of ME *cloute, clute* 'to patch' (fr. OE *clūt* 'a patch'). — *Cobbler, patcher*.

Shoubiggere. 1279.   NED: —
So: Walt. Shoubiggere 1333 *SR* 8. — *Ca:* Sim. le Shobeggere 1279 RH 417, 418.

OE *scōh* 'shoe' + a der. of *bycgan* 'to buy'. — *One who deals in shoes*. Cf FETHERBYCGER.

CHAPTER V.

METAL WORKERS.

A. Goldsmith, Gilder.

Goldsmyth, Gildsmith. 1250.   NED: c1000.
Ess: Thom. Goldsmith' 1255 *Ass* 29. Henr. le Goldsmeth 1303 2.*GDR* 13. Will. Goldsmyth 1332 *SR* 7. — *Sx:* Agnes La Goldsmyth 1318 *Ass* 41. Johanna la Goldsmyth 1327 SR 137. Ad' Goldsmyth 1332 SR 317. — *Ha:* Rob. le Goldsmyth 1333 *SR* 8. — *So:* Joh. le Goldsmyth 1327 SR 274. Thom. le Goldsmyth 1349 BBA 110. — *Wo:* Joh. Goldsmyth 1327 SR 42. Thom. Le Goldsmyth ib. 55. Thom. le *Gildsmith* 1336 OCW 74. Will. le Goldsmyth 1338 ib. 26. — *St:* Sim. le Goldsmyth 1315 9.Ass 56. Henr' le Goldsmyth 1327 SR 214. Thom. le Goldsmith 1332 SR 81. — *La:* Rob. le Goldsmyth 1325 CR 83. Henr. le Goldsmyth' 1338 *Ass* 8. Joh. Goldesmyth 1341 *SR* 4. — *Y:* Edm. le Goldsmyth' c1346 *SR* 8. — *Li:* Joh. le Goldsmyth' 1322 *Ass* 43. Hugo Goldsmyth 1327 2.*SR* 18. Alic. Goldesmyth' 1332 3.*SR* 5. — *Nf:* Rog. Goldsmiz 1250 *Ass* 6. Barth. le Goldsmyth 1315 *GDR* 29. Marg. Goldsmith 1329 *SR* 59.

OE *goldsmið*. The form *Gildsmith Wo* is influenced by *Gilder*, and the signification is perhaps the same; cf GOLDER. — *Goldsmith*.

Orfeuere. 1243.   NED: 1415.
Ess: Galfr. le Orfeuere 1285 *Ass* 48. — *Sx:* Gregorius le Orfeure 1254 FF 9. Coraldus le Orfevre 1291 ib. 157. Elias le Orfeure 1308 ib. 1. — *Ha:* Ric. le Orfeuere 1272 *Ass* 6. Sim. le Orueure 1280 *3.Ass* 26. Rob. le Orfeure 1287 *Ass* 2. — *So:* Pet. le orfeuer' 1243 Ass 216. Turstan le Orefeuere 1277 Ass 117. — *Wo:* Ric. le Orfever 1275 SR 4. Rob. Le Orfeure 1294 *Ass* 5. — *St:* Steph. le Orfevere 1272 FF 252. — *Y:* Will. le Orfeuere 1279 *Ass* 66. German Lorfeure 1329 FF 23. — *Li:* Will. le Orfeuere 1281 *1.Ass* 39. Ric. le Orfeure 1319 *Ass* 21. — *Nf:* Hunfr. Le Orfeuere 1286 *Ass* 105. John le Orfevere 1295 CDN 55. Steph. le Orfevre 1306 ib. 117.

OF *orfevre*. — *Goldsmith*.

Gilder, Golder. 1281.   NED: 1550.
Lo: Joh. le Geldere 1281 CLB (B) 8. Joh. le Gilder 1306 CLB (C) 202. Will. Goldere, tawyer 1365 PMR 29. — *Sr:* Rad. le Gelder' 1332 SR 66. — *Sx:* Joh. Golder 1296 SR 37. — *Wo:* Rich. le Guylder (?) 1319 Inq 122.

A der. of OE *gyldan* 'to gild'. The form *Golder(e)* is influenced by *gold, goldsmith;* cf Gildsmith. — *One who gilds, a gilder.*

Goldbeter. 1252. NED: 1415.
Wo: Joh. Le Goldbeter 1327 *SR* 35. — *Y:* Will. the Goldbeter 1252 FF 59. Hen. Goldbeter, major 1345 Free Y 38. Alic. Goldbeter c1346 *SR* 14. — *Li:* Nich. Goldebeter 1327 *3.SR* 2.

OE *gold* + *bēatere.* — *Gold-beater, goldsmith.*

Betere. *One who beats metals;* v. p. 102. Cf Goldbeter, Ledbeter.

Orbatour. 1305. NED: —
Wo: Alan. le Orbatour 1305 *Ass* 1. — *Y:* Joh. le Orebatour 1313 Free Y 15. Hen. le Orbatour 1331 ib. 26.

OF *orbateor* 'batteur d'or' (Godefroy). — *Gold-beater.* — Cf Will. de Popilton, *orbatour* 1277 Free Y 3.

Batour. *One who beats metals;* v. p. 102. Cf Orbatour.

Goldehoper. 1327. NED: —
Li: Joh. Goldehoper 1327 *2.SR* 1.

A der. of ME **goldhope* (fr. OE *gold* + *hōp* 'hoop'). — Prob. *a maker of hoops or rings of gold.*

Silverhewer. 1212. NED: —
Y: Rob. Silverhewer 1212 Cur 329.

ON *silfr* 'silver' + a der. of OE *hēawan.* — *One who hews silver in order to shape it.*

Finur. 1218. NED: 1489.
So: Rob. le Finur 1333 *SR* 9. — *Li:* Rad. le Finur 1218 Ass 247.

OF *fineur* 'affineur' (Godefroy). — *One who refines; a refiner of gold, silver, etc.* — Cf John Hugyn, *fynour* 1384 PMR 87 (Lo).

B. Coiner, Seal-Maker, Engraver.

Coiner. 1202. NED: c1440.
Ess: Rob. le Coner 1316 *3.GDR* 49. — *Sx:* Joh. le Conyare 1327 SR 128. — *Ha:* Thom. le Cuner 1272 *Ass* 10. Ric. le Cuner ib. 20. Will. le Cuner 1280 *3.Ass* 43. — *So:* Will. le Coiner 1327 SR 197. Joh. le Coner'

1333 *SR* 19. — *Wo:* John le Coner 1306 Reg 174. — *Li:* Rog. le *Cuinnur* 1202 Ass 65. Sim. le Coiner 1281 *2.Ass* 36 (le Cuner ib.). — *Nf:* Alex. le Cuner 1286 *Ass* 120. Joh. le Coner ib. 104.

A der. of OF *coignier, cungner* 'to stamp money, to mint'. The form *Cuinnur Li* comes fr. OF *coigneur* 'one who stamps money'. — *Coiner, minter.*

Mineter. 1296. NED: c950.
Lo: Nich. le Mineter 1303 CLB (C) 191. John le Meneter 1310 CLB (D) 184. — *Sx:* Joh. Muneter 1296 SR 16.

OE *mynetere.* — *One who coins or stamps money; moneyer.*

Monnyer. 1230. NED: a1300.
Ess: Will. Le Monnyer 1310 *4.GDR* 1. — *Lo:* Hamo le Moneur 1284 CLB (A) 161. — *Sx:* Will. le Moyner 1249 *Ass* 23. — *Ha:* Rog. le Moyner 1280 *2.Ass* 75. Joh. le Moyner ib. 64. — *Wo:* Reg. le Moyner 1332 SR 26. — *Y:* Gilb. le muneur 1230 P 287 (*monetarius* ib.). Rob. le Moinier 1297 SR 80. Steph. le Moinier 1301 SR 33. Rog. le Moyner ib. 41.

OF *monier, monnier, monnoyer* 'monnayeur, changeur' and *monnoyeur* 'celui qui fabrique de la monnaie' (Godefroy). The form *Moyner,* which seems to belong here, is not recorded in Godefroy. — *One who coins money;* also *a money-changer.* — Cf Joh. de Esynwald, *monemaker* 1400 Free Y 104 'maker of money'.

Seeler. 1327. NED: (1382).
Ess: Joh. Le Seeler 1327 *SR* 13. Reg. le Seeler 1330 CR 101 (le Sealer ib. 102).

Besides these instances some of those included under SELER, SELLER 'saddler' prob. belong here.

A der. of ME *sel, seel, seal* 'a seal' (fr. OF *seel*). — *Maker of seals.* NED has *sealer* 1382 'one who affixes a seal to a document', but this signification is not probable here. Cf the following quotation fr. Salzman (Med. Ind. 132): »Hugh le *Seler* of York made a new seal for the bishopric of Durham» (1333). — The following tradename is synonymous: John de Essex, »*selmakere*» 1311 CLB (D) 75 (Lo).

Orgraver. 1308. NED: —
Y: Rob. le Orgraver 1308 2.Wake 155. Joh. Uregrafer, barker 1416 Free Y 125.

OF *or* 'gold' + ME *graver* (v. GRAUER). — *Gold engraver.*

Grauer. 1293. NED: 1398.

La: Joh. le Grauer 1338 *Ass* 5. — *Y:* Pet. le Grauere 1293 *Ass* 34. Joh. le graver, de Beverle, pulter 1350 Free Y 44.

OE *grafere, græfere;* cf OF *graveur, graveresse.* — *Engraver, sculptor* (NED). Cf ORGRAVER and also the following surname: Adam le *Selgraver* 1332 SR 86 (Lo) 'one who engraves seals'. — *Grauer* also means 'one who digs'; »Piers le *Graver* was killed by the collapse of the pit in which he was working by himself at Silkstone in 1290» (Salzman: Med. Ind. 7).

Cyselour. 1251. NED: 1883.

Ess: Steph. le Cyselour 1285 *Ass* 31. — *Y:* Hugh le Cyselyur 1251 *Ass* 44.

OF *ciseleur.* — *Chiseller, engraver.*

C. **Maker of Clocks.**

Orloger. 1311. NED: [1368].

Ess: Adam le Orloger 1311 CR 36. Thom. Orloger 1319 *SR* 8, 1327 *SR* 5. — *Sx:* Sim. Orologer 1332 SR 229. — *Li:* Cecilia Le Orloger 1328 *Ass* 3.

OF *orlogier.* — *Clock-maker.*

Clocker. 1292. NED: —

La: Thom. le Clocker 1292 *1.Ass* 10, 1292 *2.Ass* 11. — *Nf:* Rob. Cloker 1332 *SR* 12.

A der. of ME *clocke, clok* (v. NED *clock).* — *One who makes clocks.* — Cf Hans *Clokkemaker* 1390 PMR 176 (Lo).

D. **Copper-Smith, Brazier, Bell-Founder.**

Copersmith. 1316. NED: 1327.

Wo: Rog. le Copersmith 1316 Inq 72.

OE *coper + smið.* — *Copper-smith.* — Cf the following synonymous surname: Steph. le *Coperbeter* 1286 CLB (A) 163 (Lo).

Brounsmyth. 1296. NED: —

So: Will. Brounsmyth 1327 SR 107. — *Y:* Thom. le Brounesmyth 1296 1.Wake 239 (le Brounsmyth 1307 2.Wake 107). Rich. Brounsmyth 1317 4.Wake 201. — *Li:* Adam Brounsmyth' 1327 *1.SR* 5.

OE *brūn* 'brown' + *smið*. — *Worker in copper and brass* (Bardsley). Cf BLAKESMYTH, WHITESMYTH.

Orsmyth. 1292. NED: —
La: Rad. le Orsmyth' 1292 *1.Ass* 14, 1292 *2.Ass* 28.

OE *ārsmið* 'copper-smith, brazier'. — *A smith who works in 'ore'* (here prob. copper or brass).

Caldroner. 1269. NED: —
Y: Rog. le caldroner 1299 Free Y 8. — *Nb:* Symon Caldruner 1269 Ass 163.

OF *chalderonier, cauderonnier* 'chaudronnier'. — *Maker or seller of cauldrons.* — Cf Nich. de Storteford, »*chaudruner*» 1277 CLB (A) 15 (Lo).

Latoner. 1306. NED: 1392—3.
Ess: Ric. le Latoner 1319 *SR* 13. Joan la Latoner 1341 CR 183. John Latoner ib. 181. — *Y:* Arthurus le latoner 1325 Free Y 23. — *Li:* Godefr. le Latoner 1329 *GDR* 3. Joh. Latoner 1332 *1.SR* 19. Joh. latoner 1332 *Ass* 8. — *Nf:* Alan le Latoner 1306 CDN 112. Thom. le Latuner 1309 ib. 13. Ric. Latoner 1332 *SR* 45. Pet. Le Latoner ib. 65. Arnald le Latonner 1335 CDN 195.

A der. of ME *latoun* 'brass' (fr. OF *laton*). — *A worker in or maker of latten* (NED).

Brasier. 1327. NED: c1400.
Ess: Joh. Brasyer' 1327 *SR* 23. Will. Brasier' ib.

A der. of OE *brasian* 'to make of brass'. — *One who works in brass.*

Brasyetere. 1333. NED: —
So: Thom. le Brasgetere 1333 *SR* 31. Walt. le Brasgetere ib. 30 (le Braseyetere 1344 *Ass* 12).

OE *bræs* 'brass' + *gēotere* 'founder'. Cf OE *ārgēotere*. — *Brass-founder.*

Pannegetter. 1250. NED: —
Li: Cristin Le Pannegetter 1250 FF 76.

OE *panne* 'a pan' + *gēotere* 'founder'. — *One who casts pans.*

Panner. 1268.   NED: —

So: John le Panner 1268 Ass 47. Walt. Pannar' 1333 *SR* 33. — *Wo:* Will. le Panner 1272 Hal 40. — *Ch:* Hugh Panner 1290 Court 166.

A der. of OE *panne* 'a pan'. — Signification: = PANNEGETTER.

Foundour. 1275.   NED: 1402.

Lo: Will. le Fondur 1275 RH 424. David le Foundour 1309 CLB (D) 42. — *Y:* Joh. le foundour 1346 Free Y 40.

OF *fondeur, fundeeur.* — *One who founds or casts metal, a founder.*

Belleyetere. 1275.   NED: c1440.

So: Adam Le Belyuter' 1305 *Ass* 12. — *Wo:* Agnes le Belgietere 1275 *2.Ass* 24. Sim. le Belleyetere ib. 32. Henr. le Belleyetere ib. 25. Rich. le Bellyeter 1301 OCW 19. Rob. le Belleyeotere (undated) ib. 50. Rich. le Belleyettere 1316 Inq 73. — *St:* Will. le Belleyetere 1327 SR 214. — *Y:* Thom. le Bellegetere 1279 *Ass* 28. Rob. le Bellegeter 1283 Free Y 4. — *Nf:* Rob. le Belleyetere 1314 CDN 47. Edmund Belyeter 1344 Free L 8.

OE *belle* 'bell' + *gēotere* 'founder'. — *Bell-founder.* — Cf Hondde le *yetter* 1260 Court 21 (Ch). — The following surname, of which I have only found one instance in London, prob. also means 'bell-founder': John le *Bellere* 1338 PMR 188.

Seinter. 1197.   NED: —

Lo: Benedictus le Seintier 1197 P 166. — *Wo:* Sim. Le Seynter 1275 *2.Ass* 51 (le Seynter ib. 26). Rich. called le Seynter 1294 OCW 8. — *St:* Rich. le Seinter 1221 FF 218. Magister Mich. le Seinter 1266 4.Ass 162. — *Y:* Rob. le Seinter 1208 Cur 262. Gerardus le Seinter 1210 ib. 114.

OF *saintier* 'fondeur de cloches' (Godefroy). — *Bell-founder.* — Salzman (Med. Ind. 145—6) mentions three famous bell-founders in the 13th century who all bore this surname:[1] *Beneit le Seynter* (1216), *John le Seynter* (1250), and *Hugh le Seinter* (1252).

Moldemaker. 1335.   NED: 1780.

Y: Gilb. le moldemaker, portour 1335 Free Y 30.

ME *molde* 'mould, pattern' (fr. OF *modle*) + ME *maker*. — *Maker of moulds.* — Cf Ric. de Duffeld, *moldemaker* 1350 Free Y 45.

---

[1] But he is not aware of the real sense of this.

E. Tinker, Pewterer, Plumber.

Tynkere. 1243. NED: c1265.

Ess: Adam Tynekere 1285 *1.GDR* 15. — *Sx:* Rad. le Tyneker 1263 *Ass* 29. — *So:* Rob. le Tinker 1243 Ass 304. Will. le Tynekar 1327 SR 142. — *Wo:* Steph. le Tinekere 1275 *1.Ass* 6. Galfr. le Tinckare 1275 SR 75. Thom. le Tinekere 1276 3.Hal 5. Walt. Le Tynker 1327 SR 15. — *St:* Ph. le Tynkere 1327 SR 223. Will. le Tynkere ib. 253. Ambros' le Tynker 1332 SR 108. — *La:* Henr. le Tynekere 1292 *1.Ass* 5. Mich. le Tynker' 1292 *3.Ass* 109. Henry le Tynker 1325 CR 158. — *Y:* Elias le Tynker 1275 1.Wake 36. Rich. the Tynker 1286 3.Wake 158. Gilb. le Tincker 1314 ib. 52. — *Li:* Thom. le Tynker' 1281 *1.Ass* 10. Euerardus le Tynkere 1281 *2.Ass* 22. Joh. le Tynker 1328 *Ass* 13. — *Nf:* Alex. La Tynekere 1286 *Ass* 51. Will. le Tincker 1289 CDN 28. Iwannus Tynker' 1329 *SR* 23. Henr. Tynker' 1332 *SR* 20.

Origin uncertain. — *Tinker, one who mends pots, kettles, etc.*

Tynkeler. 1268. NED: c1175.

La: Henry le Tinkeler 1278 Ass 170. Rad. Le Tyncklere 1292 *2.Ass* 24. Elias le Tinclere 1303 *Ass* 6. John le Tynkeler 1325 CR 84. — *Y:* Rog. le Tinkelere 1268 *Ass* 24. Elias le Tynclere 1293 *Ass* 36. Alan. Tynkeler 1301 SR 57. Gilb. le Tinkeler 1309 2.Wake 215. Rich. the Tynkler 1315 3.Wake 75. Will. le Tinkeler 1343 FF 170. — *Cu:* Will. Tynkeler 1332 SR 27.

Formed on TYNKERE, with another suffix (NED). — *Tinker, worker in metal.* — This is a characteristically northern word, and, as a surname, I have only found it in *La, Y,* and *Cu.*

Peutrer. 1331. NED: 1348.

Lo: Rog. le Peautrer 1331 CLB (E) 259. Margery la Peautrer 1333 PMR 97. — *Nf:* John Peutrerer 1350 Free L 12.

AF *peautrer* = OF *peautrier* 'batteur d'étain'. The instance in *Nf* has an additional *-er*. — *Pewterer, a worker in pewter, one who makes pewter utensils* (NED).

Whitesmyth. 1309. NED: 1302.

St: Rich. le White-Smyth 1309 10.Ass 6.

OE *hwīt* 'white' + *smið*. — *Tinsmith; one who polishes metal goods* (NED).

Amelour. 1311. NED: —

Lo: John le Aumayller, goldsmith 1311 CLB (B) 32 (le Aumaillor 1312 ib. 33). — *So:* Sim. le Amelour 1344 *Ass* 13.

OF *esmailleur* 'ouvrier qui travaille en émail' (Godefroy). Cf NED *amel (aumayl)* sb (fr. AF *amail, OF *esmail*) 'enamel'. — Enameller.

Vesseler. 1249. NED: —

Sx: Rob. le Wesseler 1249 *Ass* 38 (le Vesselir 1263 ib. 49). Will. le Vesseler 1296 SR 85. Joh. le Vesseler 1305 FF 184. Rob. le Vesseler 1321 FF 45. Agnes le Vesselyr 1327 SR 114. — *Ha:* Joh. le Vesseler 1333 *SR* 8.

A der. of ME *vessele* (AF and OF *vessel, vessele*) or fr. an OF *vesselier. — *One who makes or sells vessels* (for the table and household). — This surname is common in *Sx*, but outside this county only one instance has been found (in *Ha*).

Cannere. 1305. NED: —

Sx: Joh. Canner 1332 SR 332. — *Ha:* Joh. Le Kannere 1305 *Ass* 9. — *St:* Will. le Cannere 1327 SR 241 (le Canner 1332 SR 123).

A der. of OE *canne* 'can'. — *Maker or seller of cans.*

Haneper. 1319. NED: —

Ess: Rob. le Haneper 1319 *SR* 7. Thom. Haneper ib. 20. Johanna la Hanyper 1327 *SR* 15. — *Sx:* Walt. le Henepere 1327 SR 162. Rob. le Henepere ib. (R. Haneper 1332 SR 276). — *So:* Will. Henyper 1327 SR 232. — *Li:* Reg. Heniper 1327 *2.SR* 18.

OF *hanapier* 'faiseur de hanaps'; cf OF *hanap (hanep, henep)* 'cup' (Godefroy). — *Maker or seller of hanaps or goblets.* — Cf *hanaper* 'basket' (NED 1380), which also may have given rise to the above surname (as a nickname).

Plumer. 1230. NED: 1385—6.

Ess: Thom. le Plumber 1255 *Ass* 14. Agnes la Plumer 1319 *SR* 7. Sim. le Plomer 1326 *3.GDR* 11. Sewall' le Plomer 1327 *SR* 1. — *Sx:* Jord. Le Plumer 1279 *Ass* 1. Ric. le Plomer 1296 SR 82. — *Ha:* Galfr. le Plomer 1272 *Ass* 16. Ad. le Plomer 1327 *SR* 18. Matill' la Plumer 1333 *SR* 8. Joh. le Plomere 1340 SR 6. -- *So:* Joh. le Plomer 1333 *SR* 24. — *De:* Ric. le plumber 1230 P 25. — *Wo:* Reg. le Plummer 1275 *1.Ass* 2. Hugo le Plomer 1275 SR 9. Rob. le Plummer 1304 Hal 494. Joh. Plumer 1327 SR 72. — *St:* Will. le Plumer 1248 4.Ass 111. Joh. le plummere 1327 SR 226. Will. le Plomere ib. 235. — *La:* Sim. le Plumer 1246 Ass 114. — *Y:* Elyas le Plomer 1268 *Ass* 5. Henr. le plummer 1296 Free Y 6. Ric. le Plumber 1305 *Ass* 15. Steph. le plummer 1324 Free Y 22. Pet. le Plummer c1346 *SR* 1. — *Li:* Rad. le Plumer 1281 *1.Ass* 16. Gilb. le Plomer 1317 *Ass* 4. Rad. le Plumer 1327 *2.SR* 25. Will. Plommer 1332 *2.SR* 1. — *Nf:* Pet. le Plumer 1286 *Ass* 95. Adam le Plomer 1328 CDN 143. Benedictus plumer 1329 *SR* 44. Rob. le Plomer 1332 *SR* 80.

OF *plummier, plommier, ploumier* 'plombier'. — *Plumber, one who works or deals in lead.* — *Plumer* may also mean 'a dealer in feathers', v. p. 118.

Ledbeter. 1245. NED: —
St: Walt. le Ledebeter 1333 11.Ass 43. — *La:* Jord. le Ledbetere 1292 *1.Ass* 32. Ralph le Leddebeter 1324 CR 68. Rog. le Ledbeter 1332 SR 77. Gilb. le Ledbeter 1332 *Ass* 11. Ric. le Ledebeter 1332 *Ass* 11. — *Y:* Ric. le Ledebeter 1297 SR 118. Will. Ledebeter 1301 SR 21. Rog. Ledebeter ib. 92. Ric. le Ledbeter c1346 *SR* 15. Ric. Ledebeter 1349 Free Y 44. — *Li:* Will. Le Ledbetar 1245 *Ass* 5. Joh. Ledebeter 1327 *2.SR* 21. Will. Ledbeter 1328 *Ass* 12. Pet. Ledbeter 1332 *2.SR* 13. Rob. Ledebeter 1332 *3.SR* 1. — *Nf:* Ric. le Ledbetere 1286 *Ass* 109. Ric. Ledbeter' 1332 *SR* 27.

OE *lēad* + *bēatere.* — *A worker in lead.* — This surname has only been found in the Anglian counties.

Ledsmyth. 1329. NED: —
Nf: Jacobus le Ledsmyth 1329 *SR* 31.

OE *lēad* + *smið.* — *A smith who works in lead, a plumber.*

Ledyetere. 1280. NED: —
So: Ralf Ledyetere 1280 Ass 87. Joh. Le Ledyetere 1305 *Ass* 9, bis (Le Ledyutere ib. 11).

OE *lēad* + *gēotere.* — *One who founds lead.*

Ledere. 1296. NED: c1440.
Ess: Eua le Ledere 1319 *SR* 13. — *Sx:* Gilib. le Ledere 1296 SR 51. Ric. Leder 1332 SR 285. — *Li:* Alan. le ledere 1317 *Ass* 3. Pet. le ledere 1327 *4.SR* 11. Sampson le ledere ib.

A der. of OE *lēad.* — *Plumber* (NED). — It may also mean 'one who leads or carries something; the driver of a vehicle'; cf Henr. le *Watirledere* 1332 *SR* 26 (Ess) 'one who carries water'.

Bligeter. 1332. NED: —
Li: Rad. Bligeter 1332 *3.SR* 21.

The first element corresponds to MDu *bli*, MLG *blī*, ON *blȳ* 'lead'; the second el. is OE *gēotere.* — Signification: = LEDYETERE. — Cf the MLG surname (fr. Lübeck): Joh. *blig(h)etere* (Reimpell p. 89). — It is also possible that the whole surname is of MLG origin.

F. Blacksmith, Shoeing-Smith.

Smyth. 1250.　　　　　　　　　　　　　　　　　NED: Beow.
Ess: Henr. le Smyth' 1319 *SR* 19. Rog. Le Smyth' 1327 *SR* 13. Joh. le Smith' 1332 *SR* 6. — *Sx:* Adam Le Smyth 1288 *Ass* 29. Thom' le Smyth 1296 SR 66. Emma la Smyth 1344 FF 109. — *Ha:* Ric. le Smyth 1280 *3.Ass* 26. Rog. le Smyth' 1327 *SR* 5. Lucia la Smyth' 1333 *SR* 4. — *So:* Will. le Smyth 1275 Ass 14. Walt. le Smythe 1327 SR 168. Thom. le Smyth 1333 *SR* 2. — *Wo:* Rob. Smyte 1275 SR 33. Galfr. Le Smyth' 1307 *Ass* 3. — *St:* Adam le Smith 1318 9.Ass 74. Rob. le Smyth 1327 SR 198. Adam le Smith 1332 SR 83. — *La:* Will. le Smyth 1327 *SR* 14. Henr. le Smyth' 1332 *Ass* 8. — *Y:* Rich. the Smyth 1315 3.Wake 70. Alan le Smyth 1328 FF 23. — *Li:* Joh. le Smith' 1319 *Ass* 27. Thom. Smith' 1327 2.*SR* 1. Hugo le Smyth' 1332 2.*SR* 3. — *Nf:* Thom. le smiz 1250 *Ass* 6. Adam le Smyth 1315 *GDR* 25. Rad. Le Smyth 1332 *SR* 8.

OE *smið*. — *Smith, blacksmith, farrier.* — This surname occurs very frequently, although the Latin equivalent, *Faber*, is very common, especially in early rolls.

Feuere. 1243.　　　　　　　　　　　　　　　　　NED: 1415.
Ess: Joh. le feure 1255 *Ass* 29. Thom. Le Feuere 1327 *SR* 12. — *Sx:* Nigellus le Feure 1248 FF 119. Henr. le Feuere 1317 *Ass* 47. — *Ha:* Will. le Feure 1272 *Ass* 1. Walt. le Feuere 1327 *SR* 3. — So: Rog. le Fevere 1243 Ass 180. Joh. le Feure 1320 *Ass* 22. — *Wo:* Adam le Feuere 1275 2.*Ass* 35. Alicia la Fevere 1275 SR 16. — *St:* John le Fevre 1248 FF 242. Ric. le fevere 1327 SR 218. — *La:* Thom. le Feuer 1246 Ass 10. Ric. le Feuer' 1338 *Ass* 8. — *Y:* Rob. le Feure 1251 Ass 52. Adam le Feure c1346 *SR* 13. — *Li:* Reg. le Feuere 1248 FF 48. Rob. le Feuer 1332 *3.SR* 1. — *Nf:* Hugo le Feure 1250 *Ass* 22. Jacobus Le Feuer' 1332 *SR* 64.

OF *fevere, fevre* 'celui qui travaille le fer, forgeron' (Godefroy). — *Smith.* — This surname is frequent, especially in early rolls.— Cf the pl. n. *Faversham Ke* (*Fefresham* 811), the first element of which is supposed to be an early loan fr. L *faber*. (v. Ekwall: Trades in Engl. Pl. N. p. 84).

Ferrour. 1200.　　　　　　　　　　　　　　　　　NED: c1380.
Ess: Rog. le Ferur 1255 *Ass* 25. Will. le Ferer' 1285 *Ass* 20. Ric. le Ferour 1319 *SR* 17. Joh. Le Ferrour 1327 *SR* 1. — *Sx:* Wybertus le Ferur 1241 FF 97. Galfr. Le Ferur 1279 *Ass* 1. Joh. le Ferur 1296 SR 70. Rad. le Ferour 1327 SR 126. — *Ha:* Vmfridus le Ferur 1200 P 197. Elias le Ferrour 1327 *SR* 17. Rob. le Feror 1333 *SR* 9. — *So:* Geoffrey le Ferur 1252 FF 152. Ric. Le Ferour 1307 *Ass* 4. Nich. le Ferrour 1327 SR 125. Joh. le Ferour 1333 SR 20. — *Wo:* Rich., called Ferur 1269 Epi 36. Rob.

Le Ferrour 1307 *Ass* 5. Nich. Le Ferour 1327 SR 25. — *St:* Pet. le Ferour 1306 7.Ass 160. Ric. le ferour 1327 SR 235. Thom' le Ferour 1332 SR 108. — *La:* Adam le Ferour 1323 *Ass* 10. Joh. le Ferour 1334 *Ass* 17. — *Y:* Rob. le Ferur 1202—8 Ass 42. Ric. le Ferrour 1301 SR 121. Gilb. Ferour 1332 *SR* 5. — *Li:* Picot le Ferur 1200 P 78. Walt. le Ferur 1281 *1.Ass* 19. Joh. Le Feroure 1327 *2.SR* 10. Edm. le Ferur 1332 *3.SR* 2. — *Nf:* Galfr. le ferour 1329 *SR* 5. Rog. Ferour 1332 *SR* 9.

OF *ferreor, ferour.* — *Worker in iron, smith* (NED). — *Ferrour* is of frequent occurrence during this period.

Blakesmyth. 1333. NED: 1483.
Ha: Ric. le Blakesmyth' 1333 *SR* 4.
OE *blæc* + *smið*. — *Blacksmith.*

Watersmyth. 1333. NED: —
So: Joh. Watersmyth 1333 *SR* 30.

OE *wæter* 'water' + *smið*. — Prob. *a smith who uses a hammer driven by water.* Cf NED *water-miller* 'the owner or manager of a water-mill' (a1530).

Balismith. 1271. NED: —
Wo: Phil. le Balismit 1271 Hal 26 (le Balismid 1275 ib. 74, le Balismyth 1279 ib. 120). Joh. Balismyth 1300 ib. 404 (le Balysmyth 1304 ib. 485, le Balismyth 1306 ib. 540).

OE (Anglian) *bælg, bælig* 'bag, bellows' + *smið*. This surname has only been found in the North of *Wo*, and the Anglian form *Bali*- is therefore the form one would expect. — *'Bellows-smith', a smith who uses a pair of bellows.*

The form *bali* is not evidenced in NED in the sense of 'bellows' (the WS form of the word, ME *buli*, had this sense), but it has prob. existed, especially in the counties situated at the boundary between the WS and Anglian districts. Cf NED *belly* (for the differentiation of forms and senses).

Blowere. 1199. NED: c897.
Ess: Walt. Blauer' 1306 *2.GDR* 14. Will. le Blawer' 1319 *SR* 17. Will. Le Blowere 1327 *SR* 8. Reg. le Blawere 1332 *SR* 6. — *Sr:* Will. le Blowerre 1199 P 58. — *Sx:* Godefr. le Blower 1249 *Ass* 28. Nich. le Blowere 1263 *Ass* 36. Ric. Le Blowere 1279 *Ass* 4 (Le Blawer ib. 32). Gilib. le Blouwere 1296 SR 47. Ric. le Blower 1327 SR 167. — *Ha:* Walt. Blowere 1280 *3.Ass* 40. — *So:* Will. le Blouwar' 1327 *SR* 3. Rob. le Blouwar' ib. — *La:* Joh. le Blaer 1292 *1.Ass* 44. — *Y:* Margery the Blawer 1316 4.Wake 138. Thom.

Blauer 1332 *1.SR* 17. — *Li:* Joh. Blower 1327 *1.SR* 6. — *Nf:* Walt. le Blowere 1286 *Ass* 134. Sim. le Blowere 1295 *GDR* 11. Rog. Le Blowere 1332 *SR* 79. Ran. Le Blower' ib. 17.

OE *blāwere* 'blower'. — Signification: 1. *Bellows-blower.* 2. *Hornblower.*

Blomere. 1279. NED: —

St: Rob. le Blomere 1279 6.Ass 142. Will. le Blomere 1306 7.Ass 165. Rob. le Blomere 1307 ib. 180. Rog. le Blomere 1331 11.Ass 21. — *Y:* Adam le Blomer 1284 1.Wake 191, 1286 ib. 212. Walt. le Blomere 1293 *Ass* 83.

A der. of OE *blōma* 'ingot of iron'. — *Maker of blooms, ironworker.* — In the following example 'blomer' is the name of a trade: Joh. de Kirkeby, *blomer* 1379 Y (v. Bardsley s. v. *Bloomer*).

Mareschal. 1222. NED: 1258.

Ess: Joh. le Marescall' 1255 *Ass* 19. Thom. le Mareschal 1332 *SR* 27. — *Sx:* Steph. le Mareschal 1241 FF 95. Joh. le Mareschal 1328 *Ass* 1. — *Ha:* Ric. le Marescal 1272 *Ass* 10. Nich. le Marschal 1333 *SR* 7. — *So:* Nich. le Mareschal 1268 Ass 30. Walt. le Mareschal 1333 *SR* 13. — *Wo:* Will. le Mareschall' 1255 *Ass* 4. Joh. le Marchalt 1306 Hal 535. Thom. Mareschald 1327 SR 25. — *St:* Hugh le Mareschall 1222 4.Ass 18. Rob. le Mareschal 1327 SR 200. Joh. le Marchald 1332 SR 96. — *La:* Jacobus le Mareschal 1292 *1.Ass* 20. Adam le Marschale 1341 *SR* 4. — *Y:* Joh. le mareschall 1273 Free Y 2. Rob. le Mareschalle 1301 SR 7. Adam le Mareschall' 1332 *SR* 12. — *Li:* Alina la Mareschale 1242 FF 340. Ric. le Marchal 1332 *2.SR* 5. — *Nf:* Will. le Mareschal 1250 *Ass* 25. Sabina le Marchal 1332 *SR* 41.

OF *mareschal, marescal, marescald, marechault* (Godefroy). — Signification: 1. *One who tends horses, esp. one who treats their diseases, a farrier.* 2. *A shoeing smith* (NED). Mareschal was also the title of a high officer of state and of high military officers, but this interpretation is, of course, applicable to the surname only in exceptional cases (e. g. Earl Will. Mareschall 1220 Ass 11 *St*).

This surname is very common throughout the period.

Shosmyth. 1288. NED: 1625.

Sx: Will. Le Shosmith 1288 *Ass* 12 (Le Shosmyth ib., W. Sosmyth 1296 SR 9).

OE *scōh* 'shoe' + *smið*. NED has *shoe* in the sense of 'horseshoe' 1387. — *Shoeing-smith.*

Shouger. 1309. NED: c725.

Sr: Joh. le schoger' 1332 SR 54. — *St:* Will. Le Schouger 1309 *GDR* 3.

A der. of OE *scōgan* 'to shoe horses'; OE had *scōere* in the sense of 'shoemaker'. — *One who shoes horses* (NED).

Ferun. 1185. NED: —
Ess: Joh. le Ferrun 1274 RH 161. — *Li:* Pet. Le Ferun 1234 FF 290. — *Nf:* Walt. le Ferun 1290 CDN 31. — *Np:* Face Le Ferun 1185 P 50.

OF *ferron, feron* 'marchand de fer, forgeron' (Godefroy). — *Iron-monger, smith.*

Irmongere, Ismongere. 1165. NED: 1343.
Ess: Rob. Ysmonger' 1327 *SR* 18. Galfr. le Ismonger' ib. 24. Joh. le Irmonger 1332 *SR* 24. — *Ke:* Ailredus Ismangere 1165 P 104. — *Sx:* Isabell' le Ismangere 1249 *Ass* 32. Ernald' Le Ismongere 1288 *Ass* 19. Ric. Le Hirmongere ib. 31. Pet. Hysmongere 1296 SR 70. Will. le Ismongere 1317 *Ass* 50. Ph. le Ismongere 1327 SR 138. Joh. le Ismongar 1332 SR 243. Amelyna le Ismongar ib. — *Ha:* Euerard. Ismongere 1280 *1.Ass* 65.. Ric. le Irmongere 1305 *Ass* 16. Rob. Le Ysmanger' ib. 17. Thom. le Irmongare 1327 *SR* 9. Adam le Ismongere 1333 *SR* 4. Will. le Irmonger 1340 *SR* 6. — *So:* Joh. le Irmangere 1333 *SR* 21. — *Wo:* Nic. le Iremonger 1293 Hal 234 (le Yrenmonger 1297 ib. 375, le Irmonger 1304 ib. 474, le Irremonger 1305 ib. 502). Henr. Le Irmonger 1327 SR 56. — *St:* Elyas le Ironmongere 1294 7.Ass 22. John le Ysmonger 1306 ib. 165. Rog. le Ernmongere 1327 SR 211. — *La:* Adam le Irnemonger 1338 *Ass* 4 (le Irnemongher 1339 *Ass* 16). Henr. Irnemonger 1339 *Ass* 16. — *Y:* Galfr. le Irnemongere 1279 *Ass* 72. Joh. le Yernemanger 1332 *SR* 15. — *Li:* John le Ismonger 1249 FF 282. Millisantia Irnemanger 1327 *2.SR* 7. Will. Le Yernmanger ib. 24. Alan. Ernmanger ib. 14. Nich. Yerenmanger ib. 12. Will. Irmonger 1327 *4.SR* 3. Leticia la Irnemonger 1327 *3.SR* 2. Thom. Yrmanger 1328 *Ass* 25. Will. Irnemonger 1332 *3.SR* 2. — *Nf:* Edm. le Irinmunger 1286 *Ass* 138. Will. de Wynch le Irenmonggere 1293 CDN 48. Walt. le Yrynmongere 1294 ib. 51. Henry le Irynmongere ib. 53.

OE *īren, īsern, īsen* 'iron' + *mangere*. — *Ironmonger.*

This surname is spelt very differently in the different counties, and the following survey of all the instances found shows a distinct difference between Saxon and Anglian counties:[1]

Ess: Ismonger 3 inst., Ir- 2. *Sx:* Ismongere 25, Ir- 3. *Ha:* Ismongere 10, Ir- 12. *So:* only Irmongere. *Wo:* Iremonger 10, Iren- 5. *St:* Ironmongere 1, Ern- 1, Ys- 1. *La:* only Irnemonger. *Y:* Irenmongere 1, Yerne- 1. *Li:* Irnemanger 4, Yern- 2, Ern- 1,

---

[1] Cf Heuser (Altlondon 27): »Die altertümliche Form *ise(n)* für *ire, iron* = ae. *īsen, īren* ist eigentlich nur aus Kent bekannt und bildet daher ein scharfes Characteristicum für den Londoner Dialekt».

Ir- 3, Is- 1. *Nf:* only Irynmongere. — Some forms in the North seem to reveal Scandinavian influence; cf ON *jarn, earn* 'iron'.

G. Locksmith, Lorimer.

Locksmyth. 1255. NED: 1226.
Ess: Walt. le Loksmyth' 1255 *Ass* 9. Henr. le Locsmyt ib. 30. Pet. le Locsmyth' 1302 *2.GDR* 12. Will. Loxsmyth' 1319 *SR* 13. Joh. Loxsmyth' ib. 18. — *Wo:* Steph. le Loksmith 1301 OCW 19. — *Y:* Alan. Lock'Smyth' 1293 *Ass* 74. Will. le Loksmyth' c1346 *SR* 8. Joh. Loksmith 1350 Free Y 45. — *Li:* Will. Loksmith' 1327 *2.SR* 6. — *Nf:* Walt. Locsmyth' 1286 *Ass* 84. Katerina le loksmith' 1308 GDR 3. Joh. Locsmyth 1329 *SR* 15. Ran. Locsmyth 1332 *SR* 30. Galfr. le loksmyth ib. 33. Will. le Lochsmyt ib. 57.

OE *loc* 'lock' + *smið*. — *Locksmith*.

The locksmith also made keys, but sometimes there existed special key-smiths. In the ten counties treated in this book, however, I have not found any such surname, but in other counties I have come across a few instances of *Keyer*, which prob. means 'key-smith': Rich. le Kayer 1287 CLB (A) 169 (Lo). Will. le Keer[1] 1307 RBL 256 (Le). Rob. le Keyere 1275 RH 220 (Ke).

Lockere, Lokyere. 1221. NED: 1356.
Ess: Andr. le Lokiere 1285 *Ass* 36. Joh. le Lokere 1317 *3.GDR* 28 (le Lockere 1317 *2.GDR* 40). Will. Lokyere 1319 *SR* 7. — *Sx:* Joh. le Lokere 1263 *Ass* 47. Sim. le Lokyere 1296 SR 30. Rob. Lokyer 1332 SR 227. John le Lokyere 1346 FF 116. — *Ha:* Steph. le Lokyare 1280 *2.Ass* 57. Joh. le Loquer 1327 *SR* 5. — *So:* Ric. Le Lokyer' 1307 *Ass* 9. Nich. le Lokyere 1327 SR 211. Joh. le Loker 1333 *SR* 17. — *Wo:* Pet. le Loker 1221 Ass 615. Walt. le lokere 1275 *1.Ass* 19. Will. Le Loker 1327 SR 4. — *St:* Ran. Lokyer 1327 SR 207 (le Loker' 1332 SR 101). Joh. le Loker' 1332 SR 101. — *La:* Henr. le Lokkere 1292 *1.Ass* 6. — *Y:* Henr. Lokar 1268 *Ass* 38. Will. Locker 1301 SR 87. — *Nf:* Henr. le lokyer' 1286 *Ass* 106.

A der. of OE *loc* 'lock'. — *Locksmith*. — The form *Lokere* may also mean 'one who looks after something, a shepherd'; v. NED *looker*. Another spelling, *Louker* (e. g. Rob. le Louker 1333 *SR* 31 *So*), only admits of this interpretation.

Lokyestere. 1288. NED: (1590).
Sx: Matild. La Lokyestre 1288 *Ass* 35.

---

[1] For the spelling cf Jordan § 94; he records the form *kee* (instead of *kai*) 'key' for the adjoining county *Wa*.

The fem. correspondence to LOKYERE. — Prob. = LOKYERE. Cf, however, NED *lockster* (1590, one inst.) '? a woman who picks yarn'.

Serrur. 1255. NED: —
Ess: Hugo le Serrur 1255 *Ass* 3.
OF *serror, -our* 'serrurier' (Godefroy). — *Locksmith.*

Lokersmyth. 1255. NED: —
Ess: Hugo le lokersmyth 1255 *Ass* 6.
Prob. OE *locer, locor* 'plane' + *smið; locer* has not been found after the OE period. — *Maker of planes.*

Pundermaker. 1286. NED: —
Nf: Pet. le Pundermaker 1286 CDN 7. Will. le Pundermakere 1303 ib. 97. Rog. le Pundirmaker 1315 ib. 66 (le Pundermaker 1336 ib. 202).
ME *punder* 'auncel' (etym. not clear, v. NED *pounder*) + ME *maker*. — *Maker of auncels* (a kind of balance). — There is another surname of the same meaning of which I have found some instances in London, e. g. Thom. le *Aunseremakere* 1313 CLB (E) 20.

Lorimer. 1166. NED: a1225.
Ess: Ric. le lorimier 1198 P 137. Joh. le Lorimer 1255 *Ass* 28. Saierus le Lorymer 1341 *Ass* 11. — *Sx:* Will. le Lorimer 1249 *Ass* 34. Joh. Le Lorimer 1279 *Ass* 1. — *So:* Joh. le Lorimer 1320 *Ass* 11. Will. Lorymer 1327 SR 279. — *Wo:* Sim. le lorimer 1221 Ass 654. David le Loriner 1301 OCW 50. Nich. le Lorimare 1332 SR 26. — *St:* Will. le Lorimer 1294 7.Ass 16. — *La:* Rog. le Lorimer 1285 Ass 212. Adam Lorymer 1338 *Ass* 1. — *Y:* Hernisus le lorinner 1166 P 47. Joh. le Lorymer 1293 *Ass* 30. Galfr. le Lorimer 1301 SR 119. David le lorimer 1318 Free Y 18. — *Li:* Gilb. le Lorimer 1257 FF 144. Sim. Lorymer 1332 *3.SR* 25. — *Nf:* Rob. le Lorimer 1203 Cur 235. Joh. Lolimer 1332 *SR* 76.
OF *loremier, lorenier*. — *Lorimer, spurrier.*

Sporiere. 1288. NED: 1389.
Sx: Nich. Le Spuriere 1288 *Ass* 26. — *So:* Nich. Sporiare 1327 SR 239 (le Sporiere 1333 *SR* 26).
A der. of OE *spora, spura* 'a spur'. — *Spur-maker.*

H. Needler, Nailer, Buckle-Maker.

Nedlere. 1275. NED: 1362.

Ess: Rob. le Neidlere 1319 *SR* 6. Rob. le Nadler' 1327 *SR* 24. — *Sx:* Ric. le Nedelere 1309 *1.GDR* 6. — *So:* Andreas le Nelder' 1333 *SR* 29. Hugo le Nelder' ib. (le Neldare, mercer 1335 BBA 86). — *Wo:* Ph. Le Nedlere 1275 *1.Ass* 20 (Le Nelder' 1275 *2.Ass* 51). Nich. le Nedlere 1275 *2.Ass* 38. — *La:* Ric. le Nedlere 1292 *1.Ass* 31, 1292 *2.Ass* 20. — *Nf:* Joh. le Nedlere 1286 *Ass* 104. Edmund le Nedelere 1291 CDN 40. Adam Ston le Nedelere 1293 ib. 45.

A der. of OE *nǣdl* 'needle'. — *Needler, needle-maker*. — The form *Nadlere*, which is regular in *Ess*, is also the original form in *London*, where it is not uncommon, e. g. Rob. le *Nadlere* 1309 CLB (D) 38.

Aguiller. 1188. NED: —

Ha: Henr. Laguillier 1188 P 171. — *Y:* Tho. le Aguiller 1301 Free Y 9. — *Nf:* Edmund le Acgulyer 1288 CDN 19.

OF *aiguillier, agullier* 'celui qui fait des aiguilles' (Godefroy). — *Maker of needles*.

Pinnere. 1244. NED: c1400.

Lo: Walt. le Pinnere 1281 CLB (B) 11. — *Wo:* Adam le Pinare 1244 Inq 1. Walt. le Pinnare (printed 'Pumare') 1275 SR 1. John le Pynnare 1317 OCW 45.

A der. of OE *pinn* 'a peg, pin'. — *Pinmaker*. The pinner made not only pins but also wire articles, especially the small needles inserted in cards used in cloth dressing (1.YMB Intr. 38). — *Pinner* is common as a trade-name in Free Y: Ric. Spenser, pinner 1349 p. 44. Cf Rob. de Badby, *pinmaker* 1350 p. 45.

Wirdragher. 1313. NED: 1265.

Lo: Will. le Wirdrawiere 1320 CLB (E) 136. Rog. le Wyrdrawere 1332 ib. 286. — *Y:* Rog. le wirdragher 1313 Free Y 15. Will. le wiredragher 1326 ib. 23.

OE *wīr* 'wire' + a der. of *dragan*. — *Wire-drawer, one who makes wire*. — *Wirdragher* is common as a trade-name in Free Y: Rad. de Notingham, wirdragher 1300 p. 8. — Cf Joh. Buller, *wiresmyth* 1438 ib. 154.

Cager. 1319. NED: —
Ess: Will. Cager 1319 *SR* 13. Galfr. le Cager ib. (Cager 1327 *SR* 17).
— *Ha:* Steph. le Caggere 1327 *SR* 5, 1333 *SR* 8.

F *cagier* 'celui qui vend des oiseaux en cage; celui qui fabrique ou vend des cages' (Godefroy). — Prob. *a maker of cages*.

The form *Caggere* is uncertain; it may come fr. *cag* sb 'small cask, keg' (NED 1452) and mean 'a maker of cags'. *Cag* is supposed to be of Scandinavian origin (ON *kaggi*), and, if so, one would not expect to find the surname in *Ha*. Cf, however, Björkman (Scand. Loan-W. 243): »The distribution of the word (i. e. *cag*) in the mod. dialects does not point to Scand. origin. It may very well be a native word».

Nayler. 1273. NED: c1440.
Sx: Joh. Le Nayler 1279 *Ass* 18. — *St:* Will. le Nayllur 1297 7.Ass 42. Will. le Naylere 1327 SR 198. — *La:* Ric. le Naillere 1323 *Ass* 8. Will. le Naylor 1325 CR 158. Alex. le Nailer 1327 *SR* 4. Alcok' le Nailer 1333 *Ass* 14. — *Y:* Jacobus le nayler 1273 Free Y 2. Ric. le Neyler 1274 1.Wake 18. Rob. Nailler c1346 *SR* 1. — *Li:* Math. Nailer 1332 *2.SR* 16. Henr. Nayler 1332 *3.SR* 2.

A der. of OE *nægel* 'nail'. — *Maker of nails*.

Spiker. 1329. NED: (1884).
Nf: Rog. Spiker' 1329 *SR* 29.

A der. of ME *spike* (of doubtful origin) 'a nail'. — Prob. *a maker of spikes, nails*.

Reveter. 1313. NED: (1800).
Y: Ric. le reveter 1313 Free Y 15.

OF **rivetier, *revetier* or a der. of ME *ryvet, revette* 'a rivet' (OF *rivet*). — Prob. *a maker of rivets*. Cf NED *riveter* (1800) 'one who rivets'. — *Reveter* occurs several times as a trade-name in Free Y: Thom. de Heworth, reveter 1351 p. 47.

Douler. 1275. NED: —
Ess: Rich. le Doulier 1334 CR 128. — *Wo:* Joh. le Doulare 1275 SR 67. Rog. le Douler ib. 100. Will. Le Douler' 1327 SR 19. Will. Le Douler' ib. 47.

A der. of ME *dowle, doule* 'dowel' (of doubtful derivation). — *Maker of dowels* (a headless pin, peg, or bolt).

Bokeler. 1203. NED:—

Ess: Ric. le Bokeler 1316 *4.GDR* 6. — *Wo:* Rich. called Bokeler 1282 Epi 161 (R. le Bokeler 1283 ib. 208). — *Y:* Pet. le Bucler 1203 Cur 220. Beatricia Bokeler 1329 Free Y 26. Rob. Bokelere 1332 *SR* 3. Will. Bokelere ib. 14. — *Nf:* Ric. Le Bukler 1286 *Ass* 91 (le Bokeler ib. 142). Gregor. Bukeler 1332 *SR* 4.

OF *bouclier* 'fabricant de boucles' (Godefroy). — *Maker of buckles.* — The following surname is synonymous: John *Bokelsmyth* 1384 PMR 87 (Lo).

Botoner. 1295. NED:—

Y: Ric. le botoner 1295 Free Y 6. Joh. Botonner 1332 *SR* 10. — *Li:* Thom. le Botunner 1305 *Ass* 16 (Le Botonier ib. 10).

OF *botonier* 'fabricant, marchand de boutons' (Godefroy). — *Maker of buttons.*

I. Maker or Furbisher of Armour.

Armurer. 1280 NED: c1386.

Ess: Sim. le Armurer 1286 *1.GDR* 5. Rob. le Armurer 1340 CR 171. Nich. le Armurer 1341 *Ass* 2. — *La:* John le Armurer 1324 CR 80. — *Y:* Leonet le armorer 1322 Free Y 21. — *Li:* Adam le Armurer 1328 *Ass* 60. — *Nf:* Will. de Biltham le armurer 1300 CDN 79. Aunsell le Armurer 1323 ib. 114. Will. le Armourer 1332 *SR* 80.

AF *armurer* = OF *armurier*. — *Armourer, maker of armour.*

Hauberger. 1251. NED: 1481.

Sx: Steph. le Hauberger 1326 FF 63. — *So:* Henr. Le Hauberger 1305 *Ass* 3. — *Y:* Pet. the Hauberger 1251 FF 39.

OF *haubergier*. — *Maker of hauberks or coats of mail.*

Heumer. 1284. NED:—

Lo: Rich. le Heumer 1284 CLB (A) 86. »Mannekin» le Haumer 1298 CLB (B) 71. — *Y:* Alan. le heumer 1322 Free Y 21.

OF *heaumier, heumier* 'celui qui faisait ou vendait des heaumes, des casques' (Godefroy). — *Maker of helmets.* — Cf Joh. Tournay, *heumer* 1337 Free Y 33.

Sheldmakere. 1285. NED: 14..

Ess: Galfr. le Seldmakere 1285 *Ass* 7.

OE *sceld* 'shield' + a der. of *macian*. The spelling *seld* occurs several times in NED at this time. — *Shield-maker.*

Furbur. 1199. NED: c1415.

Ess: Adam le Forbour 1333 CR 109. — *Lo:* Rog. le Furbur 1199 P 129. — *Sx:* Rog. Le Furbur 1288 *Ass* 28. — *Ha:* Rad. le Forbour 1272 *Ass* 20. Gilb. Le Fourbur 1306 *Ass* 2. Ric. le Fourbour 1327 *SR* 17. Joh. le Furbur 1333 *SR* 8. — *So:* Walt. Le Fourbour 1307 *Ass* 6. Joh. le Furbour 1344 *Ass* 13. — *Wo:* Rog. le Furbur 1275 SR 79. — *St:* Rich. le Fourbour 1306 7.Ass 155. Will. le Forbour 1348 FF 163. — *La:* Will. Le Furbur 1300 *Ass* 3. — *Y:* Thom. le furbur 1230 P 274. Rob. le Furbur 1297 1.Wake 308. Rich. le Furbour 1331 FF 35. — *Li:* Hugo le Furbur 1327 *3.SR* 3. Will. Le Furbur 1328 *Ass* 8. Galfr. le Fourbeour 1332 *3.SR* 25. Nich. le Fourbour 1332 *3.SR* 25. — *Nf:* Ralph le Furbur 1285 CDN 3. Sim. le Fourbour 1327 CDN 137. Ric. Furbour 1332 *SR* 80.

OF *forbeor, four-, fur-* 'fourbisseur' (Godefroy). — *One who furbishes armour, weapons, etc.* — »It appears from the ordinances of the Furbishers (fourbours) in 1350 (in London) that among other articles they made pommels and hilts of swords and leather scabbards» (1.PMR 126). — Of the modern equivalent, Furbisher, I have only found one instance: Galf. le *Furbisur* c1260 RBL 117 (Le).

Rubbare. 1275. NED: 1611.

Wo: Rob. le Rubbare 1275 SR 89.

A der. of ME *rubben* 'to rub' (= LG *rubben*). — *One who rubs in order to polish something* (prob. armour).

Slykere. 1333. NED: —

Ha: Will. Slykere 1333 *SR* 1.

A der. of ME *sliken* 'to polish' (OE *-slician*). — *One who polishes, a furbisher*.

Grater. 1223. NED: 14..

Ha: Juliana la Gratour 1327 *SR* 7. Will. le Grator 1333 *SR* 3. — *Y:* John the Gratere 1223 FF 50. Ric. le Grater 1268 *Ass* 32. — *Li:* Alfredus le Grater 1321 *Ass* 41. — *Nf:* John le Grater ?1316 CDN 64.

OF *grateor, gratour* 'celui qui gratte'. This only accounts for the *Ha* forms; there may also have been an OF **gratier,* or the form *Grater* has been formed fr. the verb *grate* (OF *grater*). — *One who grates*, prob. *a furbisher*.

J. Maker of Military Engines, Swords, Knives.

Gynour, Engynour. 1191.   NED: a1300.
Ess: Will. le Engynnur 1255 *Ass* 28. Ric. le Gynour 1319 *SR* 20. Joh. Le Gynour 1327 *SR* 22. Galfr. le Gynnour 1332 *SR* 7. — *Sx:* Rad. le Gynnour 1327 SR 178. — *Ha:* Pet. le Gynneur 1280 2.*Ass* 5. — *So:* Rob. Lengynor 1327 SR 204. Ric. le Gynnour 1344 *Ass* 16. — *Wo:* Joh. le enguigniur 1221 Ass 461. Adam le Gynnur 1275 SR 16. Nich. Le Gygneour 1307 *Ass* 1. Alicia Le Gynor 1327 SR 30. — *La:* Rich. le Iniur 1246 Ass 95. Will. le Enginer 1292 *1.Ass* 42. Thom. le Engingnour ib. Will. le Genour 1324 CR 2. — *Y:* Ric. lengignur 1191 P 23 (lenginnur 1196 P 169). Joh. Genour 1332 *SR* 5. — *Li:* Will. Gynur 1281 2.*Ass* 44. Henr. Gynier 1328 *Ass* 3. Ric. le Gynur 1332 2.*SR* 2. — *Nf:* Will. lenginnur 1200 P 141. Will. le Enginnur 1286 *Ass* 74. Rob. le Ginyour 1296 *GDR* 2. Alex. Gyniour 1329 *SR* 62.

OF *engigneor, enginior* 'ingénieur, faiseur d'engins, de machines' (Godefroy). The prefix has in most cases been dropped; cf, however, NED *ginour*. — *An engineer, a constructor of military engines.*

Biller. 1275.   NED: —
Wo: Rich. Byllar 1322 OCW 97. — *Y:* Hugo le biller, pelter 1296 Free Y 6. — *Ca:* Henr. le Billere 1279 RH 457. — *Sf:* Joh. Billere 1275 RH 197.

A der. of OE *bil* 'a bill'. — *Maker of bills* (halberds or billhooks). — *Biller* occurs as the name of a trade in Free Y: Ric. de Galway, biller 1389 p. 88. — In the same roll there is also one instance of a compound: Joh. de Ireland, *whernebiller* 1389 p. 88, the signification of which is 'one who makes »quernbills»' (fr. OE *cweornbill* 'a stone chisel for dressing querns'); 'quernbill' has not been found after the OE period.

Brochere. 1225.   NED: —
Ess: Isabell' le Brokkere 1316 2.*GDR* 45. — *Lo:* Rog. le Brochere 1281 CLB (B) 10. — *So:* Hugh Brockere 1225 Ass 55. Adam Brocker 1327 SR 235. — *Wo:* Henry le Brucher 1315 OCW 143. Will. le Bruchere 1332 SR 24.

A der. of OF *broche, broke, broque* 'arme pointue' (Godefroy). — Prob. *a maker of 'broaches'* (lances, spears). Cf PLOGHBROCHER and the toponymical surname BROKER, some instances of which might belong here.

Brandwright. 1103—15.   NED: —
Ha: Spilemanus brandwirchte 1103—15 LWint 542.

OE *brand* + *wyrhta*. — *Maker of swords*. — This use of *brand* shows that it was not confined to poetry in the sense of 'sword'. Cf NED.

Exsmyth. 1299.   NED: —
Nf: Adam le Exsmyth 1299 CDN 73 (le Exsmicht 1303 ib. 94).

OE *æx* 'axe' + *smið*. — *Maker of axes*. — Cf the synonymous ON surname *Öxasmiðr* 1299 (Lind).

Clubbere. 1203.   NED: —
Ess: Rad. Clobbere 1203 Cur 3. Joh. Clobber' 1319 *SR* 21. — *Nf:* Beatrix le Clubber 1301 CDN 91. Rosa la Clubbere 1316 *GDR* 33.

A der. of ME *clubbe. clobbe* (fr. ON *klubba* 'a club'). — *Maker of clubs*. — »Under the Assize of Arms every adult man was bound to be provided with at least a coutel or knife and a 'baculus', a staff or club» (CDN, Intr.).

Cuteler. 1249.   NED: c1400.
Ess: Thom. le Cuteler 1285 *Ass* 4. Joh. le Cotiller 1301 *2.GDR* 11. Matill. le Cutiller 1319 *SR* 13. Elias le Coteler 1341 *Ass* 21. — *Sx:* Will. le cutiler' 1249 *Ass* 34. Sim. Cuteler 1296 SR 50. Alic' Cuteler 1327 SR 171. — *Ha:* Euerard. le Cuteler 1280 *2.Ass* 87. Oliuerus le Cotyler ib. Thom. le Cuteller 1333 *SR* 8. — *So:* Will. le Cuteyler 1263 FF 201. — *Wo:* Thom. le Cotiller 1275 SR 2. — *St:* Rob. le Cotiller 1294 6.Ass 297. John le Cotiller 1306 7.Ass 155. Will. le Cotiler 1327 SR 206. — *La:* Adam le Cuteler 1292 *1.Ass* 1. Walt. le Cutiller ib. 10. Joh. le Cotiler 1338 *Ass* 6. — *Y:* Rob. le Coteler 1297 SR 76. Hugo le Cotiller 1301 SR 118. Haukynus le cotoler 1313 Free Y 15. Andr. le Cotelere 1332 *SR* 7. — *Li:* Matild' la Cutiller 1275 RH 318. Nich. le Cuteler 1281 *1.Ass* 37. Will. le Cotiler 1281 *2.Ass* 36. Alan. Kotler 1332 *1.SR* 17. — *Nf:* Joh. Cuteler 1286 *Ass* 67. Rob. le Cuteler 1305 CDN 105. Rob. le Cuteler 1316 *GDR* 38.

OF *coutelier, cotelier*. — *Cutler, one who makes, deals in, or repairs knives and similar cutting utensils* (NED).

Knyfsmith. 1284.   NED: 1738.
St: Will. Knysmyt 1326 10.Ass 73 (le Knyfsmyth 1347 FF 161, 1348 12.Ass 90). — *La:* Adam *le Cutyller de Wygan (erased)* Knyfsmith 1284 Ass 194 (A. Knyfsmith *of Wygan (erased)* 1285 Ass 209).

OE *cnīf* + *smið*. — *A smith who makes knives, a cutler*.

Rasorer. 1285.   NED: —
Y: Walt. le Rasorer 1285 1.Wake 195.

OF *rasorier or a der. of ME rasor (= OF). — Prob. *a maker of razors*.

Forceter. 1311. NED: —
Ess: Rich. le Forseter de Parys 1311 CR 35, 36 (le Forceter ib. 38, 39).

OF *forcetier* 'fabricant de ciseaux de jardiniers ou de tondeurs de draps' (Godefroy). — *One who makes shears, a cutler*. — Cf Rob. *Schersmyth* 1264 Newc. Deeds 120 (Nb) 'a smith who makes shears'.

Swerdsliper. 1313. NED: 1478—9.
Y: Will. Suerdsliper 1313 3.Wake 6 (Swerdsliper ib. 16, the Swerdslyper 1316 4.Wake 110). — *Li:* Will. Swerdslyper 1328 *Ass* 12.

Perhaps fr. Scand.; cf MSw *swerdslipare*. — *Sword-sharpener*. I have found one instance of a surname in *Sx*, Laurencius *Slyper* 1332 SR 252, which may be synonymous; cf NED *slipe* vb 1390 'to polish, to sharpen'. This interpretation, however, is not certain.

Shether. 1302. NED: 1379.
Ess: Rich. le Schadere 1316 *2.GDR* 49. Walt. le Shather' 1332 *SR* 25. Rob. le Shether 1336 CR 139. — *So:* Joh. Schether 1327 SR 168 (Shether' 1333 *SR* 35). — *Y:* Henr. le schether 1302 Free Y 9. Joh. Shether 1332 *SR* 3.

A der. of OE *scǣp, scēap* 'sheath'. — *Sheath-maker*.

Chapemaker. 1350. NED: 1886.
Y: Thom. le chapemaker 1350 Free Y 45.

ME *chape* (fr. F *chape* 'the chape or locket of a scabbard') + ME *maker*. — *Maker of chapes* (the metal plate or mounting of a sheath or the sheath itself; NED). In 1466 the chapemakers of London made not only chapes but also bread-graters, shoebuckles, tin spoons, and dripping-pans (Salzman: Med. Ind. 332).

K. Maker of Bows or Arrows.

Bowyer. 1223. NED: 1297.
Ess: Jord. le Bowyere 1255 *Ass* 34. Alic. le Bowyer' 1319 *SR* 11. Andr. le Bouer' ib. 15. Joh. le Bowyere 1327 *SR* 24. — *Sx:* Pet. le Bouer 1223 FF 47. Will. le Bowyere 1279 *Ass* 24. Sim. le Bouiere 1296 SR 54. Ric.

Bouiere 1327 SR 170. Godefr. le Boghier 1332 SR 228. — *Ha:* Henr. le Bowyere 1280 *3.Ass* 40. Walt. le Boghyere 1325 *Ass* 2. Walt. le Boghier' 1340 *SR* 6. — *So:* Ric. le Bogyere 1305 *Ass* 2. Will. Bouyour 1327 SR 205. Walt. Bowyere 1339 BBA 93. — *Wo:* Rad. Bouger 1275 SR 35. Rog. Le Bouwyer' 1307 *Ass* 1. Will. Le Bowyor 1327 SR 35. — *St:* Rob. le Bowyere 1327 SR 254 (le Bower' 1332 SR 129). — *La:* Will. le Bogher 1338 *Ass* 5. — *Y:* Rob. Bouer 1297 SR 121. Will. Le Bower 1305 *Ass* 21. John the Bougher 1316 4.Wake 67. Andreas le bougher 1325 Free Y 23. — *Li:* Galfr. Bower 1327 *3.SR* 1. Hugo le Bower 1332 *3.SR* 25. — *Nf:* Joh. le Bowyere 1315 *GDR* 20. Walt. le Boweyer 1332 CDN 172.

A der. of OE *boga* 'bow'. — *Maker or seller of bows.* — This surname is common, especially in *Sx* and *Y.*

Bowewright. 1292. NED: —
La: Joh. le Boghewrichgte 1292 *1.Ass* 4 (Le Boghewrichgte 1292 *2.Ass* 4). Will. le Bouright 1324 CR 58.

OE *boga* 'bow' + *wyrhta*. — *Bow-maker*.

Bowemakere. 1281. NED: 1864.
St: Hugo le Bowemakiere 1309 *GDR* 3. — *Le:* John le Boumaker 1281 RBL 191.

OE *boga* 'bow' + a der. of *macian*. — *Maker of bows*.

Flecher. 1197. NED: c1400.
Ess: Godefr. le Flecher 1255 *Ass* 1. Will. Flecchere 1317 *3.GDR* 39. — *Sx:* Will. le Flecher 1249 *Ass* 23. Nic. Flecher 1296 SR 13. Joh. le Flecher 1329 *Ass* 64. — *Ha:* Joh. le Flecher 1272 *Ass* 16. Walt. Le Fleccher 1305 *Ass* 11. — *So:* Will. le Flecchere 1344 *Ass* 15. — *Wo:* Adam le Fleccher 1247 Inq 2. Walt. le Flecchere 1307 *Ass* 4. Rob. le Fletchare 1332 SR 24. — *St:* Rob. le Flecher 1203 3.Ass 122. Henry le Fletcher 1293 6.Ass 255. Ric. le Flecher' 1332 SR 120. — *La:* Will. le Flecher 1203 Cur 180. Rich. le Fletcher 1246 Ass 63. Steph. le Flecher 1338 *Ass* 2. — *Y:* Thom. Flecher 1207 FF 111. Jacobus le Flecher 1279 *Ass* 19. Elias the Fleccher 1317 4.Wake 184. — *Li:* Joh. le Flecher 1245 *Ass* 18. Alan. le *Flacher*' 1281 *2.Ass* 27. Joh. Fletcher 1332 *2.SR* 4. — *Nf:* Odo le flecch(er) 1197 P 245. Joh. le Flecchere 1315 *GDR* 20.

OF *flechier, flecher*. — *One who makes or deals in arrows; perhaps sometimes one who makes bows and arrows*. — Though of French origin, this name was rare in Paris. In SR 1292 there is only one instance of *Flechier*. In England, however, this surname was of common occurrence.

Aruwemakere. 1305. NED: 1681.
So: Ric. Le Aruwemakiere 1305 *Ass* 2.

OE *arwe* 'arrow' + a der. of *macian*. — *Maker of arrows*.

Arowesmith. 1278.   NED: c1400.
Ess: John le Arevesmyth 1311 CR 27 (le Arrowesmith 1312 ib. 88). Rob. le Arwesmyth 1336 ib. 139. — *St:* Rog. le Aruesmyth 1278 6.Ass 87. — *Y:* Laurence Arousmyth 1337 FF 128. Rob. Arusmyth 1343 ib. 170.

OE *arwe* 'arrow' + *smið*. — *A smith who makes arrows, especially iron arrow-heads*.

Boltsmith. 1346.   NED: —
Wo: John Boltsmith 1346 OCW 63.

OE *bolt* + *smið*. — *Maker of bolts, arrows*.

Baiounsfeuere. 1333.   NED: —
Sx: Rog. Baiounsfeuere 1333 FF 83.

OF *baion* 'flèche d'une arbalète' + *fevere* 'smith'. — *Maker of crossbow arrows*.

Tippere. 1275.   NED: (1819).
Wo: Pet. le Typpere 1275 SR 9. Henr. le Typpare ib. 14. Alex. le Typpare ib. 26. Adam le Tippar ib. 44. Ric. le Tippere ib. 47. Thom. le Tippare ib. 50. Joh. le Typper 1332 SR 23. — *St:* Will. le Tippere 1293 6.Ass 279. John le Tipper 1326 9.Ass 113. Will. le Tippere 1327 SR 209. Thom' le Typper 1332 SR 102. — *Li:* Walt. Tipper 1332 *3.SR* 13.

A der. of ME *typpe* 'to furnish with a tip' (fr. ME *typ* 'a tip' = MLG, MDu). — *A maker, or fitter on, of metal tips or mounts; prob. an arrow-header*.

CHAPTER VI.

WOOD WORKERS.

A. Sawyer, Maker of Laths or Boards.

Sawyere. 1202—8.   NED: 1350.
    Ess: Will. le Sauwyer' 1288 *1.GDR* 2. Walt. Le Sawyer 1304 *2.GDR* 14. Eua le Sawyer' 1319 *SR* 16. — *Sx:* Ric. Le Saihiere 1279 *Ass* 18. Rob. Le Sawere 1288 *Ass* 28. Walt. le Saghier 1327 SR 137. Alan. le Saghiar 1332 SR 259. — *Ha:* Joh. Le Sawyere 1280 *2.Ass* 25. Ric. le Saghiere 1327 *SR* 2. — *So:* Humfrey le Sayhare 1270 Ass 134 (le Sawyere ib. 139). Will. Saweyer 1327 SR 101. Adam le saghier' 1333 *SR* 20. — *Wo:* Will. le Sawyere 1281 3.Hal 84. Galfr. Le Sawyer 1327 SR 19. — *St:* Henry le Saghere 1313 9.Ass 42. — *Y:* Rich. le Saer 1202—8 Ass 28. Joh. le Sawere 1268 *Ass* 6. Rob. le Sahar 1297 SR 81. Ran. le Saygher 1301 SR 39. Rob. le Sagher 1332 *SR* 10. — *Li:* Will. Saghere 1327 *2.SR* 9. Rog. le Sagher 1332 *3.SR* 25. — *Nf:* Ric. le sagere 1329 *SR* 31. Will. le Sagher' 1332 *SR* 56.

    A der. of ME *saghe, sawe* 'to saw' (fr. OE **sagu, saga* 'a saw'). — *One who saws timber, boards, laths.* — This surname is most common in *So* and *Y*.

Syur. 1225.   NED: —
    So: Rog. le Syur 1225 Ass 45. Humfrey le Syur 1270 Ass 144 (le *Sawyere* ib. 139). — *Wo:* Thom. le Syour 1299 Epi 510. — *St:* Will. le Syur 1293 6.Ass 269. — *Y:* Will. le Syur 1275 1.Wake 29. Alice le Syur 1285 ib. 204. Rich. le Syur 1306 2.Wake 58. Phil. le Ciour 1316 3.Wake 102 (the Syour ib. 103). — *Nf:* Joh. le Syur 1286 *Ass* 24 (le *Sayur* ib.).

    OF *seieor, syeeur, scieur, saieur* 'scieur' (Godefroy). — Signification: = SAWYERE.

Lattewright. 1268.   NED: —
    Y: Hugo le Lattewrichte 1268 *Ass* 7.

    OE *lætt* 'lath' + *wyrhta*. — *Maker of laths.* — Cf the following trade-names in Free *Y*: Nich. Smyth, carpenter et *latclever* 1466 p. 186. Ric. Womersley, *latryver* 1597 p. 41.

Lathere. 1318. NED: 1897.

Lo: Rob. le Latthere, vintenarius 1318 CLB (E) 95. — *Sr:* Rob. le Lattar' 1332 SR 75. — *Ha:* Nich. le Lathere 1327 *SR* 17. Pet. le Latthere 1333 *SR* 3. — *So:* Ph. le Lathere 1327 *SR* 14.

A der. of OE *lætt* or **læpp-*; v. NED *lath (lathe, latthe)*. Cf OF *lateor* 'ouvrier en lattes' (Godefroy). — Prob. = LATTEWRIGHT.

Delmaker. 1274. NED: —

Wo: Thom. Delmaker 1274 Hal 54.

ME *dele* 'deal' (fr. MLG *dele* 'plank') + ME *maker*. — *Maker of deals* (planks, boards). — Cf Ric. Brock, *beam maker* 1694 RTC 190 (Ch).

Bordhewere. 1327. NED: —

St: Will. le Bordhewere 1327 SR 220. Thom' Bordhewer' 1332 SR 115.

OE *bord* 'board' + a der. of *hēawan*. — *One who hews (cleaves, makes) boards*. — The signification of the following surname is prob. the same: Henry *Burdclever* 1465 2.YMB 232. Will. *Burdclever*, skynner 1495 Free Y 220.

Bordwright. 1327. NED: —

Sx: Ric. Bordwrozte 1327 SR 188 (Bordwreghte 1332 SR 299).

OE *bord* 'board, table' + *wyrhta*. — Either = BORDHEWERE or *a maker of tables*. Cf LATTEWRIGHT. — The following surname is synonymous: Rob. *Bordmakere* 1356 CLB (G) 64 (Lo).

Tymbermongere. 1188. NED: 1275.

Lo: John »Timbermongere» 1282 CLB (A) 53. — *Sr:* Fulko le Timbermangere 1188 P 27. Gilb. Tymbermongere 1332 SR 5. — *Ha:* Laur. le Tymbirmongere 1280 *3.Ass* 43 (le Thimbermongere 1280 *2.Ass* 94).

OE *timber* + *mangere*. — *Dealer in timber*. — The following surname has a similar meaning: Rob. *Wudemonger'* 1275 RH 433 (Lo).

B. **Carpenter, Joiner.**

Carpenter. 1175. NED: c1325.

Ess: Henr. le Carpenter 1255 *Ass* 36. Thom. le Charpenter 1285 *Ass* 39. Gilb. Le Carpenter 1327 *SR* 1. — *Sx:* Rad. Carpenter 1222 FF 45. Rob. le Carpenter 1249 *Ass* 2. Will. le Carpentier 1332 SR 253. — *Ha:* Will. le

Carpenter 1272 *Ass* 16. Joh. le Charpenter 1305 *Ass* 15. Gunnyld' la Carpentire 1333 *SR* 9. — *So:* John le Carpenter 1235 FF 88. Henr. le Carpunter 1327 SR 212. Ric. le Carpanter 1333 *SR* 23. — *Wo:* Adam le Charpenter 1255 *Ass* 1. Leticia la Carpentere 1275 SR 27. Ric. Le Carpenter 1327 SR 17. — *St:* Ralph le Charpenter 1253 4.Ass 126. Steph. le Carpenter 1284 6.Ass 136. Will. le Carpenter 1327 SR 104. — *La:* David le Carpenter 1246 Ass 9. Henry le Charpenter 1285 Ass 209. Rob. le Carpunter 1338 *Ass* 8. — *Y:* Rad. Carpenter' 1175 P 181. Alan. le Carpenter 1301 SR 118. — *Li:* Walt. Carpenter 1183 P 68. Sim. le Charpenter 1245 *Ass* 26. Gilb. le Carpunter 1332 *2.SR* 3. — *Nf:* Will. le carpenter 1250 *Ass* 24. Ida la Carpentere 1295 *GDR* 9. Thom. Carpunter 1332 *SR* 53.

AF *carpenter* = OF *charpentier*. — *Carpenter*. — As is to be expected, *Carpenter* belongs to the surnames that occur most frequently.

Wright. 1214. NED: ?a695.
Ess: Walt. le Wrhyte 1316 *3.GDR* 33. Rob. le Wrighte 1319 *SR* 21. Joh. le Writhe 1327 *SR* 7. — *Sx:* Patere le Writh 1214 FF 35. Hugo Wreytche 1296 SR 31. Juliana la Werghte 1312 *2.GDR* 9. Nich. le Whergte 1327 SR 140. Joh. Wreghte ib. 188. Joh. le Worghtte 1332 SR 232. Will. le Wroghte ib. 299. — *Ha:* Joh. le Wryghte 1306 *Ass* 1. Johanna la Worghte 1333 *SR* 3. — *So:* Hugo Le Wrycht' 1305 *Ass* 9. Adam le Wrighte 1333 *SR* 15. Thom. le Worghte ib. 21. — *Wo:* Ric. le Worithte 1275 SR 84. Hug. Le Wrych' 1294 *Ass* 4. — *St:* Rich. Wryth 1297 7.Ass 44. Sim. le Wrughte 1320 10.Ass 33. Will. le Wrighthe 1327 SR 219. Ric. le Wryth 1332 SR 96 (le *Charpentir* 1327 SR 211). Ric. le Wryeth 1332 SR 110. — *La:* Thom. le Wrythe 1292 *3.Ass* 104. Adam le Wryght 1321 FF 42. Hugo le Wright 1338 *Ass* 7. — *Y:* Margery the Wricth 1306 2.Wake 57. Rob. le Wright 1332 *SR* 10. — *Li:* Will. le Wricthe 1245 *Ass* 34. Henr. le Wright' 1317 *Ass* 7. Rob. le Wryht' 1327 *2.SR* 8. Joh. le Wright 1332 *3.SR* 3. — *Nf:* Rob. le Wrighte 1286 *Ass* 120. Katerina le Wright' 1301 *GDR* 20. Thom. le Wrighte 1332 *SR* 5.

OE *wyrhta, wryhta*. — *Carpenter, joiner*. — The same person is called both *Carpenter* and *Wright* in *St*, v. above. — In early rolls this surname is generally latinized, but it occurs frequently in the 14th century. — In compounds (these are very common) *wright* has a more general sense: 'one who manufactures something'. — Of the following compound I have only found one instance: Rob. le *Briggwricht* 1230 P 104 (Lo) 'a maker of bridges'.

Joynour. 1306. NED: 1386.
Ess: Clemens Joynour 1319 *SR* 16. — *Lo:* Nich. le Joynour 1306 CLB (B) 176.

AF *joignour* = OF *joigneor* 'celui qui joint, qui fait les jointures'. — *Joiner*.

Joyntur. 1286. NED: —

Nf: Joh. Le Joyntur 1286 *Ass* 119. Walt. le Joyntur ib. Gilb. Joyntur 1329 *SR* 5 (Joynttour 1332 *SR* 57).

Godefroy has *jointeur, jointteur* in the sense 'instrument qui sert à relier les tonneaux'; it may also have meant 'joiner'. — Prob. = JOYNOUR.

Tabler. 1201. NED: —

Sx: Rad. le Tabler 1212 Cur 248. Rob. le Tabler 1229 FF 60, 1232 ib. 73. — *So:* Ralph Tabeler 1201 Ass 17.

OF *tablier* 'menuisier' (Godefroy). — *Joiner*.

Fesor. 1329. NED: —

Sx: Rich. le Fesor 1341 FF 100, 102. — *Nf:* Crist. Fesour 1329 *SR* 31.

OF *faiseor, fes-* 'celui qui fabrique, artisan' (Godefroy). — One who manufactures something, perh. = WRIGHT.

Borere. 1318. NED: 1483.

Ess: Reg. Le Boriere 1327 *SR* 15. — *Lo:* Rob. le Boriere 1318 CLB (E) 95. — *Li:* Gilb. Borer' 1327 *1.SR* 2. Mabil. Borer' ib. Henr. Borer' ib. Hugo Le Borer ib. 4, 1332 *2.SR* 6.

A der. of OE *borian* 'to bore'. — *One who bores or pierces* (NED). — *Borer* is a trade-name in the following instance: Adam Cok borer 1366 RBL 142 (Le).

Dofkotemakere. 1281. NED: —

Li: Pet. le Dofkotemakere 1281 *1.Ass* 9.

ME *dovecote* (OE **dufe*, 'dove' + *cote*) + ME *makere*. NED has *dovecote* c1425. — *Maker of dovecotes*.

Cottemakere. 1311. NED: —

Nf: Alex. le Cottemakere 1311 CDN 28.

OE *cote* + a der. of *macian*. — *A maker of cotes for doves, sheep, etc.*

C. Maker of Carts, Wheels, Ploughs.

Cartwright. 1275.   NED: 14..
Wo: Joh. le Cartwereste 1275 SR 17. Rad. le Cartwreute 1294 Hal 296.
— *St:* Will. le Cart Wrygthe 1327 SR 202. Thom. le Cartwrigte ib. 254.
Rob. Cartewryght 1348 14.Ass 73. — *La:* Ric. le Cartewrychgte 1292 *1.Ass*
42. Adam le Cartewright 1324 CR 9. Hugo le Cartewrighte 1327 *SR* 8. Ric.
le Cartwright 1332 SR 19. — *Y:* Rich. le Cartewricht 1308 2.Wake 191.
Elias the Cartwriht 1317 4.Wake 166. Henr. le cartwrith 1334 Free Y 29.
Will. Cartewryght 1345 FF 179. Joh. Cartewright c1346 *SR* 6. Constance
Cartewryght 1348 FF 15. — *Li:* Thom. le Cartewricht' 1321 *Ass* 43. Galfr.
Cartwryth' 1327 *2.SR* 22. Alan. Cartwhryt' 1332 *1.SR* 7. Joh. Cartewryght'
1332 *3.SR* 2. Rob. le Cartewright 1332 *Ass* 12.

OE *cræt* 'cart' + *wyrhta*. Cf ON *kartr* 'cart'. Note that no instance of this surname has been found in the South of England *(Ess, Sx, Ha, So)*. — *One who makes carts.*

Waynwright. 1246.   NED: c1000.
La: Will. son of Lewaynrith 1246 Ass 89. Adam le Waynwryche 1292 *1.Ass* 31. Bate le Waynwryche ib. Will. le Waynwright 1323 CR 30. Alan. le Waynwright 1332 SR 17. Ric. le Waynwright ib. 83. — *Y:* Adam the Waynwryth 1285 1.Wake 193. Alcok le Waynwrith 1306 2.Wake 54. John the Waynwricht 1314 3.Wake 43. Henry the Waynwright ib. 50. Alex. the Waynwryght 1316 4.Wake 49. Hugh the Waynwryhte ib. 120.

OE *wægnwyrhta*. — *Wagon-builder.*

Whelere. 1249.   NED: 1497.
Ess: Steph. le Weler' 1282 *2.GDR* 1. Sim. le Wheler' 1316 ib. 46. Margeria le Wheller' 1319 *SR* 18. Walt. le Wheller ib. Alex. Le Whelere 1327 *SR* 8. Joh. le Wheler 1332 *SR* 21. Rog. le Whelere ib. 30. — *Sx:* Rog. le Wewelere 1249 *Ass* 23. Thom. le Wegheler 1284 FF 130. Walt. le Wegler 1296 SR 103. Rob. Le Whegeler' 1317 *2.GDR* 16. Rog. le Wheler' 1319 *Ass* 39. Ric. le Wheler' ib. Joh. le Wheghler 1327 SR 120. — *Ha:* Henr. le Weweller' 1280 *3.Ass* 13. Adam le Whelere ib. 21. Joh. le Wheghelere 1327 *SR* 15. Thom. le Whelare ib. 18. Gunylda la Whelere 1333 *SR* 3. Rob. le Wheghelere ib. 7. — *So:* Will. Wheler 1327 SR 186. Thom. Wheler' 1333 *SR* 29. — *Wo:* Joh. le Whelare 1275 SR 21. Matilda la Whelare ib. Nich. Le Wheler 1327 SR 6. Ric. le Whelare 1332 SR 6. Ralph le Wheler 1332 OCW 30. — *St:* Ric. le Wheler' 1332 SR 84. Will. le Weler' ib. 97 (*Rotarius* 1327 SR 213). — *Y:* Will. le Weler 1301 SR 39. — *Nf:* Joh. Qweler' 1329 *SR* 48.

A der. of OE *hweogol, hweowol, hwēol* 'wheel'. — *Wheelwright, wheel-maker.* — This name is common in the South of England.

11

Whelster. 1327.   NED: —
Li: Rob. Welster 1327 *2.SR* 18.
The fem. correspondence to WHELERE. — *Wheelwright.*

Whelwright. 1274.   NED: 1281.
Ess: Walt. Welwryhte 1274 RH 160. Rog. le Whelwrighte 1319 *SR* 14. Nich. le Welwrite 1327 *SR* 24. John le Whelewriht 1337 CR 151. Will. Whelwrigth' 1341 *Ass* 18. — *Ha:* Will. le Whelwhritte 1287 *Ass* 3. Alex. Le Whelewryghte 1289 *Ass* 16. — *Wo:* Rob. Le Whelewryte 1327 SR 54 (le Welwrytthe 1332 SR 16). *Y:* Ric. Whelwright 1305 *Ass* 18. Alcok le Quelewrigh 1308 2.Wake 181. Adam Quelwrigh' c1346 *SR* 9. John Whelwryght 1346 FF 188. — *Li:* Rob. Welwristh' 1327 *4.SR* 11. Henr. Whelwreyth' 1327 *1.SR* 1. Joh. Whelwreyt' ib. 2. Will. Whelewryth' ib. 7. — *Nf:* Will. le Whelwrihte 1316 CDN 69. Rob. Le Wellewrythe 1332 *SR* 64.

OE *hwēol* 'wheel' + *wyrhta*. — *One who makes wheels and wheeled vehicles* (NED).

Whelsmyth. 1319.   NED: —
Ess: Euota Welsmyth' 1319 *SR* 16. Iuo le Welsmyth' 1327 *SR* 7.

OE *hwēol* 'wheel' + *smið*. — *One who makes wheels* (esp. the iron parts).

Rower. 1197.   NED: —
Sx: Joh. le Rouier 1327 SR 159. — *Ha:* Walt. le Roer 1272 *Ass* 12. Joh. le Roer 1280 *2.Ass* 67 (le Rower ib., le Rouwer 1280 *3.Ass* 15). — *So:* Walt. le Rowere 1278 3.Ass 158. Joh. le Roere 1307 *Ass* 7. Will. le Royare 1327 SR 140. Walt. le Royer ib. 211. — *Wo:* Rob. le Roer 1275 SR 12. Juliana la Rowere ib. 115. John le Rowere 1296 Inq 56. Will. le Rouer 1306 *Ass* 4. Hugo le Rower 1327 SR 42. — *St:* Rich. le Roher 1221 4.Ass 17. Rich. le Roer 1266 ib. 160. — *Y:* Hugh Roher 1329 FF 24. — *Sf:* Joh. le Rohier 1197 P 237.

OF *roier, rouwier, roer, rouer* 'fabricant de roues, charron' (Godefroy). — *Wheelwright.* — Cf CLB (C) p. 96 f., where it is said that the Commonalty of London owes a sum 'to Dyonisia la *Rowere*, for *wheels*' (1301).

Cf NED *rower* (1598) 'one who puts a nap on cloth'; the late appearance of this word does not make this explanation of the surname probable.

Whelmonger. 1332.   NED: —
Ess: Joh. Welmongher 1332 SR 20.

OE *hwēol* 'wheel' + *mangere*. — *One who sells wheels.*

Nawright. 1301. NED: —
Y: Adam Nawrith' 1301 SR 103. Rich. Nowright 1332 *SR* 4.

OE *nafu, nafa* 'nave' + *wyrhta*. ME *nave* seems also to have had the spelling *nove* (in *Nowright*), in which the *o* is due to the influence of *v;* cf ME *govel* (gavel), *novel* (navel), Jordan § 29. The *v* in the surname has been absorbed by the following *w*. — *Maker of naves* (the central part of a wheel).

Ploghwright. 1285. NED: 1285.
Ess: Ralph le Plouhwrihte 1334 CR 116. — *Y:* Rob. le Plogwryth 1285 1.Wake 195 (le Plogwricht 1307 2.Wake 78, le Ploghwrith 1309 ib. 192). Eudo .Plowryth' 1301 SR 90. — *Nf:* Joh. le Ploughwrighte 1316 *GDR* 33. Rob. le Plouwricte 1332 *SR* 71. Thom. le Plouwricthe ib. Alic. Plouwricthe ib. 73. Will. Plowrihte 1337 *SR* 1.

OE *plōh* + *wyrhta*. — *Maker of ploughs.*

Ploghbrocher. 1281. NED: —
Li: Will. ploghbrocher 1281 *2.Ass* 39.

ME *plogh* 'a plough' (OE *plōh*) + a der. of ME *broche* 'a tapering pointed instrument, a broach' (OF *broche*). — This surname seems to mean *a maker of ploughshares.* Cf Brochere.

D. Maker of Ships, Boats, Oars.

Shipwright, Skipwright. 1279. NED: c1000.
a. S h i p w r i g h t:
Ess: Phil. Shipwrighte 1319 *SR* 5. Ric. le Shipwrithe 1327 *SR* 2. Joh. le Shipwrighte 1332 *SR* 23. — *Sx:* Joh. Shipwerghte 1327 SR 137. Rog. le Shipwerghte 1332 SR 254. — *Ha:* Rog. Shipworghte 1327 *SR* 10. — *Y:* Joh. le schipwrith 1308 Free Y 12. — *Li:* Ric. Shipwreght' 1340 *Ass* 7. — *Nf:* Benedictus Le Schypwrytte 1286 *Ass* 68.

b. S k i p w r i g h t:
Y: Henr. le Skipwryghtte 1279 *Ass* 44 (le Skipewryhgte ib.). — *Nb:* Walt' le Skippewrytte 1279 Ass 397. Will' Skippewrytte ib.

OE *scipwyrhta*. The form *Skip-* in *Y* and *Nb* comes fr. ON *skip;* this word is not evidenced in NED. — *One who builds ships.*

Kelmaker. 1328. NED: —
Li: Eudo le Kelmaker 1328 *Ass* 13 (bis).

ME *kele* (fr. MDu *kiel* 'ship') + ME *maker*. — *Maker of 'keels'* (flat-bottomed vessels, lighters). — In the same county (and only in this) and at the same time I have found three instances of the surname *Keleman, Kelman* 'one who works on a keel or barge' (NED *keelman* 1516), e. g. Joh. Keleman 1328 *Ass* 6.

Botsmith. 1327. NED: —
Li: Ric. Bot'smith' 1327 *4.SR* 3.

OE *bāt* 'boat' + *smið*. — *A smith who makes metal fittings on boats*, or perhaps *a boat-builder*. Cf ON *Askasmiðr* (10th cent.) and *Knarrarsmiðr* both = 'ship-builder' (Lind).

Ankersmyth. 1329. NED: 1662.
Nf: Galfr. Ankersmyth 1329 *SR* 68. Joh. Ankelsmith ib.

OE *ancor* 'anchor' + *smið*. — *A smith who makes anchors*.

Orewright. 1332. NED: —
Nf: Ric. le Orewrycthe 1332 *SR* 45.

OE *ār* 'oar' + *wyrhta*. — *Maker of oars*.

Picher. 1243. NED: 1611.
So: Will. le Picher 1243 *Ass* 320. Will. Pycher 1320 *Ass* 26. — *Li:* Will. Picher 1327 *2.SR* 13. Rob. Picher 1332 *Ass* 11.

A der. of OE *(ge)pician* 'to pitch'. — *One who pitches, who covers or caulks with pitch* (NED).

E. Maker of Coffers, Boxes, Organs.

Coffrer. 1275. NED (c1330).
Ess: Ric. le Coffrer' 1285 *Ass* 5. — *So:* John le Cofrer 1275 *Ass* 21. Joh. Le Coffrer 1305 *Ass* 3. — *St:* Thom. le Cofrer 1327 SR 220.

OF *coffrier* 'faiseur de coffres' (Godefroy). — *Maker of coffers, boxes, chests*. — NED has *cofferer* (c1330) in the sense of 'treasurer', and this is, of course, also possible for the surname; cf, however, Bardsley (s. v. *Cofferer*): 'Pype-makers, wodemongers, and orgyn-makers, *Coferers*, carde-makers, and carvers'. Cocke Lorelle's Bote.

Whicchere. 1288. NED: —
Sx: Rob. Le Wiccher' 1288 *Ass* 7. Ric. le Wuchere 1296 SR 68 (Whychere 1327 SR 153). — *Ha:* Alic. la Whocchare 1327 *SR* 7. Margar. la Whocchare

ib. Rob. le Whicchere 1333 *SR* 3. — *So:* Ric. Le Wycher 1305 *Ass* 1. — *Wo:* Pet. Le Wycher 1327 SR 28.

A der. of OE *hwicce* 'chest'. — Signification: = WHICCHEWRIGHT.

Whicchewright. 1256. NED: —
So: Will. le Wycchewrichte 1256 FF 176.

OE *hwicce* 'chest' + *wyrhta*. — *Maker of 'whitches'* (chests, coffers, arks).

Kystewright. 1332. NED: —
Nf: Will. le kystewrycthe 1332 *SR* 39.

ME *kyste* (fr. ON *kista* or OE *cist*, the spelling of which may have been altered owing to ON influence) + ME *wright* (OE *wyrhta*). — *Maker of kists, coffers*.

Arkewright. 1246. NED: —
Ch: Thom. the Arkewrytte 1286 Court 225. — *La:* Gilb. de Arkewright 1246 Ass 40.

OE *arc* 'ark' + *wyrhta*. — *One who makes arks* (chests, bins).

Hucher. 1325. NED: —
Ha: Joh. le Huchere 1327 *SR* 14. — *La:* Alan le Hocher 1325 CR 106.

OF *huchier* 'menuisier' (Godefroy); cf ME *huche* 'chest' (NED 1303). — *Maker of hutches* (chests, coffers). — In SR 1292 for Paris there are 29 instances of *Huchier* (v. Géraud).

Escriner. 1280. NED: —
Ha: Ric. le Escriner 1280 *2.Ass* 21.

OF *escrinier* 'menuisier qui fait des écrins, des petits coffres' (Godefroy). — *One who makes boxes, coffers*.

Tabletter. 1281. NED: —
Lo: Pet. le Tableter 1281 CLB (B) 1. — *Nf:* Rich. le Tabletter 1333 CDN 177 (le Tableter 1336 ib. 197). — *Le:* Ric. Tableter 1318 RBL 312.

OF *tabletier* 'celui qui fait et vend des échiquiers, des damiers' (Littré). Godefroy has only the secondary sense 'porteballe, petit marchand'; cf Kusche p. 47. — *Maker of chess-boards, draught-boards, etc.*

Orgoner. 1332. NED: 1413.
Sr: Walt. le Organer 1332 SR 6. — *Nf:* Elena le Orgoner 1332 *SR* 45.

OF had *organier* as the title of a book on the organ, but prob. also in the ME sense. — *Organ-maker;* also *organ-player*.

11*

F. Turner, Maker of Spoons, Combs, Slays.

Turnour. 1199.   NED: c1400.
Ess: Rog. le Turnur 1255 *Ass* 27. Beatrix la Turnure 1285 *Ass* 48. Ric. le Turnur 1332 *SR* 13. — *Sx:* Steph. le Turnur 1222 FF 45. Will. le Turnur 1249 *Ass* 33. Thom. le Turnere 1317 *Ass* 50. — *Ha:* Will. le Turnur 1272 *Ass* 1. Maur. le Tornor 1333 *SR* 3. Joh. le Tornour 1340 *SR* 5. — *So:* Ralph le Tornur 1243 Ass 223. Nich. Le Turnour 1307 *Ass* 4. Joh. le Tornour 1333 *SR* 2. — *Wo:* Ernaldus le Tornur 1221 Ass 494. Maur. Le Turnur 1255 *Ass* 31. Will. Tourner 1327 SR 11. — *St:* Rob. le Turnur 1199 3.Ass 39. Ric. le Turnur 1327 SR 198. Ran. le Tornour 1332 SR 88. — *La:* Thom. le Turnur 1246 Ass 81. Adam le Turnur 1292 *1.Ass* 25. Joh. le Turnour 1338 *Ass* 7. — *Y:* Sim. le turnur 1230 P 279. Elyas le Turnur 1268 *Ass* 7. Will. le Turnour 1332 *SR* 6. — *Li:* Henr. le turnur 1219 Ass 116. Pet. le Turnur 1245 *Ass* 34. Thom. Le Turnur 1327 *2.SR* 11. — *Nf:* Rob. le Turnur 1286 *Ass* 94. Steph. le Turnur 1308 CDN 11. Joh. le Tornour 1332 *SR* 45.

OF *tornour, tourneour*. — *Turner, one who turns or fashions objects of wood, metal, bone, etc., on a lathe* (NED). — This name is of frequent occurrence in medieval rolls.

Keruere. 1275.   NED: c1380.
Sx: Will. Keruer 1327 SR 215. — *Ha:* Ric. le Keruere 1327 *SR* 17 (le Keruer 1340 *SR* 6). — *Li:* Ric. le Kerver 1275 RH 312, 325.

A der. of OE *ceorfan* 'to cut, carve'. — *Carver, one who carves wood, etc.* — I have found several early instances, spelt *Caruer, Charuer,* which might seem to belong here: Rob. le Caruer 1285 *Ass* 10 (Ess). Thom. le Charuer 1245 *Ass* 31 (Li). This is another surname, however, and comes fr. OF *charuier, caruier* 'ploughman'.

Sponere. 1179.   NED: c1515.
Wo: Thom. le Sponere 1221 Ass 587. — *St:* Will. le Sponere 1280 6.Ass 104. — *La:* Dobbe le Sponer 1292 *1.Ass* 10. Will. le Sponer' ib. 13. Cristiana le sponere ib. 33. Rog. le Sponer 1323 *Ass* 12. — *Y:* Rog. Lesponere 1179 P 23. Walt. le Sponer 1279 *Ass* 1. Nich. le Sponer ib. Ric. le Sponere 1293 *Ass* 40. Thom. Sponer 1301 SR 54. Will. the Sponer 1316 4.Wake 145. Rob. le Sponer c1346 *SR* 6. Adam Sponer ib. 11. Will. le Sponer ib. 3. — *Nf:* Pet. le Sponere 1286 *Ass* 140. Ralph le Sponere 1295 CDN 56. John de Blitheburgh le Sponer 1331 CDN 164.

A der. of OE *spōn* 'chip, splinter'. — *Maker of spoons*. The exact signification of this surname during this early period (first inst. as early as 1179) is not certain. *Spoon* is recorded in NED in its modern sense fr. c1340; the earliest sense was 'chip, splinter', and fr. 1316—7 NED has the sense of 'roofing-shingle'. It is therefore possible that *Sponere* originally meant 'one who makes shingles' or perhaps 'one who covers roofs with shingles'. It is noteworthy that this surname has not been found in the South of England. Cf ON *spánn* 'splinter, shingle, spoon'.

Ladeler. 1284. NED: (1643).
Ch: Rob. the Ladelere 1286 Court 221. — *Y:* Hugh the Ladeler 1285 1.Wake 205 (le Ladeler ib. 206, le Ladelere 1293 *Ass* 33). — *Li:* Ric. Ladeler 1332 *3.SR* 25.

A der. of OE *hlædel* 'ladle'. — *Maker of ladles.*

Cuillerer. 1214. NED: —
Sx: Rad. le Cuillerer 1214 FF 35.

OF *cuillerier* 'fabricant de cuillers' (Godefroy). — *Maker of spoons.*

Peniur. 1275. NED: —
Bk: Joh. le Peynur 1279 RH 347. — *Li:* Eborardus Penier 1275 RH 314. — *Nf:* Thom. le Peniur 1275 RH 505.

OF *peigneor* and *peignier* 'fabricant de peignes' (Godefroy). — *Maker of combs.*

Hornere. 1275. NED: 1421—2.
Ha: Henr. le Hornere 1333 *SR* 8. Ric. le Horner 1340 *SR* 7. — *So:* Ric. le Hornere 1307 *Ass* 8. — *Wo:* Will. le Hornare 1275 *SR* 1. Joh. le Horner' 1307 *Ass* 5. Adam le Hornere 1337 OCW 45. — *St:* John le Hornere 1341 14.*Ass* 57. — *La:* Ric. Le Hornhere 1292 *2.Ass* 37. — *Y:* Cecil' le Hornere 1293 *Ass* 66. Walt. Horner 1301 SR 28. Ric. le horner, pistor 1310 Free Y 13. Adam le Horner c1346 *SR* 9. — *Li:* Will. le Horner 1281 *1.Ass* 35 (le Hornnere 1281 *2.Ass* 35). Godefr. Horner 1328 *Ass* 3. — *Nf:* Walt. le Hornere 1315 CDN 61. John le Horner 1329 ib. 147.

A der. of OE *horn*. — *Maker of horn spoons, combs, etc.*; also *a horn-blower.*

Slaywright. 1250. NED: —
Ess: Henr. le Sleywrithe 1327 *SR* 16 (le Sleyghwrithe Dupl. 15). Rob. le Sleywrihte 1334 CR 130. — *So:* Reg. Sleywryght' 1327 *SR* 30. — Nf: Walt. le slegwrechte 1250 *Ass* 28. Joh. Le Sleywrycht 1286 *Ass* 90. Will. le Sclaywryhte ib. 99. Nich. le Slaywrite ib.

OE *slege* 'slay, stroke' + *wyrhta*. — *Maker of slays* (an instrument used in weaving). Cf Joh. Whyt, *slaymaker* 1389 Free Y 89.

Slayare. 1311. NED: (1881).
Ess: Will. Slayare 1311 CR 39.

Prob. a der. of OE *slege* 'slay, stroke'. — Signification: = SLAY-WRIGHT. — I have found two instances of another surname, *Slayman*, which seems to have the same signification: Henr. Slayman 1279 RH 412 (Ca). Thom. Slayman 1383 CLB (H) 227 (Lo).

Spyndeler. 1236. NED: —
Lo: John Spyndeler 1369 CLB (G) 243. — *Sx:* Will. le Spinlere 1236 FF 87.

A der. of OE *spinel* 'a spindle'. — *One who makes spindles* (a spinning instrument).

G. **Cooper, Hooper.**

Coupere. 1181. NED: c1415.
Ess: Will. le Copere 1255 *Ass* 23. Ric. le Cupere 1285 *Ass* 28. Galfr. le Cuppere 1319 *SR* 10. Alic. le Couper 1319 *SR* 17. Walt. Le Couper 1341 *Ass* 22. — *Sx:* Rad. le Cupere 1249 *Ass* 26. Joceus le cupere 1296 SR 17. Thom' le Copere 1327 SR 114. Henr' le Coupere ib. 141. Reg. le Cupere 1332 SR 289. — *Ha:* Rob. le Cupere 1200 P 201. Ric. le Cupare 1280 *2..Ass* 21. Henr. le Copere ib. 69. Eua la Coupere 1327 *SR* 9. Steph. le Coupare 1333 *SR* 2. — *So:* Joh. Le Coppere 1307 *Ass* 4. Will. le Cuppare 1333 *SR* 16. Henr. le Coupere ib. 17. — *Wo:* Will. Couper 1270 Hal 2. Adam le Cupere 1275 SR 49. Joh. Copere ib. 58. Thom. Le Coupar 1327 SR 65. Sim. le Couper 1332 SR 11. — *St:* Nich. le Couper 1276 RH 116. Gilb. le Cupere 1300 7.Ass 66. Rob. le Coupere 1327 SR 226. Ric. le Coupere 1332 SR 93. — *La:* Henr. le Cupere 1292 *1.Ass* 31. Rog. le Couper 1323 *Ass* 25. Joh. le Couper 1334 ib. 17. — *Y:* Emma le Cupere 1260 Ass 100. Rog. le Cupere 1268 *Ass* 46. Pet. le Coupere 1293 *Ass* 43. Will. le coupper 1295 Free Y 6. Will. le Couper c1346 *SR* 5. — *Li:* Sim. Le Cupere 1231 FF 236. Gregor' le Cuper 1305 *Ass* 16 (le Couper ib.). Joh. Couper 1327 *2.SR* 9. Thom. Le Coper ib. 25. Amisia le Couper 1332 *2.SR* 7. — *Nf:* Selide le Copere 1181 P 91 (le Cupere 1182 P 72). Rog. le Copere 1250 *Ass* 25. Edm. le Coupere 1286 *Ass* 39. Rog. koppere 1329 *SR* 38. Joh. Cupper' 1332 *SR* 48. Ric. le Cupere ib. 60.

Origin not certain; prob. fr. med. L *cuparius, cuperius* 'cooper'; cf MDu *cuper*. — *Maker or seller of casks, buckets, and tubs.*

Sometimes the spellings *Coppere, Cuppere* occur; these may also be derived from ON *koppari* 'a maker of cups or small vessels'. According to Lindkvist (Anglia 50, p. 371) this ON word is the first element of the following street-name in York: *Coppergate* (1120—35, 1337), *Cuppergate* 12th cent., *Cupergate* c1300; now *Coppergate*. — Cf Joh. de Kendale, *copper* 1296 Free Y 6.

Though not evidenced in NED until c1415, *Coupere* occurs very frequently during this early period.

Cuppestere. 1280.   NED: —
Ha: Johanna la Cuppestere 1280 *3.Ass* 35. — *Wo:* Walt. Le Coppester 1327 SR 43.

The fem. form of COUPERE (*Cupere*). — Signification: = COUPERE.

Keuer. 1292.   NED: —
La: Reynerus le Keuere 1292 *1.Ass* 6 (Le Kevere 1292 *2.Ass* 8). Rich. le Keuer 1324 CR 13, 1325 ib. 144, 145.

A der. of OE $c\bar{y}f$ 'tub'; v. NED *keeve, kive*; the latter form represents the regular development of the OE form; the other form, which apparently forms part of the surname, is a dialectal development: $\bar{y} > \bar{e}$. This change has sometimes taken place in *WMl*, e. g. in *Meaford, St, Metford, Db*, both fr. OE *gemȳþu* 'junction of streams' (Ekwall, Lectures). — *Maker or seller of tubs.*

Cuver. 1250.   NED: —
Sx: Will. le Cuuiar' 1332 SR 231. Joh. Cuuer ib. 318. — *Nf:* Alex. le Cuuyer 1250 *Ass* 12 (bis). Will. le Cuver 1289 CDN 27.

A der. of ME *cuve* 'cask, vat' (fr. OF *cuve*), or OF **cuvier*; cf OF *cuvelier* 'cooper', fr. *cuvele* 'small cask'. — *Cooper.*

Tuneler. 1334.   NED: —
Y: Galfr. le thuneler 1334 Free Y 29.
OF *tonnelier*. — *Cooper.*

Hopere, Hoppere. 1228.   NED: 1552.
Ess: Salom' le Hoppere 1255 *Ass* 33. Joh. le Hoppere 1285 *Ass* 43. Will. le Hoppere 1332 *SR* 21. — *Sx:* Joh. le Hoppere 1249 *Ass* 22. Maur' le Hoppere 1296 SR 30. Ric. Hoper 1332 SR 295. — *Ha:* Henr. le Hoppere 1272 *Ass* 7. Joh. le Hopere 1280 *2.Ass* 83. Nigellus le Hoppare 1327 *SR* 1. — *So:* Godfrey le Hopere 1228 FF 71. Adam le Hopere 1277 Ass 101. Ric.

Le Hoppere 1305 *Ass* 4 (Le Hoper' ib.). Will. le Houpere 1320 *Ass* 20. Lucas le Houpere 1327 SR 249. Henr. le Hopere 1333 *SR* 4. Joh. le Opare ib. 31. — *Wo:* Gilb. le Hopere 1275 SR 5. Hawisia la Hopere ib. 20. Nich. le Hopere 1306 *Ass* 3. Hugh le Hoper 1317 OCW 45. Henr. le Hoppar 1332 SR 9. — *La:* Hugo le Hoppere 1292 *1.Ass* 18. — *Y:* Ralph le Hoppere 1251 Ass 62. Nigellus le Hopper c1346 *SR* 8. — *Li:* Rob. le Hoppere 1245 *Ass* 48. Walt. Hoper 1327 *2 SR* 7. Will. Hoper ib. — *Nf:* Sim. le hoppere 1286 *Ass* 111. Beatrix le Hoppere 1295 *GDR* 9. Walt. Hoper' 1332 *SR* 74.

A der. of OE *hōp* 'hoop'. — *Maker of hoops, cooper*.

The form spelt *Hoppere* is most common in all counties, except in *So*, where *Hopere* occurs very frequently (I have recorded 55 instances there, but only 3 *Hoppere*). *Hoppere* may also mean 'leaper, dancer' (NED c1375); cf the fem. form *hoppestere* 'female dancer', which already occurs in OE. — Some instances of this surname may be explained as toponymical surnames, v. p. 198.

The first element of the pl. n. *Hopperton* (*Hopretone* DB, *Hoperton*' 1203 FF) is explained by Prof. Ekwall (Trades in Engl. Pl. N.) as OE **hōpere* 'hooper'.

Payler. c1296—7. NED: —

Wo: Ralph le Payller c1296—7 OCW 17. Nich. le Payler, undated, ib. (the Paillare, undated, OCW 139).

A der. of ME *payle, paille* 'a pail' (of uncertain origin). — *Maker or seller of pails*.

Kittewright. 1275. NED: —

Y: Ric. le Kittewritt' 1275 1.Wake 38.

ME *kitt(e)* (fr. MDu *kitte* 'a wooden vessel made of hooped staves') + *wright* (OE *wyrhta*). — *Maker of kits* (tubs, milking-pails).

Tunwright. 1246. NED: —

La: Hugh le Tunewrith 1246 Ass 106. Will. le Tonwright 1324 CR 9 (de Tunwright ib. 142). — *Y:* Thom. le Tunwrith' 1279 *Ass* 78.

OE *tunne* 'a tun' + *wyrhta*. — *Maker of tuns*.

Tunnere. 1280. NED: —

Ha: Will. le Tunnere 1280 *2.Ass* 37 (le Tuniere 1280 *1.Ass* 24). Rob. le Tonnere 1327 *SR* 6. — *So:* Walkelinus Tonere 1333 *SR* 17. Will. le Tonyer ib. 31. Rob. le Tunare 1344 *Ass* 6. Walt. le Tonnare ib. 5.

A der. of OE *tunne* 'a tun'. — Prob. = TUNWRIGHT.

Tankarder. 1319. NED: —
Ess: Rob. Tankarder 1319 *SR* 3. — *Sr:* Joh. Tankarder 1332 SR 25. Walt. tankarder ib.

A der. of ME *tankard* 'a large tub-like vessel used for carrying water, etc.' (= MDu *tanckaert*). — *One who makes or sells 'tankards' or tubs.*

Meysemakere. 1332. NED: —
Nf: Vyncent' Meysemakere 1332 *SR* 45.

ME *meise* fr. OF *meise* 'barrel for herrings' + ME *makere*. — *Maker of 'meases'*, here evidently in the OF sense, which is not recorded in *NED* (v. *mease*, 1469, 'a measure for herrings').

H. Maker of Baskets or Sieves.

Skepper. 1281. NED: 1499.
Li: Walt. le Skeppere 1281 *1.Ass* 20. Hugo le Skepher 1327 *3.SR* 1 (le Skepper 1332 *3.SR* 25). Rad. le Skepher 1327 *3.SR* 1. Rog. le Skepper 1328 *Ass* 47. Ric. Skepper 1329 *GDR* 2. — *Nf:* Joh. Skepper 1332 *SR* 48.

A der. of ON *skeppa* 'basket, bushel'. — *A maker of skeps or baskets.*

Busseler. 1243. NED: —
So: Rich. le Busselar 1243 Ass 282. — *Li:* Pet. Boseler 1305 *Ass* 9.

OF *boisselier* 'fabricant de boisseaux' (Godefroy). — *Maker of vessels (baskets) holding a bushel.*

Lepmaker. 1338. NED: 1360—1.
Nf: John le Lepmaker 1338 CDN 215.

OE *lēap* 'basket' + a der. of *macian*. — *Maker of baskets.*

Paniermaker. 1310. NED: 1472.
Ess: Rad. le Paniermakier' 1310 *4.GDR* 1.

ME *panier* 'a basket' (OF *paniere*) + ME *maker*. — *Maker o panniers.*

Corbiller. 1225. NED: —
So: Rob. Corbiller 1225 Ass 45.

OF *corbeillier* 'Korbmacher' (Tobler); Godefroy has only *cor beilleor*. — *Maker of baskets.*

Siuyere. 1275.   NED: c1440.

Ess: Walt. le Syuiere 1283 *1.GDR* 8. Will. Le Syuier 1300 *2.GDR* 10. Thom. le Siuyere 1312 CR 72. — *Sx:* Rob. le Syuyer 1327 SR 133 (le Seuyar 1332 SR 246). Ric. le Suwyar 1332 SR 230. Rog. Suuyer ib. 307. — *Ha:* Rob. le Suuyere 1327 *SR* 7. Walt. le Seuyare ib. 10. Relicta le Seuyare ib. 8. Joh. le Suuyere 1333 *SR* 1. Math. le Syuiere ib. 2. Will. le Syuyere ib. — *So:* Rich. Le Syuier 1305 *Ass* 13. Rob. Le Syuyer' ib. (Le Syueare ib. 10). Ric. le Suuiare 1344 *Ass* 8. — *Wo:* Gena la Siuegar 1275 *2.Ass* 40. — *St:* Laur. Le Siuiger 1308 *GDR* 2. — *Y:* Rob. le Siuyer 1305 *Ass.* — *Li:* Sim. le Siuier 1281 *1.Ass* 33.

A der. of OE *sife* 'sieve'. Some forms with *-u-* (*Suuyer*) occur in *Ha, Sx,* and *So*; NED has no such spelling of *sieve*. — *Sieve-maker.*

Syvewright. 1301.   NED: —

Y: Laur. Syffewrythe 1301 SR 48. Will. Syffewryth' ib. 77. Joh. le Syvewryct' ib. 85. Gilb. Syuewryct' ib. 23.

OE *sife* 'sieve' + *wyrhta*. — *Maker of sieves.*

Syveman. 1298.   NED: —

Y: Rich. le Syveman 1298 2.Wake 32 (the Syveman ib. 38).

OE *sife* 'sieve' + *mann*. — Prob. = SIUYERE, but the signification may also be 'one who uses a sieve'.

I. Maker of Hurdles or Palings.

Hirdler. 1279.   NED: 1874.

Ess: Christina la Herdler 1334 CR 129 (Cristina Herdler 1346 ib. 214). — *Nf:* Henr. le Hirdler' 1332 *SR* 70 (H. Horn le hirdeler 1332 CDN 167). — *Ca:* Gilb. le Herdlere 1279 RH 426.

A der. of OE *hyrdel* 'hurdle'. — *Hurdle-maker.*

Flekewynder. 1327.   NED: —

Li: Joh. Flekewynder 1327 *4.SR* 7 (le Flekewynder 1328 *Ass* 60, Flekewinder ib.).

ME *fleke* 'flake' (prob. fr. ON *flake, fleke* 'hurdle') + ME *windere* (fr. OE *windan*). — *One who makes flakes, wattled hurdles.*

Flekeman. 1292.   NED: —

La: Rob. le Flekeman 1292 *1.Ass* 18.

ME *fleke* 'flake' (v. above) + ME *man*. — Signification: = FLEKEWYNDER.

Paleser. 1315. NED: [1368—9].
Y: Rog. Paleser 1315 4.Wake 39. Henr. Bryg al(ia)s Palaser 1414 Free Y 122.

A der. of OF *palis, paleis* 'palissade'. — *Maker of palings or fences.*

J. Maker of Spades or Besoms.

Spadere. 1332. NED: (1647).
Ess: John le Spadere 1336 CR 139. — *Sr:* Joh. Spadier' 1332 SR 93.

A der. of OE *spadu, spade,* or *spada* 'spade'. — Prob. *a maker of spades.* Cf NED *spader.*

Besmere. 1263. NED: —
Sx: Joh. le Besmere 1263 *Ass* 46 (Le Besmere 1288 *Ass* 21).

A der. of OE *besma* 'besom'. — *Maker of besoms.* — Cf MG *besemer* 'Besenmacher' (Bücher).

Burstlere. 1319. NED: —
Ess: Will. le Bustler' 1319 *SR* 21. Rob. Le Burstelere 1327 *SR* 14 (le Burstelere 1341 *Ass* 9, le Bustler ib. 4, le Burstlere ib.).

A der. of ME *brustel, burstyll,* etc. (perh. fr. OE **brystl*); v. NED *bristle* sb. — Prob. *one who makes brushes of bristles.*

K. Maker of Charcoal, Potash, Tinder.

Coliere. 1172. NED: c1350.
Ess: Galfr. le Coliere 1255 *Ass* 27. Rob. le Coyler' 1319 *SR* 13. Will. Le Coliere 1327 *SR* 9. — *Sx:* Henr. le Colier 1249 *Ass* 28. Galfr. le Kolyhere 1296 SR 75. Clemens le Coliar 1332 SR 227. — *Ha:* Walt. le Coliere 1272 *Ass* 13. Pet. le Colyare 1327 *SR* 7. Will. le Colyere 1333 *SR* 1. — *So:* Bernardus le Coliere 1172 P 72. Andr' Le Coliere 1307 *Ass* 8. Sim. le Coliar' 1333 *SR* 31. — *Wo:* Rad. le Colier' 1275 *1.Ass* 6. Will. le Collier' 1275 SR 59. Ric. Le Colier 1327 SR 4. — *St:* Rich. le Colyere 1261 4.*Ass* 148. Ric. le Colyere 1327 *SR* 216. — *La:* Ad. le Coylyer 1292 *1.Ass* 10. Joh. le Colier 1334 *Ass* 18. — *Y:* Rob. le Coliere 1268 *Ass* 42. Agnes le Colier 1297 1.Wake 262. Rog. Colyer 1332 *SR* 19. — *Li:* Rob. Colyer 1281 *2.Ass* 35. Rad. le Colier 1340 *Ass* 21.

A der. of OE *col* 'coal'. — *Maker of wood charcoal; charcoal seller.* — This surname occurs frequently in all counties, except in

Nf, where I have found no instance; in this county, however, there occur many instances of a similar surname, *Culyour, Colyour* (e. g. Rich. le Culyour 1291 CDN 42), but this is apparently of French origin (OF *cueilleor* 'tax-collector').

Carboner. 1275.   NED: —
So: John le Carboner 1277 Ass 101. — *Wo:* Adam le Carboner 1275 SR 45. Ric. le Carboner ib.

AF **carbonner,* OF *charbonnier* 'celui qui fait ou vend du charbon' (Godefroy). — *Maker or seller of charcoal.*

Askebrenner. 1278.   NED: —
Sx: Thom. Asborner 1332 SR 295. — *La:* Rob. le Eskebrenner 1278 Ass 171. — *Y:* Hugo le Askebrennere 1279 *Ass* 58. Will. the Askebrenner 1308 2.Wake 161. John Askebrenner 1309 ib. 201. Rich. le Askebrenner ib. 210. Adam le Askebrenner ib. 211. — *Cu:* Rich. Askbrinner 1332 SR 29. Rob. Askbrinner ib.

ON *aska* 'ashes' + a der. of ON *brenna* or OE *brinnan* 'to burn'. — The *Sx* form is native: OE *asce* + a der. of *beornan.* It is not certain, however, that this instance belongs here; it may very well be a toponymical surname, derived from the river *Ashburn Sx.* — *Maker of potash.*

Potash was made from the ashes of wood, bushes, weeds, or straw, and an important process in the manufacture was the burning of these ashes, hence the origin of the surname. For a detailed description of the making of potash, v. VH Ess vol. II p. 372—5.

Dethewright. 1299.   NED: —
Ess: Joh. le Dethewright' 1299 *2.GDR* 8 (Le Dedewrithe 1327 *SR* 19, le Dedewrighte Dupl.).

OE *dȳð* 'fuel, tinder' + *wyrhta;* the first element has only been found in OE. — The signification of this surname seems to be *one who makes tinder.*

Turber. 1219.   NED: —
Li: Bonifacius le Turber 1219 Ass 354.

OF *tourbier* 'celui qui extrait, qui prépare la tourbe' (Godefroy). — *One who makes peat.*

CHAPTER VII.

MASONRY AND ROOFING WORKERS.

A. Mason, Plasterer, Painter.

Mason. 1170. NED: c1205.
 Ess: Walt. le Masun 1274 RH 162. Nich. le Masoun 1319 *SR* 17. Will. le Machoun 1327 *SR* 5. Wm. le Maschaun 1334 CR 121. — *Sx:* Rob. le macun 1249 *Ass* 2. Galfr. le Mazun 1263 *Ass* 29. Ric. Machun 1296 SR 4. Henr' le Masson 1332 SR 322. — *Ha:* Adam le Mazun 1272 *Ass* 5. Henr. Le Maschun 1305 *Ass* 11. Rob. le Masson 1327 *SR* 3. Joh. le Machon 1333 *SR* 4. — *So:* Rich. le Mazun 1243 Ass 138. Math. Le Mazoun 1307 *Ass* 6. Will. le Machon 1333 *SR* 1. Joh. le Macoun 1344 *Ass* 13. — *De:* Ric. le Macun 1170 P 102. — *Wo:* Joh. le maszun 1221 Ass 642. Nich. Le Mazun 1275 *1.Ass* 18. Thom. Le Mason 1327 SR 40. — *St:* Thom. le Mazun 1227 *4.Ass* 53. Alan. le Machun 1308 *GDR* 2. Adam le Masun 1327 SR 239. — *La:* Henry le Mazun 1246 Ass 75. Thom. le Machun 1292 *1.Ass* 23. Hankin le Masoun 1332 SR 55. — *Y:* Walt. le Mazun 1251 Ass 65. Thom. le Masoune 1301 SR 14. Sim. le Mazon ib. 119. Joh. le Mazon c1346 *SR* 2. — *Li:* Walt. le Macun 1202 FF 43. Hugo le Mazun 1245 *Ass* 20. Ric. Le Machun 1327 *1.SR* 7. Joh. le Mazoun 1332 *3.SR* 4. — *Nf:* John le Maschun 1285 CDN 1. Rog. le Mazoun 1286 *Ass* 9. Thom. le mason 1329 *SR* 2. Symon le Mazon 1332 *SR* 43.

 ONF *machun,* or cent. OF *masson, maçon.* — *Mason.* — This surname is very common in medieval rolls. — Cf Rad. de Holdernesse, *rughmason* 1379 Free Y 78 'a mason building only with unhewn stone' (NED 1444).

Wallere. 1221. NED: c1440.
 Ess: Ric. Le Wallere 1327 *SR* 5. Edm. le Wallere 1341 *Ass* 16. — *Sx:* Adam le Wallere 1325 *Ass* 14. Rob. le Waller' ib. Will. Waller 1332 SR 278. — *Ha:* Adam le Walere 1280 *2.Ass* 73. — *So:* Walt. le Waller 1327 SR 203 (le Wallere 1333 *SR* 8). — *Wo:* Joh. le Waller' 1221 Ass 540. — *Y:* Thom. le Wallere 1268 *Ass* 34. Will. Waller 1332 *SR* 7. — *Li:* Rad. Waller 1332 *3.SR* 24. — *Nf:* Joh. Waller 1332 *SR* 52.

 A der. of ME *walle* 'to furnish with walls' (OE **weallian*). — Signification: = WALMAKERE.

Walmakere. 1286.　　　　　　　　　　　　　　　　NED: —
Nf: Alan. Le Walmakere 1286 *Ass* 110.

OE *wall, weall* 'a wall' + a der. of *macian*. Cf OE *weallwyrhta* 'mason'. — *One who builds walls.*

Plastrer. 1281.　　　　　　　　　　　　　　　　NED: 1393.
Sx: Joh. le Plastrere 1322 *Ass* 30. Nich. le Plastrer 1327 SR 134. Will. le Plastrer ib. — *Ha:* Pet. le Plastrer 1333 SR 8, 1340 SR 6. — *Y:* Hugo le Playstrer 1293 *Ass* 103. Henr. le Plastrur 1305 *Ass* 13. — *Li:* Benedict. le Plastrer' 1281 *1.Ass* 7. Reg. le Plasterer 1328 *Ass* 59.

OF *plastrier* 'plasterer'. — *Plasterer, one who plasters buildings.*

Dauber. 1263.　　　　　　　　　　　　　　　　NED: [c1300].
Ess: Ric. le Daubere 1285 *Ass* 48. Walt. Dobere 1319 *SR* 9 (le Daubere 1327 *SR* 3). Math. le Dober' 1319 *SR* 13. Joh. Daubere 1320 *2.GDR* 33. Joseph Douber 1346 CR 204. — *Sx:* Joh. le Daubour 1263 *Ass* 26. Petr' le Dober' 1296 SR 47. Will. le Dobur ib. 81. Pet. le Daber 1332 SR 291. Rog. le Daber ib. Rob. Daubur ib. 226. — *So:* Will. le Daubor 1333 *SR* 17. Will. le Daubour 1344 *Ass* 16. — *Wo:* Rich. the daubour 1305 OCW 113. — *St:* Will. le Daubor 1327 SR 223. — *La:* Galfr. Dauber 1292 *1.Ass* 46. Henr. le Daubere ib. 43. Adam le Dauber 1326 CR 75. Will. le Dauber 1334 *Ass* 18. — *Y:* Will. le Daubur 1268 *Ass* 24. Alan. le Daubere 1293 ib. Adam le Douber 1301 SR 106. Ad. le Daubour 1305 *Ass* 10. Thom. Douber 1332 *1.SR* 18. — *Li:* Rad. le Daubur 1281 *1.Ass* 26. Rob. Dauber' 1327 *1.SR* 8. Ric. le Dauber' 1332 *2.SR* 9. — *Nf:* Joh. le Daubur 1286 *Ass* 115. Joh. Daubur 1329 *SR* 66. Walt. Le Dauber' 1332 *SR* 42.

AF *daubour* (med. L *daubator* 'whitewasher, plasterer'); OF **daubier* or a later der. of the verb, OF *dauber* 'to whitewash, plaster'. — *Dauber, plasterer.*

Gyssere. 1333.　　　　　　　　　　　　　　　　NED: —
Ha: Alicia la Gyssere 1333 *SR* 4.

OF *gippier, gissier* 'celui qui fait des ouvrages de maçonnerie avec le gypse' (Godefroy). — *Gypsum worker, plasterer.*

Chalkere. 1275.　　　　　　　　　　　　　　　　NED: (1865).
Ess: Rob. le Chalkere 1292 *2.GDR* 2. — *Wi:* Thom. le Chalker 1275 RH 242. — *Y:* Rob. Chalker 1297 SR 123. Will. Chalker ib.

A der. of OE *(ge)cœlcian* 'to whiten'; only found in OE. — *One who whitewashes.*

Whytere. 1280. NED: —
Ess: Andrew le Whytere 1310 CR 11 (Andr. le Whyter' 1315 *3.GDR* 31).
Rich. le Wyter 1310 CR 14. John Whyter 1346 CR 206. — *Sx:* Ric. Whiter
1327 SR 127. — *So:* Thom. le Whittere 1320 *Ass* 13 (le *Whitter'* ib., le
Whittere ib. 2). — *Wo:* Joh. le Wytere 1275 SR 88.

A der. of OE *hwītian* 'to become or make white'. — *One who whitewashes*; perhaps also *a bleacher*.

Peyntour. 1240. NED: 1340.
Ess: Henr. le Peyntur 1303 *2.GDR* 13. Cristiana le Peyntour 1319 *SR* 1.
Joh. le Peyntour 1341 *Ass* 8. — *Sx:* Cristian Peyntur 1296 SR 22. Steph.
le Peyntour 1327 SR 183. — *Ha:* Joh. le Peyntur 1280 *2.Ass* 63. Will. le
Payntour 1327 *SR* 4. — *So:* Rad. Le Peyntour 1320 *Ass* 8 (le Peyngtour
ib. 11). — *Wo:* Will. Peynter 1302 Hal 448. Thom. Le Peyngtour 1305 *Ass* 3.
Ric. le Peyntur 1306 Hal 529. Joh. Le Peyntr' 1327 SR 35. — *St:* Thom.
le Peyntour 1306 7.Ass 165. — *La:* Margeria le Peintour 1292 *3.Ass* 109. —
Y: Rich. the Paintur 1240 FF 87. Alicia le Peyntur 1293 *Ass* 24. Alex. le
payntour 1350 Free Y 45. — *Li:* Joh. le Peyntur 1245 *Ass* 28. Will. le
Penntur' 1281 *1.Ass* 22. Joh. Le Paintoure 1327 *2.SR* 15. Henr. le Peyntour
1328 *Ass* 11. Rob. le Peyntour 1332 *3.SR* 25. Eua Payntour 1340 *Ass* 7. —
Nf: Pet. Le Peyntur 1286 *Ass* 104. Rog. le Peyntour 1308 CDN 4. Rad. le
Peyntour 1332 *SR* 57.

AF *peintour*, OF *peintour, -tor*. — *Painter*.

B. Thatcher, Tiler, Slater.

Couerour. 1225. NED: 1393.
Ess: Joh. le Cuuerour 1285 *Ass* 36. Ric. Le Couerour 1327 *SR* 6. Rog.
le Couerour 1337 CR 154. — *Sx:* Will. le Couerur 1225 FF 52. Math. le
Coueur 1288 *Ass* 36. Steph. Coureour 1327 SR 134. — *Ha:* Rob. le Cuuerur
1272 *Ass* 25. Joh. le Couerur 1280 *2.Ass* 51. Ric. le Coueror 1280 *3.Ass* 38.
— *Wo:* Will. le Coverur 1275 SR 14. Hugo Le Couerour 1307 *Ass* 4. —
La: Rog. le Cuuerur 1246 Ass 77. — *Y:* Geoffrey le Cuverur 1260 Ass 88.
Rad. le Couerur 1268 *Ass* 29. Rob. le Couerur 1279 *Ass* 73. Thom. le
Coverur 1298 2.Wake 51. — *Li:* Wido le Couerour 1287 *Ass* 5. — *Nf:* Pet.
le coueur 1250 *Ass* 13. Joh. Le Couerur 1286 *Ass* 91.

OF *couvreor, cov-* 'ouvrier qui fait les couvertures, les toits des maisons' (Godefroy). — *One who covers or roofs buildings*. — Common as a trade-name in Free Y, e. g. Rob. de Duffeld, *couvereour* 1382 p. 80.

Thecchere. 1275. NED: c1440.

Ess: John le Thecetere 1311 CR 37. Gilb. le Thecchere 1312 CR 69. Galfr. le Thechere 1324 *3.GDR* 18. Walt. le Theccher' 1327 *SR* 16. Will. le Thecchere 1332 *SR* 20. — *Sx:* Will. Thechere 1279 *Ass* 12. Rog' le Theccher 1327 SR 140. Ric. le Thecher ib. 154. Rob. le Thecchar 1332 SR 230. Rad. le Thecchar ib. 240. — *Ha:* Thom. le Thecchere 1327 *SR* 11. Walt. le Thecchare ib. 5. Joh. le Thechere 1333 *SR* 3. Henr. le Thechere ib. 4. Ad. le Thecchere ib. 5. — *So:* Ric. Thecchar' 1307 *Ass* 4. Phil. le Thetcher 1327 SR 135. Joh. Theccher' 1333 *SR* 15. Thom. le Thechere 1344 *Ass* 14. Rad. le Thechere 1345 BBA 101. — *Wo:* Joh. le Thacchere 1275 SR 65. Nich. Thecchere 1306 *Ass* 2. Rog. Le Thacher 1327 SR 2. Ric. Le Thacher ib. 13. Joh. Le Thacher ib. 21. — *St:* Will. le Thatchere 1327 SR 236. — *Li:* Thom. le Thacchere 1328 *Ass* 3. — *Nf:* Nich. le thacherer 1286 *Ass* 28. Rob. le Thechere ib. 41.

A der. of OE *peccan* 'to cover', later 'to thatch'. The form *Thachere*, which corresponds to the modern form, seems to be Anglian; I have not found any such instance in *Ess, Sx, Ha,* and *So.* — *Thatcher, one who thatches houses* (with thatch or other material). — This surname belongs chiefly to the South of England, where it is common; it does not occur at all in the North. Cf THEKER and THACKER.

Thacker. 1316. NED: 1420.

La: Ric. le Thakker 1332 *Ass* 14. — *Y:* Rich. the Thaker 1316 4.Wake 60. — *Li:* Will. Le Thaker 1327 *1.SR* 1. Rad. Thaker 1328 *Ass* 3 (Thacker ib.). Gilb. le Thakkere ib. 47. Galfr. le Thakkere ib. Thom. Thacker' 1332 *1.SR* 8. Ran. Thaker 1332 *3.SR* 16.

Prob. OE **pæccere* fr. *pacian* 'to thatch'. — *One who covers roofs with thatch, a thatcher* (NED).

Thakestere. 1295. NED: c1340.

Nf: Elena la Thakestere 1295 *GDR* 6. Rad. Thakestere 1329 *SR* 10. Henr. le Thakestere 1332 *SR* 39. Rob. Thakster' ib. 47. Rog. Thakester' ib. 73. Joh. Taxther ib. 72.

The fem. form of THACKER. — Signification: = THACKER.

Theker. 1199. NED: 14..

St: Walt. filius Thecker 1199 *Ass* 35. — *Y:* Joh. le Theker 1293 *Ass* 53 (le Theckere ib. 72). Will. le Theker 1297 SR 50. Ralph the Theker 1313 *3.Wake* 5. Gilb. the Theker 1315 *4.Wake* 22. Matilda the Theker 1316 *4.Wake* 134. Thom. the Theker ib. 151. Maud the Theker 1317 ib. 193. — *Li:* Rob. le Thekere 1281 *2.Ass* 18. Alex. Theker 1327 *2.SR* 14. Matild. Theker ib. 16. Ran. Theker ib. 10. Anabill. thekker' 1327 *4.SR* 10. Rob. Le Theker 1327 *1.SR* 3. Gilb. Thecker 1332 *1.SR* 5. Lina Theckere ib. 18.

A der. of ON *pekja* 'to cover'. Cf NED *theek* vb. — *One who roofs buildings* (with various materials).

Streulegger. 1260. NED: —
Y: Nich. le Streulegger'¹ 1260 Ass 137.

OE *strēaw* 'straw' + a der. of *lecgan* 'to lay'. — *One who thatches houses with straw.* — Cf NED: *layer* 1382 (spelt *legger, leier* at this time) 'one who lays stones, a mason'. This is evidently the right explanation of the following surname: Rich. *Leggere* de Croydone 1377 CLB (H) 72 (Lo); prob. also Ric. Le *Leger* 1306 *Ass* 4 (Wo). — Cf the following trade-name: Joh. de Knyghton *leger* 1354 RBL 94 (Le).

Redere. 1275. NED: c1440.
Ess: Joh. le Redere 1285 *Ass* 25. — *La:* Joh. le Reder 1332 SR 59. Ric. le Reder 1332 *Ass* 12. — *Nf:* Sim. le Reidere 1275 RH 456. Nich. le Redere 1286 *Ass* 28. Steph. le Redere ib. 82. Will. le Reder 1322 CDN 109. Rad. Le Reder' 1332 *SR* 49. Joh. le Reder' ib. 57. Thom. le Reder' ib. 71. Godefr. Le Reder' ib. 80.

A der. of ME *redyn* 'to thatch with reed' (fr. OE *hrēod* 'reed'). — *One who thatches with reeds, a thatcher* (NED). — The following surname may have the same meaning: Norchinus le *Redman* 1332 SR 102 (La).

Salzman (Med. Ind. p. 174) says that »in the fifteenth century 'redethek' (reed thatch) was one of the peculiarities of Norwich». This seems to have been the case much earlier; note that I have found this name almost only in *Nf* (12 inst). Cf Prompt. P. p. 368 (prob. written in *Nf*). *Redare* of howsys: calamator, arundinarius, canarius.

Ledtheker. 1305. NED: —
Y: Thom. Ledtheker (bis) 1305 *Ass* 22.

ME *led* (OE *lēad*) + ME *theker* (v. THEKER). — *One who covers or roofs buildings with lead.* — Cf the synonymous MG surname: Luder *Blydecker,* Bremen 1446 (Carstens p. 95).

Tyghelere, Tiulur. 1230. NED: ?a1300.
Ess: Hugo le Tygelere 1301 *2.GDR* 11. Walt. le Teyller' 1319 *SR* 15. Will. le Tielere 1327 *SR* 4 (le Tiller', Dupl.). Walt. le Teilere 1332 *SR* 20.

---

¹ Printed *Strenlegger'*.

Sx: Steph. Le Tygeler' 1288 *Ass* 20. Ric. le Tyghelere 1296 SR 13. Will. Teglere 1327 SR 155. Nich. Thigheler ib. 182. Rob. le Tyghelar 1332 SR 236. — *Ha:* Will. le Tyulur 1280 *3.Ass* 26. Thom. le Tyghelere ib. 20. Gilb. le Tighelere 1327 *SR* 18. Joh. le Tyghelare 1333 *SR* 5. — *So:* Joh. Le Tygheler' 1307 *Ass* 4. Rob. le Tiegheler 1327 SR 187 (le Tyghelere 1333 *SR* 23). Ric. le Tyghelere 1333 *SR* 25. — *Wo:* Walt. le Tywlare 1275 SR 2. Thom. le Tiwelur ib. 79. Adam le Towelar' ib. 25. — *Y:* Ric. le Tylere 1293 *Ass* 47. Agn. le Tulere ib. Michael le Teuler 1297 SR 152. Steph. le Teuler 1301 SR 106. Ran. le tughler 1313 Free Y 15. Alic. Tygheler 1332 *SR* 17. — *Li:* Nic. tyulur 1230 P 301. Thom. Tyler 1317 *Ass* 12. Will. tylere 1327 *4.SR* 7. Beat. tylere ib. Ric. Le Tyler 1327 *1.SR* 1. Hugo le Tygler 1328 *Ass* 50 (le Tiglerer ib. 53). — *Nf:* Sim. Le Tyeler' 1286 *Ass* 88. Joh. Tulur ib. 121. Geoffrey de Tyweler 1294 CDN 51. Joh. le Tylere 1314 *GDR* 20.

    1. A der. of OE *tigule, tigele* 'a tile', or fr. the verb, ME *tile*, formed fr. this. 2. OF *tieuleor; tieulier, tiewelier, tuiweliere, tiuelier, tuilier* 'fabricant de tuiles' (Godefroy). Cf FULLERE, FULUR. — *Tiler, one who covers buildings with tiles;* also *a tile-maker* (NED). — This surname is common in *Li, Y,* and *Ess,* but no instance has been found in *St* and *La.*

Heliere. 1280.   NED: c1450.

    Ha: Gilb. le Helyere 1280 *3.Ass* 35. Rog. le Heliare 1333 *SR* 9. Gilb. le Heliere ib. 8. — *So:* Will. le Heliere 1320 *Ass* 23. Michel le Helier 1327 SR 103. Adam le Heliere ib. 121. Hugo le Helier ib. 162. Joh. le helyere 1333 *SR* 28. Will. le Heliar' ib. 30.

    A der. of OE *helian* 'to hide', later 'to cover, to roof'. — *Slater or tiler* (NED).

Sclater, Sclatter. 1255.   NED: 1379.

    Wo: Thom. le Sclatere 1255 *Ass* 36. Thom. le Sclattere 1276 3.Hal 36. Will. le Slatere 1280 Hal 158 (le Sclattere 1293 ib. 233). Pet. Le Slattere 1307 *Ass* 3. Joh. Le Sclatter 1327 SR 72. — *La:* Joh. le Sclater 1327 *SR* 8. Adam le Sklater 1332 SR 81. Will. le Sclater 1338 *Ass* 8. — *Y:* Thom. slater 1297 SR 119. Walt. le Sklater 1301 SR 17. Rob. the Sklatter 1314 3.Wake 43. Sim. Sklater 1332 *SR* 19. Adam le Sclatter c1346 *SR* 15.

    A der. of ME *sclate, sklate, slate* 'slate' (OF *esclate*) or ME *sclat, slatt* 'slat' (OF *esclat*). NED has *slatter* 1379 and *slater* 1408. — *One who lays slates.* — This surname has only been found in *Wo, Y,* and *La.*

Sklatemanger. 1332.   NED: —

    Y: Rob. Sklatemanger 1332 *SR* 18.

    ME *sklate* (OF *esclate*) 'slate' + ME *manger.* — *Seller of slates.*

CHAPTER VIII.

STONE, CROCKERY, AND GLASS WORKERS.

A. Miner, Quarrier, Stone-Cutter.

Minour. 1212.   NED: c1275.
Ess: Thom. Le Mynur 1301 *2.GDR* 11. Joh. le Minur 1302 ib. 12. — *So:* Rich. le Minnor 1327 SR 205. Rob. Minor ib. 247. Ric. Minour 1344 *Ass* 7. — *La:* Will. le Minour 1326 CR 162. — *Y:* Rog. the Minour 1314 *3.*Wake 39. Margery Mynur 1340 FF 146. — *Li:* Adam le Miner 1212 Cur 210.

OF *mineor, mineur.* — *One who works in a mine;* also *a soldier who undermines a fortress.*

Marberer. 1230.   NED: 1457.
Ess: Reg. le Marbrer 1230 P 153. — *Ha:* Joh. le Marberer 1287 *Ass* 3, 2.

OF *marbrier* 'artisan qui scie et polit le marbre' (Godefroy). — *A quarryman or hewer of marble; one who carves, or works in, marble* (NED).

Quarreur. 1275.   NED: c1375.
Ha: Will. le Quarour 1327 *SR* 3. Walt. Quarer 1333 *SR* 1. — *Wo:* Henr. le Quarreur 1275 SR 47. Cristina la Quarreur ib. 109. — *La:* Will. le Quarreur 1292 *1.Ass* 42. — *Y:* Will. le Quareour 1279 *Ass* 71. — *Li:* Rob. le Quarreur 1287 *Ass* 10. Thom. le Quarreour 1328 *Ass* 4. Ric. le quarreour 1332 *2.SR* 8.

OF *quarreour, -ieur; quarrier.* — *One who quarries stone, a quarryman.*

Perour. 1255.   NED: —
Ess: Rob. le perer 1255 *Ass* 9. Joh. Periere 1327 *SR* 5. — *Sx:* Ric. Le Perur 1288 *Ass* 19. Rog. Le Perur ib. 18. Rob. Le Perrer ib. 34. Joh. le Perour 1327 SR 157. — *Nf:* Rob. le Perere 1286 *Ass* 124.

OF *perrier* and *perrieur* 'carrier' (Godefroy). — *One who quarries stone.*

Stonhewere. 1292. NED: 1579—80.
La: Joh. le Stonhewere 1292 *1.Ass* 46. — *Y:* Rog. le Stonhewer c1346 *SR* 7.

OE *stān* 'stone' + a der. of *hēawan*. — *Stone-cutter, one who quarries stone.*

Vershewere. 1276. NED: —
So: John le Wers Hewere 1276 Ass 64 (le Wershewere, Dupl., le Wershewere 1277 Ass 128).

OE *fers* 'a verse' (ME *vers, wers*) + a der. of *hēawan*. — *Prob. one who makes verse inscriptions on stone.*

Pavour. 1281. NED: 1426—7.
Lo: Will. le Pavour 1281 CLB (B) 14. — *Wo:* Henr. Le Paveor 1327 *SR* 35.

OF *paveur*. — *Pavior, one who paves or lays pavements.*

Werkman. 1236. NED: c888.
Sx: Will. le Werkman 1236 FF 86. Will. Le Werkman 1288 *Ass* 28. Ric. le Werkman 1327 SR 128. — *Ha:* Ric. le Werkeman 1322 *Ass* 2. — *Y:* Hugo Werkeman 1301 SR 59. Henr. Werkman 1332 *SR* 17. — *Li:* Will. Werkeman Mazon 1328 *Ass* 8. Joh. le Werkemanne 1332 *3.SR* 25.

OE *weorcmann*. — *Workman, operative.*

Marlehewer. 1327. NED: —
St: Will. le Marlehewere 1327 SR 205 (le Marlehewer' 1332 SR 100). Joh. le Marlehewere' 1327 SR 205 (le Marlehewer' 1332 SR 100).

ME *marle* 'marl' (fr. OF *marle*) + ME *hewer*. — *One who hews or quarries marl.*

Marlere. 1275. NED: 1808.
Sx: Ric. Le Marler 1288 *Ass* 1. Nich. le Marlere 1327 SR 204. — *So:* Payn le Marler' 1277 Ass 99. Steph. le Marlar 1327 SR 106. Will. Marlar ib. 265. — *Wo:* Hugo le Merlere 1275 SR 43. — *La:* Henr. le Marler 1323 *Ass* 26. Rich. le Marler 1324 CR 34.

A der. of ME *marle* 'marl' (fr. OF *marle*). — Signification: = MARLEHEWER.

B. Lime-Burner, Tile-Maker.

Lymbrenner. 1305.   NED: 1329.
  Li: Will. le Limbrenner 1305 *Ass* 13 (le Lyngbrenner ib. 21, le Linbrenner ib. 22). Thom. Le lymbrennere 1319 *Ass* 23. Rad. le Lymbrenner 1332 *2.SR* 1 (Lymberner' 1340 *Ass* 7). Thom. le Lymbrenner 1332 *2.SR* 1 (Lymberner 1340 *Ass* 4).

OE *līm* 'lime' + a der. of OE *beornan* or ON *brenna* 'to burn'. — *Lime-burner, one who makes lime by burning lime-stone.* — As the name of a trade: Hugh de Hecham, »*lymbrennere*» 1329 CLB (E) 241 (Lo). I have found one instance of another, apparently synonymous, surname, *Limwright:* Hugo le Limwryte 1279 RH 352 (Bk).

Lymer. 1290.   NED: 1611.
  Sx: Ric. le Lymar' 1327 SR 138. — *Ha:* Joh. le Lymare 1327 *SR* 18. Aumsilius le Lymare 1333 *SR* 9. — *Y:* Walt. Lymer 1293 *Ass* 93. — *Li:* Steph. le Lymer 1329 *GDR* 2. — *Nf:* Rog. de Biltham le Lymer 1290 CDN 33.

A der. of OE *līm* 'lime'. — Prob. = LYMBRENNER. The sense may also be 'one who whitewashes'. v. NED *limer*.

Kylner, Kyller. 1288.   NED: —
  Ess: Ran. le Killer' 1319 SR 9. Alex. killere 1332 *SR* 30. — *Sx:* Ric. Le Kyller' 1288 *Ass* 31. — *Ha:* Joh. le Killere 1327 *SR* 17. Johanna la Kyllere 1333 *SR* 9. Rob. le Killere ib. — *La:* Will. le Kylnere 1292 *1.Ass* 44 (le Kilnere ib. 13). — *Li:* Rob. Kilner 1305 *Ass* 21. Will. Kylner 1327 *1.SR* 8. Henr. le Kilner' 1327 *3.SR* 1. Will. Kylner 1332 *2.SR* 10.

A der. of OE *cylene* 'kiln'. The assimilation of $ln > ll$ already began in the OE period. To judge from the above instances, this would, at this time, have taken place only in the Saxon counties. This agrees fairly well with the forms of MILNER, q. v., of which there are only a few instances spelt *Miller* in the Anglian counties, with the exception, however, of *Nf*, where this form is common.

One who attends to a kiln; one who burns lime, tiles, etc. The form *Kyller* may perhaps also mean 'one who kills, a butcher'.

Brenner, Berner. 1280.   NED: c1380.
  Ess: Sim. Le Bernere 1327 *SR* 5. — *St:* Jord. le Brenner 1280 6.Ass 103, 106.

A der. of OE *beornan* or ON *brenna* 'to burn'. — Signification: = LYMBRENNER; also 'one who burns bricks or charcoal'. — Some early instances (e. g. Rob. le *Bernier* 1191 P 9) do not belong here, but come from OF *brenier, bernier* 'keeper of hounds'.

Tywelwright. 1280.   NED: c1000.
Ha: Sim. le Tywelwyrgh' 1280 *2.Ass* 86 (le Tywelwrighte 1280 *3.Ass* 34).

OE *tigelwyrhta* 'brickmaker, potter'. The spelling of the first element is influenced by OF *tieule* 'a tile'. Cf similar forms under TYGHELERE. — *Maker of tiles.* — Cf Joh. le sauscer, *teghlemaker* 1352 Free Y 47. Joh. Hardy, *tieghelfourmer* 1400 ib. 104.

C. Potter, Glazier.

Pottere, Potier. 1197.   NED: a1100.
Ess: Joh. le Potier 1197 P 73. Joh. le Potyr 1285 *Ass* 50. Emma le Potter 1319 *SR* 5. Hugo le Pottere 1327 *SR* 4. Joh. le Pottere 1332 *SR* 30. — *Sx:* Thom. le Potter' 1263 *Ass* 47. Rob. le Pottere 1279 *Ass* 22. Mich. le Pottere 1296 SR 27. Joh. le Potter 1332 SR 309. — *Ha:* Walt. le Pottere 1280 *2.Ass* 81. Thom. Le Potyare 1306 *Ass* 2. Benedicta la Potyere 1327 *SR* 6. Ric. le Pottare 1333 *SR* 2. — *So:* Geoffrey le Poter 1253 Ass 423. Geruas' Le Potter' 1305 *Ass* 10. Rad. le Pottar' 1333 *SR* 12. — *Wo:* Sim. le poter 1221 Ass 605. Marg' la Pottere 1275 *1.Ass* 11. Ric. Le Pottere 1307 *Ass* 2. Gilb. Le Pottar 1327 SR 31. — *St:* Rob. le Poter 1269 4.Ass 175. Ric. le Pottere 1327 SR 214. Gilb. le Potter' 1332 SR 110. — *La:* John le Potter 1246 Ass 63. Rob. le Pottere 1292 *1.Ass* 16. Rog. le Potter 1338 *Ass* 1. — *Y:* Ric. le Potter 1279 *Ass* 52. Clemens Potter 1301 SR 58. Rob. Potter 1332 *SR* 6. — *Li:* Alex. le Poter 1263 FF 206. Rog. le Potter 1281 *2.Ass* 57. Alan. Le Potter 1327 *2.SR* 25. Margaret. Pottere 1332 *3.SR* 8. — *Nf:* Alfwinus le pottere 1198 P 92. Rad. le potier 1250 *Ass* 7. Maur. le pottere 1286 *Ass* 82. Ric. le Potter' 1332 *SR* 67.

1. Late OE *pottere.* 2. OF *potier* 'potter'. NED has only the native form. — *Maker of pots, or of earthenware vessels;* also *a maker of metal pots;* the potter was sometimes also a bell-founder. — The first sense is represented by the following trade-name: Ric. Beverlay, *erthpotter* 1426 Free Y 139. — The French form is common in early rolls, but later the native word becomes prevalent.

Potmaker. 1297.   NED: 1535.
Y: Rich. le Potmaker 1297 1.Wake 288 (le Potmakere ib. 290).

Late OE *pott* + a der. of OE *macian.* — *Potter.*

Crockere. 1275. NED: c1315.

Sx: Henr. le Crokere 1288 *Ass* 38. Ric. Crockere 1296 SR 35. Ric. le Crokker' 1319 *Ass* 39. Joh. Crockere 1332 SR 229. — *Ha:* Will. Crockere 1305 *Ass* 16. Galfr. le Crokkere 1327 *SR* 19. Will. le Crokkere 1333 *SR* 8. Alicia la Crokkere ib. 9. — *So:* Edw. Le Crockere 1305 *Ass* 7 (Le Crokere ib.). Joh. le Crocker 1327 SR 181. Adam le Crockere 1333 *SR* 26. Rog. le Crokker' ib. 27. Walt. le Crockere 1350 BBA 111. — *Wo:* Joh. le Crockare 1275 SR 19. — *Nf:* Will. Croker' 1329 *SR* 42.

A der. of OE *croc(c)* or *crocca* 'an earthen pot'. — *Potter.*

Dischere. 1275. NED: 1304.

So: Walt. le Dissher 1327 SR 126. — *Wo:* Pet. le Dissare 1275 SR 4. Will. le Disscher 1296 OCW 41 (le Disschare 1302 ib. 81). — *Y:* Ric. Dysser 1301 SR 17. Adam Le Dischere 1305 *Ass* 1.

A der. of OE *disc* 'plate, bowl'. — *Maker or seller of dishes* (NED).

Boller. 1316. NED: 1415.

So: John le Bouller 1316 FF 56. Joh. Boller' 1333 *SR* 10. — *St:* Rob. le Boller' 1332 SR 108. — *Y:* Henr. le Boller c1346 *SR* 12. — *Li:* Will. Boller 1327 *3.SR* 3.

A der. of OE *bolla* 'bowl'. — *A maker or seller of bowls.* — *Boller* is common as a trade-name in Free Y: Joh. Foune, *boller* 1334 p. 30. In London: Rog. Caury, »*bollere*» 1276 CLB (B) 262.

Urnere. 1327. NED: —

Ha: Henr. le Vrnere 1327 *SR* 17 (le Vrnere 1333 *SR* 8, le Vrnare 1340 *SR* 7).

A der. of ME *vrne* (OF *urne*) 'urn', or there may have been an OF **urnier.* — *One who makes or sells urns.*

Verrer. 1185. NED: 1415.

Ess: Rob. le Verer 1274 RH 140. Matthew le Verrer 1310 CR 7. Gilb. le Verrer 1312 CR 88. Cristina la Verrer' 1327 *SR* 4. Steph. Le Verrer ib. 17. Joh. le Veriere 1332 *SR* 8. — *Sx:* Math. le Verir 1279 *Ass* 27. — *Wi:* Fulko le Verrier 1185 P 194. — *So:* Ric. le verour 1333 *SR* 9. Rob. le verour ib. — *Wo:* Rich. le Verrer 1293 Inq 46. Thom. the Verrour 1340 OCW 143. — *St:* Will. le Werrer 1327 SR 235 (le Verrer 1332 SR 83). — *La:* Thom. le Verrer 1292 *3.Ass* 40. — *Y:* Andrew le Verrer 1231 FF 144. Walt. le verrour 1313 Free Y 15. -- *Li:* Joh. le Verrour 1327 *3.SR* 3. Will. le Verrour ib. Walt. le Verrur 1332 *3.SR* 25. — *Nf:* Jord. called le Verrer 1290 CDN 31. Will. le Verer 1301 ib. 91. Galfr. le Verrer 1306 ib. 117. Sim. le Verrer 1332 *SR* 39.

AF *verrer;* OF *verrier* and *verrieur* 'verrier' (Godefroy). — *Worker in glass, glazier.*

Glaswright, Glasenwright. 1301.   NED: c1440.

a. G l a s w r i g h t:
Ess: Mariota la Glaswrithe 1311 CR 31. Steph. Glaswrighte 1319 *SR* 13. Wm. le Glaswrihte 1337 CR 154. — *So:* Joh. Glaswort 1333 *SR* 30. — *Y:* Joh. le Glasewrith' 1301 SR 118. Walt. Glasewrith' ib. Thom. le Glasewrith' ib. 119. — *Nf:* Sim. Glaswryghte 1350 Free L 12.

b. G l a s e n w r i g h t:
Lo: Joh. le Glasenwiche 1332 SR 76. — *Li:* Will. le Glasenwright 1329 *GDR* 4 (le Glasenwryght', bis, 1332 *Ass* 14). — *Le:* Will. le Glasenwryghte 1345 RBL 63.

OE *glæs* 'glass' or *glæsen* adj. + *wyrhta*. NED has *glassenwright* 1500—20. — *Glazier, glass-maker.* — *Glasenwright* is common as a trade-name in Free Y, e. g. Joh. de Preston, glasenwreght 1361 p. 56.

Glasyer. 1316.   NED: 1385.
Ess: Joh. le Glasiere 1316 *3.GDR* 33. Thom. Glasyer' 1319 *SR* 17. Will. le Glasyer' ib. 18. Rob. le Glasyer' 1327 *SR* 16. — *Ha:* Joh. le Glasier 1323 *Ass* 8.

A der. of OE *glæs* 'glass'. — *Glass-maker.*

Glasman. 1327.   NED: 1597—8.
St: Ric. le Glasmon 1327 SR 208, 1332 SR 89. Thom. le Glasmon 1327 SR 209. Sim. le Glasemon 1332 SR 89. Rich. le Glasemon 1342 12.Ass 8.

OE *glæs* 'glass' + *mann*. — *Glazier, dealer in glass-ware*

CHAPTER IX.

PHYSICIAN, BARBER.

A. Physician, Surgeon, Veterinary.

Leche. 1249.   NED: c900.
Ess: Juliana le Leche 1292 *2.GDR* 2. Rog. le Lache 1333 CR 106. John le Lache 1336 CR 142. — *Sx:* Lambertus le Leche 1249 *Ass* 39. Felic' la Leche 1327 SR 128. Ric. le Leche 1332 SR 232. — *Ha:* Rog. Le Leche 1280 *2.Ass* 80. Galfr. Le Lech' 1305 *Ass* 13. Eufemia la Leche 1333 *SR* 8. — *So:* Will. le Leche 1279 Ass 200. Thom. le Leche 1333 *SR* 23. Joh. le Leche 1344 *Ass* 16. — *Wo:* Adam le Leche 1275 *2.Ass* 52. Will. le Leeche 1293 Hal 249. Agnes la Leche 1307 Hal 579. Joh. Le Leche 1327 SR 34. — *St:* John Leche 1261 4.Ass 148. Walt. le Leche 1299 7.Ass 52. Steph. le Leche 1332 SR 95. — *La:* Thom. le Leche 1285 Ass 204. Rich. le Leche 1332 FF 84. — *Y:* Amabel le Leche 1298 2.Wake 23. John le Leche ib. 26. Adam le Leche c1346 *SR* 6. — *Li:* Joh. Le Leche 1320 *Ass* 35. Thom. Leche 1332 *2.SR* 13. — *Nf:* Ad. Le Leche 1286 *Ass* 139. Joh. le Leche 1310 *GDR* 11. Anastacia Le Leche 1332 *SR* 49.

OE *lǣce* 'leech, physician'. As is seen above, this name, which is of frequent occurrence, is always spelt *Leche,* except in *Ess,* where another form, *Lache,* also occurs; the proportion between these two spellings in this county is the following: 27 inst. of *Lache* and 3 inst. of *Leche.* Besides in *Ess,* I have only found the form *Lache* in *Hu:* Agnes le Lache 1294 CR Ramsey 222. — Physician.

Lecher. 1272.   NED: c1374.
Ha: Walt. le Lecher 1272 *Ass* 24.

A der. of ME *leche* 'to cure' (fr. OE *lǣce* 'physician'). — One who 'leeches'; a physician.

Fisicien. 1269.   NED: a1225.
St: Magister John le Fisicien 1269 4.Ass 170. — *Li:* Joh. le Fisicien 1281 *1.Ass* 37.

ME *fisicien* fr. OF *fisicien.* — Physician.

Surgen. 1255. NED: 13..

Ess: Thom. le Surigien 1255 *Ass* 33. — *Y:* Gilb. le Surrugien 1279 *Ass* 8. — *Li:* Will. le Surgen 1328 *Ass* 59. — *Nf:* Ran. de Morle le Sursyen 1288 CDN 19.

AF *surgien, sur(r)igien,* OF *serurgien.* — *Surgeon, medical man.* — Cf the extended form: Will. Rydale, *surgener* 1422 Free Y 133.

Mareschal. *One who treats the diseases of horses, a farrier;* v. MARESCHALL p. 144.

Smerer, Shepsmerer. 1279. NED: 1632.

Y: Joh. le Smerer 1279 *Ass* 55. Joh. le Shepsmerere 1293 *Ass* 78.

(OE *scēp* 'sheep' +) a der. of OE *smerian* 'to smear'. — *One who smears sheep with a salve of tallow and tar to kill vermin.*

Greser. 1327. NED: 1641.

Li: Rob. le Greser 1327 *3.SR* 3, 1332 *3.SR* 25.

A der. of ME *greese* 'to smear with grease, to apply a salve of tallow and tar to sheep' (fr. ME *grese* sb, OF *graisse*). — Signification: = SMERER.

B. Barber, Blood-Letter.

Barber. 1250. NED: c1320.

Ess: Ric. le Barbur 1255 *Ass* 13. Galfr. le Barber 1332 *SR* 21. Nich. le Barbour 1341 *Ass* 12. — *Sx:* Joh. le Barbur 1270 FF 70. Rad. le Barber 1279 *Ass* 32. Ric. le Barber 1332 SR 293. — *Ha:* Rob. le Barbur 1280 *2.Ass* 91. Adam le Barber 1327 *SR* 17. Will. le Barbour 1340 *SR* 4. — *So:* Walt. le Barbur 1268 Ass 46. Alex. Le Barbour 1305 *Ass* 13. Henr. le Barbur 1327 SR. 220. — *Wo:* Sim. le Barber 1262 Inq 6. Rog. le Barbour 1306 *Ass* 3. Rob. Le Barber 1327 SR 41. — *St:* Henry le Barbur 1277 6.Ass 92. Nich. le Barber 1306 7.Ass 165. Will. le Barber 1327 SR 206. — *La:* Rob. le Barber 1323 *Ass* 24. Ad. le Barbour 1338 *Ass* 1. — *Y:* Joh. le Barber 1279 *Ass* 71. Wunirus le barber 1318 Free Y 18. Joh. le Barbour c1346 SR 8. — *Li:* Rob. le Barbur 1281 *1.Ass* 36. Joh. Le Barbur' 1327 *1.SR* 1. Cecil' Barber 1332 *2.SR* 8. — *Nf:* Ric. le Barbur 1250 *Ass* 7. John le Barber 1305 CDN 101. Thom. le Barbour 1316 *GDR* 37.

AF *barbour,* OF *barbeor* (NED); the form *Barber* comes from OF *barbier.* This spelling (*Barber*) is, accord. to NED, rare before 1500; but as surnames both *Barber* and *Barbour* are very

numerous, though the latter form seems to be the most common.
— *Barber, hairdresser.* Formerly the barber was also a regular practitioner in surgery and dentistry (NED). — The barber often acted as a blood-letter, and in the time of Edward I there were strict regulations for the barbers of London in this respect (v. Lib. Alb. Intr. 53).

Blodleter. 1256. NED: c1000.
Ha: Adam le Blodeleter 1280 *2.Ass* 49. — *So:* Rob. le Blodleter 1256 FF 177. Hugo le Blodleter 1327 SR 280. — *La:* Amaria le blodletere 1292 *1.Ass* 3 (le Blodletere ib. 38, Le Blodletere 1292 *2.Ass* 3).

OE *blōdlǣtere.* — *Blood-letter, one who lets blood.*

Bledere. 1293. NED: 1788.
Y: Will. le Bledere 1293 *Ass* 33. — *Li:* Wydo Bledder 1327 *2.SR* 18.

A der. of OE *blēdan* 'to bleed'. — *One who draws blood, a blood-letter.*

Ventoser. 1279. NED: c1340.
Ess: Joan la Ventoser 1311 CR 47. — *Li:* Matill' Ventuser 1340 *Ass* 18. — *Hu:* Ric. le Ventoser 1279 RH 615.

AF *venteuser* (F *ventouseur*). — *Cupper, one who performs the operation of cupping* (NED).

Soukere. 1301. NED: (1382).
Ha: Will. Le Soukere 1305 *Ass* 6 (le Sokere ib. 16). — *So:* Rob. le Sokere 1327 SR 221. Joh. le Souker' 1333 *SR* 33. — *La:* Adam le Seuker 1323 CR 38. Rog. le Suker 1332 SR 36. Rog. le Suker 1333 *Ass* 14. Joh. le Suker 1338 *Ass* 7. — *Y:* Will. Souker 1301 SR 65.

A der. of OE *sūcan* 'to suck'. — Prob. *a blood-letter.* — NED has *sucker* 1382, but not in this sense. Cf NED *blood-sucker*: 1387 'an animal which sucks blood', 1561 'one who draws or sheds the blood of another'.

EXCURSUS.
TOPONYMICAL SURNAMES.

As has already been mentioned in the Introduction, I have considered it suitable to include in this volume another group of surnames, which I have called TOPONYMICAL SURNAMES. By this term I mean names that are derived from or compounded with place-names or topographical elements (e. g. brook, hill, wood, etc.). The first type ends in *-er*, e. g. *Douner* 'one who lives on or near a certain down', and the second type is a compound, the last element of which is *man*, e. g. *Crassedalman* 'a man who is from Crassedal'. These surnames, which are interesting, especially with regard to their occurrence, are very like the other names treated in this book; it is often difficult — sometimes impossible — to decide if a name is a toponymical surname or a surname of occupation.

No serious attention has hitherto been paid to this group of surnames; no collection of them has been made, and, above all, their geographical distribution has been quite unknown. The type ending in *-er* has been mentioned in passing by Prof. Mawer for the county of Sussex (Probl. of Pl. N. Study p. 67 f.).

Toponymical surnames do not only occur in England, they are also common in Germany, and they seem to have come into use at about the same time. The same types are also found there, and they are formed from place-names or topographical elements: *Strittmatter, Furtwängler, Altenburger, Vogelbacher*, etc. fr. pl. n.: *Zipfler, Ebner, Saumer, Strasser, Gasser*, etc. fr. top. el. (v. Götze p. 16 ff.); *Buschman, Berneman, Winkelman, Kerkman, Lubekeman*, etc. (v. Carstens p. 62 ff.). These surnames do not occur in the same proportion in the whole of Germany: the *-er* type is very common in the South, while very few instances have been found in the North; the names ending in -*man* are of more general occurrence, and have been found most frequently in Bremen.¹ This distribution is very like that in England.

The English appellatives ending in -*er* and formed from pl. n. have been examined by Langenfelt. He has found several instances in ME derived from foreign pl. n., but only one, *Londoner*, from English pl. n. (p. 122). He thinks that the ending -*er* is of Flemish origin. However this may be, the surname type is certainly a native formation. It is difficult to tell exactly what has given rise to these names. There is another group of surnames, however, without the aid of which they would probably never have come into existence, viz. the type (John) *atte Broke, atte Hille*. These names are extremely common, especially in the South of England. The signification is exactly the same as that of the corresponding names in -*er* and -*man*. One might therefore think that these surnames (atte Broke, etc.) became so common, that the need of variety was felt. The model on which the new names were formed may have been words like the following: OE *wudere* 'wood-man, wood-carrier', OE *dīcere* 'one who digs ditches', ME *parkere* 'park-keeper'; ME *wodeman* 'huntsman; one who looks after the trees in a wood; *an inhabitant of the woods*', etc. The 'wudere' lived in a wood, and the 'parkere' in or near a park, etc.; this circumstance may have facilitated the development of the present surnames.

Of the 128 toponymical surnames treated in the following, eight are evidenced in NED: *fenner* 1844 'an inhabitant of the fens'; *laker* 1798 'a visitor to the English lakes'; Yorkshire *wolder* 1765 'an inhabitant of the Yorkshire wolds'; *dalesman* 1769 'a native or inhabitant of a dale'; *hillman* c1830 'an inhabitant of a hill-country'; *fen-man* 1610 'an inhabitant of the fens'; *marshman* 1573 'a dweller in a marshy county'; *woldsman* 1765 'a dweller in the wolds'.

The present surnames have been found almost exclusively in *subsidy rolls*; the instances found in other documents are proportionately few. From this we may infer that the persons who bore

¹ For further information about these surnames in Germany v. Socin (p. 353 ff.), Götze (p. 15 ff.), Koberne (p. 23 ff.), Reimpell (p. 71 f.), Carstens (p. 60 ff.), Mahnken (p. 95), Nüske (p. 99), Bähnisch (p. 48, 62).

these surnames lived in the country and probably were farmers. One seldom finds these names in towns, except in later rolls, when they had become hereditary.

The time, counties, and rolls that have been examined are the same as before. Sometimes, however, exceptions have been made in order to get a better view of the occurrence of the names. Thus, for instance, names from a few other counties have also been collected (esp. *Surrey*).

Besides the surnames treated here, others might also have been included, e. g. *Kepere, Kyrker, Compere, Stappere, Wodere,* etc.; *Capelman, Coteman, Curtman, Dykeman, Wodeman,* etc. These names, however, generally admit of another more probable interpretation. Completeness has not been aimed at in this Excursus. Of the names included some may be explained in other ways, but the interpretation given here has been considered most probable.

A. **Surnames Ending in -ER.**

As has already been mentioned, this type of surnames consists of a der. of a topographical element or a place-name. The ending is *-er*, sometimes *-ier* (but never the fem. ending *-ester*). The topographical elements are identical with the above-mentioned names preceded by *atte*.[1] The most usual significations of them are as follows (ranged after frequency): enclosure, pasture, piece of land; hill; fen, marsh; river, lake; tree (beech, oak, etc.); valley; wood; gate, stile; road; cross. The names are all of native (or ON) origin, except two, which are French: *Barrer, Valer*.

The difference between topographical elements and place-names is not great during this early period, and it is difficult to distinguish them. There are not many instances of the present surnames that are derived from real place-names. The following names probably belong here: *Ashburner, Berlondere, Glyndere, Redlondere, Rysebrigger*; perhaps also *Mulgatere*.

There is a great difference in frequency between the two types *atte Halle* and *Haller*; the latter is very rare as compared

---

[1] also *del, de la, in the, binethe,* etc.

with the former. In the subsidy rolls for *Sx,* for instance, there occur 100 inst. of *atte Halle,* but only one inst. of *Haller*; further 72 *atte Felde,* 1 *Felder*; 45 *atte Forde,* 1 *Forder,* etc. Sometimes, however, several instances have been found of the names in *-er,* but, as a rule, only one or two examples have been included from each county.

The geographical distribution of the surnames in *-er* is interesting; the case is that they do not occur in the whole of England. They are only common in the South; most instances have been found in *Sx* and many also in the adjoining counties (*Sr, Ha*). They occur in all the Saxon counties dealt with, but not in the same proportion: in *So* I have only found 11 (different) surnames, in *Wo* 8, in *Ess* 5, and in *Lo* 6 (these six are all after 1350). They are not restricted to the South of England, however; they also occur, though sparingly, in *East Midland*: in *Nf* 6 surnames have been found (Kerere, Dellere, Hoker, Holere, Lyther, Wyker); in *Ca* 3 (Cumber, Ponder, Solier); in *Hu* 2 (Ponder, Solier), and in *Db* one (Hower).[1] In West Midland and the North surnames in *-er* do not seem to have existed; no instance has been found in these counties.

When did the present surnames arise? No examples have been found in OE, nor in the first century of the ME period. To judge from my material they begin to come into use in the first half of the 13th century. The first instances that I have found are the following: *Wyker* 1225, *Barrer* 1230, *Baller* 1243, *Kerere* 1250, *Valer* 1263. At the end of the century they become common, and the frequency increases in the 14th century. In later rolls (15th—16th cent.) certain of these names are found in abundance in the South of England, and many have survived to the present day.

The signification of these surnames in *-er* is exactly identical with that of the type *atte Broke* ('at the Brook') i. e. 'one who lives at a certain brook' (etc.). This is proved by the fact that the same person is sometimes called by both these surnames. Thus *Ric. Holmer* (1327 SR 181 *Sx*) appears as *Ric. atte Holme* in 1332 (SR 310). I have found eight other such instances in *Sx:* Walt.

---

[1] For the last three counties (*Ca, Hu,* and *Db*) only a few rolls have been examined; more names can probably be found in other documents.

le Barrer' 1327 SR 127 (*atte Barre* 1296 SR 95). Hugo *le Broker* 1327 SR 157 (*atte Broke* 1296 SR 55). Rad. *le Fanner* 1327 SR 146 (*atte Fanne* 1332 SR 260). Rob. *Haller* 1332 SR 326 (*atte Halle* 1327 SR 214). Rob. *Lyncher* 1332 SR 254 (*atte Linch* 1327 SR 136). Rob. *le Lotyer* 1296 SR 24 (*atte Lote* 1327 SR 192). Rad. *Puriere* 1327 SR 147 (*atte Purye* 1332 SR 260). Will. *le Soliar* 1332 SR 243 *(ate Sole* 1327 SR 121).

For all the surnames in *-er* (and also in *-man*) that are formed from topographical elements, corresponding »*atte* names» have been found (though not denoting the same person), either in the same county or in others.

Ashburner. v. ASKEBRENNER, p. 174.

Bachiere.
Ha: Will. le Bachiere 1280 2.*Ass* 87.
Prob. fr. OE *bæce* 'stream, brook'.

Baller.
So: Adam le Baller 1243 Ass 272. Henr. le Baller' 1333 *SR* 30. Walt. le Ballere ib. 8.
ME *ball* 'a rounded hill'. »The word *ball,* used to denote a rounded hill, is confined to Somerset and Devon» (Pl. Soc. De p. 211). This surname (and also the corresponding *atte Balle*) is common in *So.*

Barrer.
Sx: Gilb. Barrer 1230 FF 58. Walt. le Barrer' 1327 SR 127.
OF *barre* 'a bar'.

Bechere.
Sx: Walt. Bechere 1359 FF 148.
OE *bēce* 'a beech'.

Berghere.
Ha: Will. le Berghere 1327 *SR* 11.
OE *beorg* 'a mountain, hill'.

Berlondere.
Sr: Joh. Berlondere 1332 SR 8.
I have not found any corresp. pl. n. in *Sr,* but there is one in *Sx: Burlands Copse* (*Berlond* 1450); v. Pl. Soc. Sx p. 209.

Bourere.
Lo: John Bourere, »turnour» 1400 CLB (I) 19. — *Sr:* Will. le Bourere 1332 SR 68. — *Sx:* John Bourere 1375 FF 179.

OE *būr* 'a bower, dwelling, cottage'.

Brecher.
Sr: Ric. le Brecher' 1332 SR 26.

OE *bræc* 'strip of newly cultivated land'.

Brigger.
Lo: John Brygger 1418 CLB (I) 174. — *Sr:* Joh. Brugere 1332 SR 8. — *Sx:* Walt. Bregger 1327 SR 208. Will. Brugger 1332 SR 270. — *Ha:* Ric. le Briggere 1327 *SR* 4. — *So:* Walt. le Briggere 1327 SR 173.

OE *brycg* 'a bridge'.

Broker.
Ess: Ric. Broker' 1319 *SR* 10. — *Sr:* Joh. le Broker' 1332 SR 24. — *Sx:* Will. Brokere 1296 SR 74. Joh. le Brouker 1327 SR 116 (le Broker 1332 ib. 240). — *Ha:* Ric. le Brokere 1327 *SR* 9. — *So:* Joh. le Broker' 1333 *SR* 29.

OE *brōc* 'a rivulet'.

Bromere.
Lo: John Bromer 1466 CLB (F) 295. — *Sx:* Rob. Bromere 1327 SR 133.

OE *brōm* 'broom'.

Kerere.
Nf: Henr. la Kerere 1250 *Ass* 23.

ME *kerr, ker* 'a pond, bog' (of ON origin); v. NED *carr*.

Cliver.
Sx: Ric. Clyuyr 1327 SR 121.

OE *clif* 'a cliff, rock'.

Clouser.
Sx: Will. Clouser 1444 FF 256.

OE *clūs* 'enclosure'.

Knapper.
Sx: Will. Knapper 1360 FF 151.

OE *cnæpp* 'top, summit of a hill'.

Knoller, Kneller.
Ess: Will. Cnoller 1319 SR 2. — *Sx:* Ric. Le Cnollere 1279 *Ass* 1. Will. Kneller 1327 SR 162 (Knoller 1332 SR 276).

1. OE *cnoll* 'hill-top, hillock'. 2. OE **cnyll*, a side-form of OE *cnoll* (Pl. Soc. Sx 169).

Crofter.
So: John le Crofter 1285 FF 264.
OE *croft* 'a small enclosed field or pasture'.

Crosser.
Ha: Pet. le Crossir 1327 *SR* 1.
OE *cros* 'a cross'.

Cruchere.
Lo: John Crowchere, vintner 1405 CLB (I) 42. — *Sx:* Will. Cruchere 1296 SR 77. — *Ha:* Adam le Cruchere 1327 *SR* 3.
OE *crūc* 'a cross'.

Cumber.
Sr: Pet. Comber' 1332 SR 32. — *Sx:* Will. le Cumbere 1263 *Ass* 20. Henr' le Coumbar 1332 SR 237. — *Ha:* Walt. le Cumbere 1280 2.*Ass* 62. — *So:* Ric. Le Cumber' 1307 *Ass* 9. — *Wo:* Will. le Cumbar' 1275 2.*Ass* 23. — *Ca:* Ric. le Cumbere 1279 RH 502.
OE *cumb* 'valley'. Cf COMBERE p. 82.

Dellere.
Nf: Rad. Dellere 1275 RH 526.
OE *dell* 'deep hollow or vale'.

Dennere.
Lo: John Denner 1384 PMR 85. — *Sx:* John Dennere 1408 FF 221.
OE *denn* 'a woodland pasture for swine'.

Douner.
Sx: Rad. le Douner' 1327 SR 123.
OE *dūn* 'hill'.

Fanner.
Ess: Will. le Fanner 1285 *Ass* 33. — *Sx:* Rad. le Fanner 1327 SR 146.
OE *fenn, fœnn* 'a fen'.

Felder.
Sr: Joh. le ffelder' 1332 SR 65. — *Sx:* Galfr' le Felder 1327 SR 155.
OE *feld* 'field'.

Forder.
Sx: Will. Forder 1327 SR 181. — *Ha:* Ad. le Fordere 1327 *SR* 11.
OE *ford* 'a ford'.

Frithere.
Ha: Ric. le Frithere 1327 *SR* 14.
OE *fyrhðe* 'a frith, a wood of some kind'.

Gatier.
Sr: Will. le Gatier' 1332 SR 29.
OE *geat* 'gate'.

Glyndere.
Sx: Henr. Glyndere 1325 *Ass* 17.
Glynde, pl. n. in *Sx.*

Grenare.
Sr: Joh. le Grener'[1] 1332 SR 13. — *Ha:* Will. le Grenar 1327 *SR* 5. — *Wo:* Will. le Grenare 1332 SR 2.
OE *grēne* 'a green'.

Grovere.
Sr: Rob. le Grouere 1332 SR 13. — *Sx:* Will. Grouar 1332 SR 327. — *Ha:* Joh. le Grouare 1327 *SR* 18.
OE *grāf* 'grove'.

Haccher.
Sr: Thom. Haccher' 1332 SR 3. Will. Hecchere ib. 72.
OE *hæc, hec* 'a hatch or gate'.

Haller.
Sr: Rob. Haller 1332 SR 23. — *Sx:* Rob. Haller 1332 SR 326.
OE *heall* 'a hall'.

Hammer.
Sr: Joh. le Hammer' 1332 SR 25. — *Sx:* Alic' Relicta Hammer' 1296 SR 61.
OE *ham(m)* 'a ham or pasture ground'.

Heggere.
Sr: Joh. Heggere 1332 SR 74. — *Sx:* Henr' le Hegger 1327 SR 157. — *So:* Walt. le Eggere 1333 *SR* 18.
OE **hecg, hegg* 'hedge'.

---
[1] Printed *Greuer'*.

Hether.
Sr: Henr. le Hether 1332 SR 45. — *Wo:* Joh. Le Hether 1327 SR 68.
OE *hǣð* 'a heath'.

Hider.
Sx: Rob. le Hider' 1309 *1.GDR* 4.
OE *hīd* 'a hide or measure of land'.

Hilder.
Sx: Will. le Hilder' 1332 SR 261.
OE *hylde*, *hielde 'a slope'.

Hoker.
Lo: Will. Hokere 1417 CLB (I) 173. — *Sr:* Joh. le Hoker 1332 SR 28. — *Sx:* Joh. le Hoker 1327 SR 148 (le Houker 1332 SR 261). — *Nf:* Will. Le Hoker' 1332 *SR* 81.
OE *hōc* 'a hook'; here prob. used of a bend in a stream.

Holere.
Ess: Ad. le Holyer' 1319 *SR* 18. Adam Holiere 1332 *SR* 19. — *Wo:* Rob. le Holare 1275 SR 4. — *Nf:* Joh. Holere 1295 *GDR*.
OE *hol* 'a hole or hollow place, a cavity'.

Holmer.
Sr: Ric. le Holmare 1332 SR 18. — *Sx:* Joh. Holmar' 1296 SR 77. — *Ha:* Will. le Holmere 1340 *SR* 4.
Prob. ME *holm* (OE *holen*) 'holly'; the corresp. *atte Holme* is very common in *Sx*.

Holter.
Sx: Ric. le Holtar' 1327 SR 129.
OE *holt* 'a wood, copse'.

Hopere.
Sr: Rob. le Hopere 1332 SR 15.
For further instances v. HOPERE p. 169. — OE *hop* 'a piece of enclosed land in the midst of fens or marshes'.

Howere.
So: Rob. Le Howere 1305 *Ass* 8. — *Db:* Henr. le Hower 1327 SR 83.
OE *hōh* 'a projecting ridge of land'; v. NED *hoe*.

Hullere.

Ess: Sam. le heller' 1332 *SR* 21. — *Sr:* Ric. le Huller 1332 SR 49. — *Sx:* Rad. le Hullere 1327 SR 162. Alex. Heller 1332 SR 283. — *Ha:* Rog. le Hullare 1333 *SR* 5.

OE *hyll* 'a hill'.

Hurner.

Sx: Ralph Hurner, chaplain 1380 FF 185.

OE *hyrne* 'a corner'.

Lakere.

Sx: Adam Lakyare 1391 FF 199. — *Ha:* Will. le Lakere 1325 *Ass* 1.

OE *lacu* 'stream, watercourse'.

Laner, Loner.

Wo: Thom. le lonere 1281 Hal 161.

For instances spelt *Laner*, v. LANER p. 90. — OE *lane, lone* 'a lane'.

Lyghere.

Sr: Will. le Lyghere 1332 SR 23. — *Sx:* Sim. Lyger 1296 SR 79.

OE *lēah* 'a lea or tract of open land'.

Lyncher.

Sx: Rob. Lyncher 1332 SR 254.

OE *hlinc* 'rising ground, a ridge'.

Lyndere.

Sx: Ric. le Lyndere 1327 SR 175. Alex. le Lyndere ib.

OE *lind* 'a lime-tree'.

Lyther.

Sr: Will. le lythyer' 1332 SR 32. — *Nf:* Rad. le Lythere 1295 CR Ramsey 173.

OE *hliþ* 'a slope'.

Lotyer.

Sx: Rob. le Lotyer 1296 SR 24.

OE *hlot* 'lot, portion'; perhaps = *gehlotland* 'land appointed by lot'.

Meriere.

So: Thom. Le Meriere 1320 *Ass* 8.

OE *mere* 'lake, pond'.

Mersher.
Sx: Will. le Mersher 1327 SR 126.
OE *mersc* 'a marsh'.

Morer.
Wo: Joh. le Morrer 1332 SR 9.
OE *mōr* 'waste land, barren land'.

Mountere.
Ha: Joh. Le Mountere 1305 *Ass* 7. Will. le Mountere 1327 *SR* 18. Henr. le Montare 1333 *SR* 9. — *So:* Rich. le Monter 1327 SR 217.
OE *munt* 'a mount, hill'.

Mulgatere.
Sx: John Mulgatere 1342 FF 103.
Prob. OE *mylen* 'mill' + *geat* 'gate'.

Pender.
Sx: John Pender 1405 FF 219.
OE *pynd* 'enclosure' (v. Pl. Soc. Sx p. 200).

Penner.
So: Joh. le Penner 1327 SR 202.
OE *penn*, 'pen, enclosure'.

Piler.
Sr: Thom. Piler' 1332 SR 39. — *So:* Joh. le Piler 1327 SR 219. Will. le Piler' 1333 *SR* 30.
OE *pīl* 'pile or stake'.

Pyriere.
Sx: Will. le Pyriere 1327 SR 155. Rad. Puriere ib. 147.
OE *pirie, pyrie* 'a pear-tree'.

Polare.
Ha: Will. le Poulere 1327 *SR* 4. — *Wo:* Rob. le Polare 1275 SR 78.
OE *pōl* or *pūl* 'a pool'.

Ponder, Punder.
Ess: Joh. le Ponder 1327 *SR* 22. — *Sx:* Ric. le Pundere 1296 SR 71. — *Ca:* Will. le Pondere 1279 RH 579. — *Hu:* Sym' Ponder 1279 RH 627.

ME *ponde, pounde* (OE **pund*) 'cattle enclosure' or 'pond'. — *Punder* Sx may also be = PENDER.

Putter.
Sr: Will. Putter'[1] 1332 SR 23. — *Sx:* Ric. Putter' 1327 SR 134.
OE *pytt* 'pit'.

Redlondere.
Sx: Will. Redlondere 1383 FF 189.
There are six pl. n. *Redland(s)* in *Sx;* v. Pl. Soc. Sx.

Rysebrigger.
Sr: John Rysebrigger 1497 SR 108.
Rysbridge pl. n. in *Sr*.

Rudere.
Ha: Ric. le Rudere 1333 *SR* 9.
OE **rīed, *rȳd* 'clearing' (Pl. Soc. Sx 378).

Seer.
Sx: Ph. Seer 1332 SR 277.
OE *sǣ* 'sea'.

Solier.
Sx: Will. le Soliar 1332 SR 243. — *Ca:* Cecil' le Soliere 1279 RH 425.
— *Hu:* Angnes Soliere 1279 RH 660.
OE *sol* 'muddy or miry pool'.

Stapeler.
Sx: Ric. Stapeler 1327 SR 120.
OE *stapol* 'post, pillar'.

Styghelere.
Sr: Will. le stygheler 1332 SR 35. — *Sx:* Rog. Styghelere 1423 FF 236.
OE *stigel* 'stile'.

Streter.
Sx: Joh. Streter 1332 SR 273. Asselyna Streter ib.
OE *strǣt* 'a street'.

Strodere.
Sr: Joh. le stroder' 1332 SR 4. — *Sx:* Joh. le Strodere 1320 *2.GDR* 25.
OE *strōd* 'marshy land'.

---

[1] Printed *Pucter'*.

Thorner.
Sx: Thom. Thorner 1426 FF 239. John Thorner ib.
OE *þorn* 'thorn-bush'.

Tyer.
Sx: John Tyer 1423 FF 237.
OE *tēag* 'an enclosed piece of land, enclosure'.

Valer.
Sx: Nich. le Valer 1263 *Ass* 44. — *Wo:* Rich. le Valer 1314 Inq 41.
OF *val* 'vale, valley'.

Wegheletere.
Ha: Rob. le Wegheletere 1327 *SR* 12.
OE *weggelǣte* 'a place where two or more roads meet'.

Weldere.
Ha: Will. le Weldere 1333 *SR* 3.
OE *weald* (WS) 'weald, forest'.

Wellere.
The spelling of this surname coincides with WELLERE 'salt-boiler', q. v. — OE *wielle, wella* 'a well'.

Wyker.
Sx: Joh. Wyker' 1327 SR 173. — *So:* Walt. le Wykere 1225 Ass 48. — *Nf:* Ad. le Wykere 1286 *Ass* 82.
OE *wīc* 'dwelling, village, farm'; later 'enclosed piece of ground'.

Wysher.
Ess: Elias le Wissere 1332 *SR* 19. — *Sx:* Will. le Wyssere 1296 SR 23.
OE *wisc* 'damp meadow, marsh'.

Wythier.
Sx: Joh' Wythiar' 1327 SR 157 (le Withier 1332 SR 271).
OE *wīþig* 'willow'.

B. Surnames Ending in -MAN.

The surnames that end in -*man* are not so common as those ending in -*er*; I have found 44 names of the former kind (84 in -*er*), and usually only a few instances of each. The distribution is also different: it is true that they chiefly occur in the same counties as those in -*er* (most instances in *Sx*), but they have also been found in other parts of England. In *the North:* in *Y* 6 surnames (Daleman, Herdewykman, Holtbyman, Tankerlayman, Waldman, Wyllesthorpman); in *Cu* 5 (Crassedalman, Haltounman, Hicdouneman, Multonman, Scaffolman). In *East Midland:* in *Li* one (Kerman); in *Nf* 2 (Delman, Welleman). In *West Midland* only one inst. — which, moreover, is not certain — has been found in *La* (Briggeman).

Real place-names occur as the first elements only in *Y* (4 inst.) and *Cu* (5 inst.). In the other counties the first elements are always topographical and identical with those that form part of the names in -*er*, with which these names in -*man* are synonymous. The other type (fr. pl. n.), however, means 'a man who is from the place in question', or possibly — if the place is small — 'a man who lives there'.

I have noted two instances in which the same person has two surnames, one in -*man* and the other consisting of the corresponding »*atte* name»: John *Vanneman* 1336 CR 149 *Ess* (atte *Vanne* 1330 ib. 105). Joh. *Strodeman* 1327 SR 214 *Sx* (atte *Strode* 1332 SR 325).

The present surnames probably began to appear at about the same time as those in -*er*, but I have not found any names quite so early. The first instances are: *Croucheman* 1255, *Delman* 1286, *Brokman* 1296, *Hidman* 1296.

Becheman.
Sr: Will. Becheman 1332 SR 8. Joh. Becheman ib. 57.
OE *bēce* 'beech'.

Bourman.
Sx: Will. Bourman 1327 SR 187.
OE *būr* 'a bower, dwelling, cottage'.

Briggeman.
Sr: Joh. brugeman 1332 SR 66. — *Sx:* Joh. Brygeman 1296 SR 83. — *So:* Ric. Brigeman 1333 *SR* 6. — *La:* Rob. le Briggeman 1292 *1.Ass* 21.

OE *brycg* 'a bridge'. — Cf NED *bridge-man* 'the keeper of a bridge' 1648.

Brokman.
Ess: Thom. Brokman 1319 *SR* 20. — *Sx:* Steph. Brokman 1296 SR 103. — *Wo:* Will. Brokeman 1332 SR 24.

OE *brōc* 'a rivulet'.

Kerman.
Li: Bened. Kerman 1327 *2.SR* 13.

ME *kerr, ker* 'a pond, bog'.

Crassedalman.
Cu: Ad. Crassedalman 1332 SR 55.

Crossdale pl. n. in *Cu*.

Croftman.
Sx: Matill Croftman 1327 SR 167.

OE *croft* 'a small enclosed field or pasture'.

Crossman.
So: Phil. Crosman 1327 SR 236.

OE *cros* 'a cross'.

Crucheman.
Ess: Ric. Crucheman 1255 *Ass* 31. Sim. Croucheman 1332 *SR* 22. *Sr:* Rad. Croucheman 1332 SR 4. — *Sx:* Joh. Croucheman 1327 SR 195.

OE *crūc* 'a cross'.

Daleman.
Y: Will. Daleman 1301 SR 20.

OE *dæl* 'valley'.

Delman.
Nf: Rob. la Delman 1286 *Ass* 128.

OE *dell* 'deep hollow or vale'.

Deneman.
Sr: Adam Deneman 1332 SR 73. — *Sx:* Will. Deneman 1327 SR 165.

OE *denu* 'valley'.

Fanneman.
Ess: John Vanneman 1336 CR 149.
OE *fenn, fœnn* 'a fen'.

Gateman.
Sx: Will. Gateman 1296 SR 71. — *Wo:* Ric. Yatemon 1307 Hal 556.
OE *geat* 'gate'.

Gorman.
Sx: Will. Gorman 1296 SR 63. Steph. Gorman 1327 SR 144.
Prob. OE *gāra* 'a gore or triangular piece of land'.

Haltounman.
Cu: Rich. Haltounman 1332 SR 12.
The corresponding pl. n. exists in other counties (*Nb, Y,* etc.), but not in *Cu.* Cf the surname Rich. *de Halton* in the same roll.

Herdewykman.
Y: Adam le Herdewykman 1297 1.Wake 285.
Hardwick pl. n. in *Y.* Cf the surname Will. *de Herdwyke* SR 1301 *Y.*

Herstman.
Sx: Will. Herstman 1327 SR 177.
OE *hyrst* 'a hillock or grove'.

Hetheman.
Ess: John Hetheman 1351 CR 220.
OE *hǣð* 'a heath'.

Hicdouneman.
Cu: Adam Hicdouneman 1332 SR 12.
I have not found the corresp. pl. n.; it may have been *Highdown.*

Hidman.
Ess: John Hydman 1346 CR 206. — *Sx.* Will. Hydman 1296 SR 43.
OE *hīd* 'a hide or measure of land'.

Hokman.
Sx: John Hokman 1402 FF 214.
OE *hōc* 'a hook'; v. HOKER.

Holtbyman.
Y: Henr. Holtbyman, milner 1407 Free Y 111.
Holtby pl. n. in *Y*.

Hulleman.
So: Rog. Hulman 1327 SR 128.
OE *hyll* 'a hill'.

Hurneman.
So: Will. Hurnneman 1327 SR 120.
OE *hyrne* 'a corner'.

Laneman.
Sx: Ric. Laneman 1327 SR 122.
OE *lane* 'a lane'.

Leyman.
Sx: Will. Leyman 1327 SR 182.
OE *lēah* 'a lea or tract of open land'.

Loteman.
Sx: Lenota Loteman 1296 SR 29. Will. Loteman 1332 SR 304.
OE *hlot*; v. Lotyer.

Mereman.
Sx: Will. Mereman 1332 SR 242.
OE *mere* 'lake, pond' or *(ge)mǣre* 'boundary, landmark'.

Mershman.
Sx: Rob. Mersman 1296 SR 22. — *So:* Rich. Merischman 1327 SR 188.
OE *mersc* 'a marsh'.

Multonman.
Cu: John Multonman 1332 SR 32.
There is a pl. n. *Moulton* in *Y*, but not in *Cu*. Cf the surname Al. *de Multon* in the same roll.

Okman.
Sx: Rob. Okman 1296 SR 81.
OE *āc* 'oak'.

Pilman.
So: Will. Pilman 1327 SR 280.
OE *pīl* 'pile or stake'.

Piryman.
Ess: Pet. Pyriman 1319 *SR* 15. — *Lo:* Rich. Pyriman 1379 CLB (H) 134. — *Sr:* Joh. Puryman 1332 SR 74. — *Sx:* Joh. Piryman 1296 SR 103. — *So:* Adam Puryman 1327 SR 125.

OE *pirie, pyrie* 'a pear-tree'.

Putman.
Sx: Henr' Putman 1296 SR 98. — *So:* Will. Putman 1333 *SR* 5.
OE *pytt* 'pit'.

Scaffolman.
Cu: Adam Scaffolman 1332 SR 53.

The corresp. pl. n. has not been found. Cf the surname John de *Scaffoll* in the same roll.

Sloman.
Sx: Will. Sloman 1327 SR 189. Joh. Sloman ib.

OE *slōh, slō* 'a piece of soft, miry, or muddy ground'. Cf *Slough Green*, Pl. Soc. Sx.

Stighelman.
Sx: Joh. Stighelman 1327 SR 121. Walt. Stighelman ib. 174.
OE *stigel* 'stile'.

Strodeman.
Sx: Joh. Strodeman 1327 SR 214. Steph. Stroudman 1332 SR 326.
OE *strōd* 'marshy land'.

Tankerlayman.
Y: Rog. Tankerlayman, boucher 1387 **Free** Y 86.
Tankersley, pl. n. in *Y.*

Trandelman.
Sx: Joh. Trandelman 1327 SR 122.

OE *trendel, trœndel* 'a circle, ring', here prob. 'a circular meadow' or the like.

Waldman.
Y: Thom. Waldman 1349 Free Y 43.
OE *wald* (Anglian) 'wold, forest'.

Welleman.
Nf: Sim. le Welleman 1308 CDN 5. Nich. Welleman 1332 *SR* 13.
OE *wella* 'a well'.

Wyllesthorpman.
Y: Joh. Wyllesthorpman, pestour 1366 Free Y 63.
Wilsthorpe, pl. n. in Y.

A List of Compound Surnames.

-BATOUR:	Orbatour.
-BETER:	Coperbeter, Flaxbeter, Goldbeter, Ledbeter, Wodebetere, Wolbetere.
-BIGGERE:	Fetherbycger, Shoubiggere.
-BYNDER:	Bokbynder.
-BREDERE:	Haryngbredere.
-BREYDER:	Lacebreyder.
-BRENNER:	Askebrenner, Lymbrenner.
-BREWERE:	Alebrewere.
-BROCHER:	Ploghbrocher.
-KARTERE:	Heryngkartere.
-KERNERE:	Smerekernere.
-CLEVER:	Burdclever.
-DRAGHER:	Wirdragher.
-DRAPER:	Lyndraper.
-FEUERE:	Baiounsfeuere, Orfeuere.
-GRAVER:	Orgraver, Selgraver.
-HEWERE:	Bordhewere, Fleshhewere, Marlehewer, Silverhewer, Stonhewere, Vershewere.
-HOPER:	Goldehoper.
-YETERE:	Belleyetere, Bligeter, Brasyetere, Ledyetere, Pannegetter.
-LEGGER:	Streulegger.
-LETER:	Blodleter.
-LITTSTER:	Corklittster.
-MAKER:	Aketonmaker, Aruwemakere, Aunseremakere, Belgmakere, Bokmakere, Bordmakere, Botelmaker, Bowemakere, Callemaker, Candelmaker, Kelmaker, Chalunmaker, Chapemaker, Chesemakere, Clokkemaker, Cordemaker, Cottemakere, Delmaker, Dofkotemakere, Elymaker, Flourmakere, Gourdmaker, Hayremaker, Hodemaker, Lepmaker, Maltmakere, Medemaker, Meysemakere, Melemakere, Moldemaker, Netmaker, Oylemaker, Paniermaker, Potmaker, Pouchemaker, Pundermaker, Quyltmaker, Saucemaker, Seggemaker, Sheldmakere, Strengmakere, Walmakere.
-MAKESTERE:	Kallemakestere.
-MAN:	Butterman, Candelman, Capman, Chapman, Cheseman, Clothman, Elyman, Fetherman, Flaxman, Flekeman, Glasman, Hauerman, Honyman, Laxman, Lekman, Lynman, Meleman, Mustardman, Oilman, Pakeman, Panierman, Redman, Sakman, Saltman, Sherman, Syveman, Slayman, Smereman, Tailman, Wademan, Waxman, Werkman.

-MARTER:	Bukmarter.
-MONGERE:	Bukmongere, Ketmongere, Chesemonger, Clothmangere, Cornmongere, Fethermongere, Fishmongere, Flaxmongere, Fleshmongere, Garlekmongere, Gosmanger, Heymongere, Henmongere, Heryngmongere, Hermonger, Horsmongere, Irmongere, Lusmonger, Madermanger, Maltmongere, Melemongere, Otmongere, Sklatemanger, Smeremongere, Taylmongere, Tymbermongere, Waxmongere, Whelmonger, Wolmongere, Wudemonger.
-MONGESTERE:	Bredmongestere
-POLLARE:	Felpollare.
-SELLER:	Clothseller.
-SLIPER:	Swerdsliper.
-SMITH:	Ankersmyth, Arowesmith, Balismith, Blakesmyth, Bokelsmyth, Boltsmith, Botsmith, Brounsmyth, Knyfsmith, Copersmith, Exsmyth, Goldsmyth, Hudsmyth, Ledsmyth, Lokersmyth, Loksmyth, Orsmyth, Schersmyth, Shosmyth, Watersmyth, Whelsmyth, Whitesmyth.
-SNITHER:	Lakensnither.
-TAWYERE:	Whittawyere.
-TEWERE:	Whittewere.
-THEKER:	Ledtheker.
-TOWERE:	Whittowere.
-WASHERE:	Skynwashere.
-WEBBE:	Poghwebbe, Sakwebbe.
-WIFE:	Flaxwife, Silkwife.
-WYNDER:	Flekewynder.
-WOMAN:	Silkwoman.
-WRIGHT:	Arkewright, Bordwright, Bowewright, Brandwright, Briggwright, Cartwright, Chesewright, Kystewright, Kittewright, Culewright, Dethewright, Glaswright, Hayrwright, Lattewright, Limwright, Nawright, Orewright, Ploghwright, Shipwright, Syvewright, Slaywright, Tywelwright, Tunwright, Waynwright, Whelwright, Whicchewright.
-WRYNGERE:	Chesewryngere.

INDEX OF SURNAMES.

K has been indexed under *C*, and *Y* under *I*. The surnames that are only mentioned in a note under another name have been *italicized*.

Aketonmaker	114	Berner	183	Bowyer	154
Aguiller	148	Besmere	173	Braceresse	79
Alebrewere	78	Betere	102, 134	Brayder	86
Aluminour	130	Biller	152	Brandwright	152
Amelour	139	Blacker	108	Brasier	137
Ankersmyth	164	Blacchere	109	Brasyetere	137
Arkewright	165	Blacchester	109	Brasur	78
Armurer	150	Blakesmyth	143	Brecher	195
Arowesmith	156	Blakestere	109	*Bredmongestere*	52
Aruwemakere	155	Blechere	109	Brenner	183
Askebrenner	174	Bledere	189	Brewere	77
Ashburner	194	Bleykestere	109	Brewstere	78
Aunseremakere	147	Blextere	109	Briggeman	204
		Bligeter	141	Brigger	195
Bakere	61	Blodleter	189	*Briggwright*	159
Bakestere	61	Blomere	144	Broker	195
Bachiere	194	Blowere	143	Brochere	152
Badger	94	Bokbynder	129	Brokman	204
Bagger	94	Bokeler	150	Brokur	54
Baiounsfeuere	156	*Bokelsmyth*	150	Brogour	54
Balismith	143	Bokmakere	129	Broyer	58
Baller	194	Bolenger	62	Bromere	195
Barber	188	Boller	185	Brounsmyth	136
Barkere	121	Boltere	59	Bucher	73
Barrer	194	Boltsmith	156	Bukmarter	75
Bastere	124	Bordhewere	158	Bukmongere	75
Batour	102, 134	*Bordmakere*	158	Budiner	75
Becheman	203	Bordwright	158	Bulgere	127
Bechere	194	Borere	160	*Burdclever*	158
Beauderer	123	Botelmaker	128	Burser	127
Belger	128	Botoner	150	Burstlere	173
Belgmakere	127	Botsmith	164	Busseler	171
Belleyetere	138	Boukere	109	Buterer	68
Bellere	138	Bourere	195	Butterman	67
Beltere	125	Bourman	203		
Berghere	194	Bowemakere	155	Cager	149
Berlondere	194	Bowewright	155	Caldroner	137

Callemaker	117	Kyller	183	Couraour	123
Kallemakestere	117	Kylner	183	Courcheuer	118
Caller	117	Cyrer	73	Courtener	93
Candeler	72	Cyselour	136	Coussur	111
Candelmaker	73	Kystewright	165	Crassedalman	204
Candelman	73	Kittewright	170	Criblur	59
Caneuacer	92	Cliver	195	Crockere	185
Cannere	140	*Clokkemaker*	136	Crofter	196
Caperoner	116	Clocker	136	Croftman	204
Capiere	116	Clothere	89	Crosser	196
Capiestere	116	*Clothman*	89	Crossman	204
Capman	116	Clothmangere	89	Crucheman	204
Carboner	174	*Clothseller*	90	Cruchere	196
Carder	83	Clouser	195	Cuillerer	167
Cardestere	83	Cloutere	132	Culewright	114
Carpenter	158	Clubbere	153	Cumber	196
Cartwright	161	Knapper	195	Cunreyour	123
Keyer	146	Knedere	62	Cuppestere	169
Ceynturer	125	Kneller	195	Cusyner	64
Keller	117	Knyfsmith	153	Custere	96
Kelmaker	163	Knoller	195	Cuteler	153
Kembere	83	Cobelere	132	Cuver	169
Kembestere	83	Coke	63	Daleman	204
Kerere	195	Cokeler	118	Dauber	176
Kerman	204	Coffrer	164	Deye	67
Kerner	68	Coyfer	116	Deyer	104
Keruere	166	Coiner	134	Deyster	105
Ketmongere	74	Coliere	173	Dellere	196
Keu	64	Combere	82	Delmaker	158
Keuer	169	Combestere	82	Delman	204
Chalkere	176	*Coperbeter*	136	Deneman	204
Chaloner	96	Copersmith	136	Dennere	196
Chalunmaker	97	Corbiller	171	Dethewright	174
Chapeler	116	Corker	108	Dyer	104
Chapemaker	154	Corklittster	108	Dischere	185
Chapman	51	*Cordemaker*	86	Dofkotemakere	160
Chappere	55	Corder	86	Doghere	62
Chaucer	115	Cordewaner	130	Douler	149
Chaundeler	72	Cornmongere	60	Douner	196
Chesemakere	66	Corser	55	Draper	89
Cheseman	66	Corueyser	131	Dreyster	102
Chesemonger	66	Cosere	55	Drovere	55
Cheser	66	Cottemakere	160	Dubbere	113
Chesewright	66	Couchur	97		
Chesewryngere	67	Couerour	177	Elymaker	70
Kydiere	54	Coupere	168	*Elyman*	70

Engynour	152	*Furbisur*	151	Haltounman	205
Escriner	165	Furbur	151	Haltrere	87
Escriueyn	129	Furmager	67	Hammer	197
Especer	68	Furner	62	Haneper	140
Exsmyth	153	Fuster	124	*Haryngbredere*	86
				Hasteler	64
Fanneman	205	Gannoker	80	Hattere	115
Fanner	196	*Garleker*	69	Hauberger	150
Fariner	60	Garlekmongere	69	Hauerman	60
Felder	196	Gateman	205	Hekelere	82
Feliper	113	Gatier	197	Heggere	197
Felpollare	123	Gaunter	126	Heymongere	55
Feltere	98	Gelyner	76	Heliere	180
Ferrour	142	Gilder	133	Henmongere	76
Ferun	145	Gildsmith	133	Herdewykman	205
Fesor	160	Gynour	152	*Heryngkartere*	77
Fetherbycger	118	Girdeler	125	Heryngmongere	77
Fetherman	118	Girdelester	125	*Hermonger*	99
Fethermongere	118	Gyssere	176	Herstman	205
Feuere	142	Glasenwright	186	Hetheman	205
Feutrer	98	Glasyer	186	Hether	198
Filour	84	Glasman	186	Heumer	150
Finur	134	Glaswright	186	Heustere	106
Fishmongere	76	Glyndere	197	Hicdouneman	205
Fisicien	187	Glouere	126	Hider	198
Flaoner	64	Goldbeter	134	Hidman	205
Flaxbeter	81	Goldehoper	134	Hilder	198
Flaxere	81	Golder	133	Hirdler	172
Flaxman	81	Goldsmyth	133	Hoker	198
Flaxmongere	92	Gorman	205	Hokman	205
Flaxwife	81	Gosere	76	*Hodemaker*	117
Flekeman	172	Gosmanger	76	Hodere	117
Flekewynder	172	Gourdmaker	128	Holere	198
Flecher	155	Grater	151	Holmer	198
Fleshhewere	74	Grauer	136	Holtbyman	206
Fleshmongere	74	Grenare	197	Holter	198
Flourmakere	58	Greser	188	Honyman	69
Forceter	154	Gryndere	58	Hopere	169, 198
Forder	197	Grocer	52	Hoppere	169
Foundour	138	Grovere	197	Hornere	167
Frithere	197			Horsmongere	55
Fruter	70	Haccher	197	Hosiere	115
Fullere	100	Hayremaker	98	Howere	198
Fullester	100	Hayrere	99	Huckere	54
Fulun	100	Hayrwright	99	Huckestere	53
Fulur	100	Haller	197	Hucher	165

Hudsmyth	117	Lyner	91	Mineter	135
Hulleman	206	Lyneter	81	Minour	181
Hullere	199	Lynger	91	Moldemaker	138
Hurneman	206	Lynman	81	Moliner	58
Hurner	199	Litester	105	*Mongestere*	52
Hurrer	116	Lyther	199	Monnyer	135
		Lockere	146	Morer	200
Yetter	138	Lokersmyth	147	Mouner	57
Irmongere	145	Lokyere	146	Mountere	200
Ismongere	145	Lokyestere	146	Muleward	57
		Locksmyth	146	Mulgatere	200
Joynour	159	Loner	199	Multonman	206
Joyntur	160	Lorimer	147	Mustarder	65
		Loteman	206	Mustardman	65
Lacebreyder	86	Lotyer	199		
Lakensnither	91	Luminur	130	Nayler	149
Lacer	86	Lusmonger	77	Nawright	163
Lakere	199			Nedlere	148
Ladeler	167	Macecrer	75	Netmaker	87
Laneman	206	Macegre	75	Nettere	87
Laner	90, 199	*Madermanger*	108		
Lathere	158	Madrer	108		
Latoner	137	Madster	108	Okman	206
Lattewright	157	Malter	79	Oylemaker	70
Launder	110	Maltestere	79	Oyler	70
Lavender	110	*Maltmakere*	79	Oilman	70
Laxman	77	*Maltmongere*	79	Orbatour	134
Leker	69	Mangere	52	Orewright	164
Leche	187	Marberer	181	Orfeuere	133
Lecher	187	Marchaunt	51	Orgoner	165
Lekman	69	Mareschal	144, 188	Orgraver	135
Ledbeter	141	Marlehewer	182	Orloger	136
Ledere	141	Marlere	182	Orsmyth	137
Ledyetere	141	Mason	175	Otmongere	60
Ledsmyth	141	Mattere	97		
Ledtheker	179	Medemaker	79	Packere	85
Leggere	179	Meysemakere	171	Pakeman	54
Leyman	206	Melemakere	58	Pacher	113
Lepmaker	171	Meleman	60	Payler	170
Lyghere	199	Melemongere	60	Payndemeynere	62
Lymbrenner	183	Mercer	92	Paleser	173
Lymer	183	Mereman	206	Pallere	93
Limwright	183	Meriere	199	Paniermaker	171
Lyncher	199	Mersher	200	Panierman	54
Lyndere	199	Mershman	206	Pannegetter	137
Lyndraper	91	Milner	56	Panner	138

Parcheminer	128	Quarreur	181	Seeler	135
Parmenter	111	Quernestere	59	Seer	201
Pavilloner	92	Quilter	96	Seggemaker	97
Pavour	182	*Quyltmaker*	96	Segger	98
Peddere	53			Seinter	138
Pedelare	53	Rasorer	153	Seler	124
Peyneresse	83	Redere	179	*Selgraver*	136
Peyntour	177	Redlondere	201	Seller	124
Peleter	125	*Redman*	179	Semere	112
Pellere	93	Regrater	53	Semester	112
Pender	200	*Retundur*	104	Serrur	147
Peniur	167	Reveter	149	Setere	93
Penner	200	Ridelere	59	Sewere	112
Perour	181	Ridelestere	59	Sewstere	111
Pessoner	76	Rischere	98	Sheldmakere	150
Pestur	61	Rysebrigger	201	Shepper	112
Peutrer	139	Rollere	129	Sheppestere	112
Picher	164	Ropere	85	Shepsmerer	188
Pilchere	126	Ropestere	85	Sherere	103
Piler	200	Rower	162	Sherman	103
Pilman	206	Rubbare	151	Shether	154
Pinnere	148	Rudere	201	Shipwright	163
Pyriere	200			Shosmyth	144
Piryman	207	Sacker	94	Shoubiggere	132
Plastrer	176	Sachere	94	Shouger	144
Ploghbrocher	163	Sakman	94	*Silkwife*	93
Ploghwright	163	Sakwebbe	94	Silkwoman	93
Plumer	118, 140	Sadelere	123	Silverhewer	134
Poker	96	Saltere	70	Siuyere	172
Pocheler	96	Saltman	71	Syur	157
Poghwebbe	95	Sartour	111	Syveman	172
Polare	200	*Saucemaker*	65	Syvewright	172
Poller	103	Sauoner	72	Slayare	168
Ponder	200	Sauser	65	*Slayman*	168
Porer	69	Sawyere	157	Slaywright	167
Potager	64	Scaffolman	207	Slykere	151
Potier	184	Skepper	171	*Slyper*	154
Potmaker	184	*Scherestere*	103	Sloman	207
Pottere	184	*Schersmyth*	154	Slopere	114
Pouchemaker	95	Skynnere	119	Smerekernere	68
Poucher	95	Skynwashere	123	Smereman	68
Puleter	75	Skipwright	163	Smeremongere	68
Punder	200	Sklatemanger	180	Smerer	188
Pundermaker	147	Sclater	180	Smyth	142
Purser	127	Sclatter	180	Smokere	114
Putman	207	Scriueyn	129	Solier	201
Putter	201	Scriuener	130	Sopere	71

Sopestere	72	Teynturer	105	Ventoser	189
Sorter	84	Teler	90	Verrer	185
Soukere	189	Teseler	102	Vershewere	182
Soutere	131	Tesere	83	Vesseler	140
Spadere	173	Tewere	122	Vineter	79
Specker	132	Thacker	178	Vyntener	80
Spexter	132	Thakestere	178		
Spicer	68	Thecchere	178	Wademan	107
Spiker	149	Theker	178	Wadere	106
Spyndeler	168	Thorner	202	Wadester	107
Spinnere	84	Throwere	84	Waferer	63
Sponere	166	Tyer	202	Wayder	106
Sporiere	147	Tyghelere	179	Waynwright	161
Stapeler	201	Tymbermongere	158	Walkere	101
Stepere	110	Tynkeler	139	Waldman	207
Stikkere	74	Tynkere	139	Wallere	175
Styghelere	201	Tipelere	80	Walmakere	176
Stighelman	207	Tippere	156	Wanter	126
Stonhewere	182	Tyssur	88	Waschere	110
Strenger	86	Tisterer	89	Wasteler	63
Strengmakere	87	Tystour	89	Watersmyth	143
Streter	201	Tiulur	179	Waxman	73
Streulegger	179	Tywelwright	184	Waxmongere	73
Strodeman	207	Tonsur	104	Webbe	87
Strodere	201	Tosere	83	Webbere	88
Suour	131	Toukere	101	Webbester	88
Surgen	188	*Touestre*	122	Wegheletere	202
Swerdsliper	154	Towere	122	Weldere	202
		Trandelman	207	Welleman	208
Tabler	160	Trauenter	54	Wellere	71, 202
Tabletter	165	Trender	86	Werkman	182
Taillour	110	Trymmere	112	Weuere	88
Tailman	99	Trinder	86	Whelere	161
Taylmongere	99	Trucker	55	Whelmonger	162
Tankarder	171	Tundur	104	Whelsmyth	162
Tankerlayman	207	Tuneler	169	Whelster	162
Taneresse	119	Tunnere	170	Whelwright	162
Tannere	119	Tunwright	170	Whicchere	164
Tannestere	119	Turber	174	Whicchewright	165
Tanur	119	Turnour	166	Whytere	177
Tapener	97	Upholdere	113	Whitesmyth	139
Tapicer	93	Upholdestere	113	Whittawyere	122
Taseler	102	Urnere	185	Whittewere	122
Tauerner	80			Whittowere	122
Tawyere	121	Valer	202	Wyker	202
Teyntur	106	Vendur	53	Wygger	63

Wyggester	63	*Wodebetere*	107	Wolmongere	90
Wyllesthorpman	208	Wodeman	107	Wright	159
Wympler	117	Wodere	106	Wringer	67
Windere	84	Wodester	107	Wrytere	130
Wirdragher	148	Wolbetere	101	*Wudemonger*	158
Wysher	202	Wollere	90		
Wythier	202	Wollestere	90		

EB 273